Sermons and Treatises
by
SAMUEL WARD, B.D.,
SYDNEY SUSSEX COL., CAMBRIDGE; PREACHER OF IPSWICH

With Memoir
By THE REV. J. C. RYLE , B. A .,

THE BANNER OF TRUTH TRUST

THE BANNER OF TRUTH TRUST
3 Murrayfield Road, Edinburgh EH12 6EL
P.O. Box 621, Carlisle, Pennsylvania 17013, USA

*

First published 1636.
Here reprinted from the James Nichol edition of 1862.
First Banner of Truth Trust reprint 1996.
ISBN O 85151 697 1

*

Printed and bound in Great Britain by
The Bath Press, Bath

CONTENTS.

MEMOIR OF SAMUEL WARD.

THE writer whose sermons and treatises I have undertaken to preface by a historical memoir, is one comparatively unknown to most readers of English theology. This is easily accounted for. He wrote but little, and what he wrote has hitherto never been reprinted. Owen, Baxter, Gurnal, Charnock, Goodwin, Adams, Brooks, Watson, Greenhill, Sibbes, Jenkyn, Manton, Burroughs, Bolton, and others, have been reprinted, either wholly or partially. Of Samuel Ward, so far as I can ascertain, not a word has been reprinted for more than two hundred years.

How far Samuel Ward's sermons have deserved this neglect, I am content to leave to the judgment of all impartial students of divinity into whose hands this volume may fall. But I venture the opinion, that it reflects little credit on the discretion of republishers of old divinity that such a writer as Samuel Ward has been hitherto passed over. His case, however, does not stand alone. When such works as those of Swinnock, Arrowsmith on John i., Gouge on Hebrews, Airay on Philippians, John Rogers on 1 Peter, Hardy on 1 John, Daniel Rogers on Naaman the Syrian (to say nothing of some of the best works of Manton and Brooks), have not been thought worthy of republication, we must not be surprised at the treatment which Ward has received.

As a Suffolk minister, and a thorough lover of Puritan theology, I should have been especially pleased, if it had been in my power to supply full information about Samuel Ward. I regret, however, to be obliged to say that the materials from which any account of him can be compiled are exceedingly scanty, and the facts known about him are comparatively few. Nor yet, unhappily, is this difficulty the only one with which I have had to contend. It is an unfortunate circumstance, that no less than three divines named

" S. Ward " lived in the first half of the seventeenth century, and were all members of Sydney College, Cambridge. These three were, Dr Samuel Ward, master of Sydney College, who was one of the English commissioners at the Synod of Dort, and a correspondent of Archbishop Usher;—Seth Ward, who was successively Bishop of Exeter and Salisbury ;—and Samuel Ward of Ipswich, whose sermons are now reprinted. Of these three, the two "Samuels" were undoubtedly the most remarkable men ; but the similarity of their names has hitherto involved their biographies in much confusion. I can only say that I have done my best, in the face of these accumulated difficulties, to unravel a tangled skein, and to supply the reader with accurate information.

The story of Samuel Ward's life is soon told. He was born at Haverhill, in Suffolk, in the year 1577, and was eldest son of the Rev. John Ward, minister of the gospel in that town.* He was admitted a scholar of St John's College, Cambridge, on Lady Margaret's foundation, on Lord Burghley's nomination, November 6. 1594, and went out B.A. of that house in 1596. He was appointed one of the first fellows of Sydney Sussex College in 1599, commenced M.A. 1600, vacated his fellowship on his marriage in 1604, and proceeded B.D. in 1607.

---

* John Ward, the father of Samuel Ward, appears to have been a man of considerable eminence as a minister and preacher. Fuller (in his Worthies of Suffolk) says that the three sons together would not make up the abilities of their father. The following inscription on his tomb in Haverhill church is well worth reading :—

JOHANNES WARDE.

Quo si quis scivit scitius,
Aut si quis docuit doctius,
At rarus vixit sanctius,
Et nullus tonuit fortius.

Son of thunder, son of ye dove,
Full of hot zeal, full of true love ;
In preaching truth, in living right,—
A burning lampe, a shining light.

LIGHT HERE.   STARS HEREAFTER.

John Ward, after he with great evidence
and power of ye Spirite, and with much fruit,
preached ye gospel at Haverill and Bury in
Suff. 25 yeares, was heere gathered to his fathers.

WATCH.   Susan, his widdowe, married Rogers, that   WARDE.

worthy Pastor of Wethersfielde. He left 3 sonnes,
Samuel, Nathaniel, John, Preachers, who for
them and theirs, wish no greater blessing
than that they may continue in beleeving
and preaching the same gospel till ye coming
of Christ. Come, Lord Jesus, come quicklye.

WATCH.   Death is our entrance into life.   WARDE.

Nothing is known of Ward's boyhood and youth. His entrance on the work of the ministry, the name of the bishop by whom he was ordained, the date of his ordination, the place where he first began to do Christ's work as a preacher, are all things of which apparently there is no record. His first appearance as a public character is in the capacity of lecturer at his native town of Haverhill. Of his success at Haverhill, Samuel Clark (in his 'Lives of Eminent Persons,' p. 154, ed. 1683), gives the following interesting example, in his life of Samuel Fairclough, a famous minister of Kedington, in Suffolk. :—

'God was pleased to begin a work of grace in the heart of Samuel Fairclough very early and betimes, by awakening his conscience by the terror of the law, and by bestowing a sincere repentance upon him thereby, and by working an effectual faith in him ; and all this was done by the ministry of the word preached by Mr Samuel Ward, then lecturer of Haverhill. Mr Ward had answered for him in baptism, and had always a hearty love to him. Preaching one day on the conversion of Zaccheus, and discoursing upon his four-fold restitution in cases of rapine and extortion, Mr Ward used that frequent expression, that no man can expect pardon from God of the wrong done to another's estate, except he make full restitution to the wronged person, if it may possibly be done. This was as a dart directed by the hand of God to the heart of young Fairclough, who, together with one John Trigg, afterwards a famous physician in London, had the very week before robbed the orchard of one Goodman Jude of that town, and had filled their pockets as well as their bellies with the fruit of a mellow pear tree.

'At and after sermon, young Fairclough mourned much, and had not any sleep all the night following; and, rising on the Monday morning, he went to his companion Trigg and told him that he was going to Goodman Jude's, to carry him twelve pence by way of restitution for three pennyworth of pears of which he had wronged him. Trigg, fearing that if the thing were confessed to Jude, he would acquaint Robotham their master therewith, and that cor-poral correction would follow, did earnestly strive to divert the poor child from his purpose of restitution. But Fairclough replied that God would not pardon the sin except restitution were made. To which Trigg answered thus : " Thou talkest like a fool, Sam ; God will forgive us ten times, sooner than old Jude will forgive us once." But our Samuel was of another mind, and therefore he goes on to Jude's house, and there told him his errand, and offered him a shilling, which Jude refusing (though he declared his forgiveness of the wrong), the youth's wound smarted so, that he could get no rest till he went to his spiritual father Mr Ward, and opened to him the whole state of his soul, both on account of this particular sin and many others, and most especially the sin of sins, the original sin and depravation of his nature. Mr Ward received him with great affection and tenderness, and proved the good Samaritan to him, pouring wine and oil into his wounds, answering all his questions, satisfying his fears, and preaching Jesus to him so fully and effectually that he became a true and sincere convert, and dedicated and devoted himself to his Saviour and Redeemer all the days of his life after.'*

From Haverhill, Samuel Ward was removed, in 1603, at the early age of twenty-six, to a position of great importance in those days. He was appointed by the Corporation of Ipswich to the office of town preacher at Ipswich, and filled the pulpit of St Mary-le-Tower, in that town, with little intermission, for about thirty years. Ipswich and Norwich, it must be remembered, were places of far more importance two hundred and fifty years ago, than they are at the present day. They were the capital towns of two of the wealthiest and most thickly peopled counties in England. Suffolk, in particular, was a county in which the Protestant and evangelical principles of the Reformation had taken particularly deep root. Some of the most eminent Puritans were Suffolk ministers. To be chosen town preacher of a place like Ipswich, two hundred and fifty years ago, was a very great honour, and shews the high estimate which was set on Samuel Ward's ministerial character, even when he was so young as twenty-six. It deserves to be remarked that Matthew Lawrence and Stephen Marshall, who were among his successors, were both foremost men among the divines of the seventeenth century.

The influence which Ward possessed in Ipswich appears to have been very considerable. Fuller says, 'He was preferred minister *in*, or rather *of*, Ipswich, having a care over, and a love from, all the parishes in that populous place. Indeed, he had a magnetic virtue (as if he had learned it from the loadstone, in whose quali-

---

* I think it right to remark that Clark, in all probability, has erred in his *dates* in telling this story. He says that Fairclough was born in 1594, and that the event he has recorded took place when he was thirteen years old. Now, in 1607 Ward had ceased to be lecturer of Haverhill. Whether the explanation of this discrepancy is that Fairclough was born before 1594, or that he was only nine years old when he stole the pears, or that Ward was visiting at Haverhill in 1607 and preached during his visit, or that Fairclough was at school at Ipswich and not Haverhill, is a point that we have no means of deciding.

ties he was so knowing,) to attract people's affections.' * The history of his thirty years' ministry in the town of Ipswich, would doubtless prove full of interesting particulars, if we could only discover them. Unhappily, I can only supply the reader with the following dry facts, which I have found in an antiquarian publication of considerable value, entitled, ' Wodderspoon's Memorials of Ipswich.' They are evidently compiled from ancient records, and throw some useful light on certain points of Ward's history.

Wodderspoon says—' In the year 1603, on All-Saints' day, a man of considerable eminence was elected as preacher, Mr Samuel Ward. The corporation appear to have treated him with great liberality, appointing an hundred marks as his stipend, and also allowing him £6 : 13 : 4 quarterly in addition, for house rent.

' The municipal authorities (possibly, because of obtaining so able a divine) declare very minutely the terms of Mr Ward's engagement. In his sickness or absence he is to provide for the supply of a minister at the usual place three times a week, ' as usual hath been." " He shall not be absent out of town above forty days in one year, without leave ; and if he shall take a pastoral charge, his retainer by the corporation is to be void. The pension granted to him is not to be charged on the foundation or hospital lands."

' In the seventh year of James I., the corporation purchased a house for the preacher, or rather for Mr Ward. This house was bought by the town contributing £120, and the rest of the money was made up by free contributions, on the understanding that, when Mr Ward ceased to be preacher, the building was to be re-sold, and the various sums collected returned to those who contributed, as well as the money advanced by the corporation.'

' In the eighth year of James I., the corporation increased the salary of Mr Ward to £90 per annum, " on account of the charges he is at by abiding here." '

' In the fourteenth year of James I., Mr Samuel Ward's pension increased from £90 to £100 yearly.'

' The preaching of this divine being, of so free and puritanic a character, did not long escape the notice of the talebearers of the court ; and after a short period, spent in negotiation, Mr Ward was restrained from officiating in his office. In 1623, August 6th, a

---

* I suspect that Fuller's remarks about the loadstone refer to a book, called ' Magnetis Reductorium Theologium,' which is sometimes attributed to Samuel Ward of Ipswich. But it is more than doubtful whether the authorship of this book does not belong to Dr Samuel Ward, the principal of Sydney College, of whom mention has already been made.

record appears in the town books, to the effect that " a letter from the king, to inhibit Mr Ward from preaching, is referred to the council of the town." '

About the remaining portion of Ward's life, Wodderspoon supplies no information. The little that we know about it is gleaned from other sources.

It is clear, from Hackett's life of the Lord Keeper Bishop Williams (p. 95, ed. 1693), that though prosecuted by Bishop Harsnet for nonconformity in 1623, Ward was only suspended temporarily, if at all, from his office as preacher. Brook (in his 'Lives of the Puritans,' vol. ii. p. 452), following Hackett, says, that ' upon his prosecution in the consistory of Norwich, he appealed from the bishop to the king, who committed the articles exhibited against him to the examination of the Lord Keeper Williams. The Lord Keeper reported that Mr Ward was not altogether blameless, but a man easily to be won by fair dealing ; and persuaded Bishop Harsnet to take his submission, and not remove him from Ipswich. The truth is, the Lord Keeper found that Mr Ward possessed so much candour, and was so ready to promote the interests of the church, that he could do no less than compound the troubles of so learned and industrious a divine. He was therefore released from the prosecution, and most probably continued for some time, without molestation, in the peaceable exercise of his ministry.' Brook might here have added a fact, recorded by Hackett, that Ward was so good a friend to the Church of England, that he was the means of retaining several persons who were wavering about conformity, within the pale of the Episcopal communion.

After eleven years of comparative quiet, Ward was prosecuted again for alleged nonconformity, at the instigation of Archbishop Laud. Prynne, in his account of Laud's trial (p. 361), tells us that, in the year 1635, he was impeached in the High Commision Court for preaching against bowing at the name of Jesus, and against the Book of Sports, and for having said ' that the Church of England was ready to ring changes in religion,' and ' that the gospel stood on tiptoe ready to be gone.' He was found guilty, was enjoined to make a public recantation in such form as the Court should appoint, and condemned in costs of the suit. Upon his refusal to recant, he was committed to prison, where he remained a long time.

In a note to Brook's account of this disgraceful transaction, which he appears to have gathered out of Rushworth's Collections and Wharton's Troubles of Laud, he mentions a remarkable fact about Ward at this juncture of his life, which shews the high esteem in which he was held at Ipswich. It appears that after his suspension the Bishop of Norwich would have allowed his people another minister in his place; but 'they would have Mr Ward, or none!'

The last four years of Ward's life are a subject on which I find it very difficult to discover the truth. Brook says that, after his release from prison, he retired to Holland, and became a colleague of William Bridge, the famous Independent minister of Yarmouth, who had settled at Rotterdam. He also mentions a report that he and Mr Bridge renounced their Episcopal ordination, and were reordained,—'Mr Bridge ordaining Mr Ward, and Mr Ward returning the compliment.' He adds another report, that Ward was unjustly deposed from his pastoral office at Rotterdam, and after a short interval restored.

I venture to think that this account must be regarded with some suspicion. At any rate, I doubt whether we are in possession of all the facts in the transaction which Brook records. That Ward retired to Holland after his release from prison, is highly probable. It was a step which many were constrained to take for the sake of peace and liberty of conscience, in the days of the Stuarts. That he was pastor of a church at Rotterdam, in conjunction with Bridge, —that differences arose between him and his colleague,—that he was temporarily deposed from his office and afterward restored,— are things which I think very likely. His reordination is a point which I think questionable. For one thing it seems to me exceedingly improbable, that a man of Ward's age and standing would first be reordained by Bridge, who was twenty-three years younger than himself, and afterward reordain Bridge. For another thing, it appears very strange that a man who had renounced his episcopal orders, should have afterwards received an honourable burial in the aisle of an Ipswich church, in the year 1639. One thing only is clear. Ward's stay at Rotterdam could not have been very lengthy. He was not committed to prison till 1635, and was buried in 1639. He 'lay in prison long,' according to Prynne. At any rate, he lay there long enough to write a Latin work, called 'A Rapture,' of which it is expressly stated that it was composed during his imprisonment 'in the Gate House.' In 1638, we find him buying a house in Ipswich. It is plain, at this rate, that he could not have been very long in Holland. However, the whole of the transactions at Rotterdam, so far as Ward is concerned, are involved in some obscurity. Stories against eminent Puritans were easily fabricated and greedily swallowed in the seventeenth century. Brook's assertion that Ward died in Holland, about 1640, is so entirely desti-

tute of foundation, that it rather damages the value of his account
of Ward's latter days.

Granting, however, that after his release from prison Ward retired
to Holland, there seems every reason to believe that he returned
to Ipswich early in 1638. It appears from the town books of
Ipswich (according to Wodderspoon), that, in April 1638, he purchased the house provided for him by the town for £140, repaying
the contributors the sum contributed by them. He died in the
month of March 1639, aged 62; and was buried in St Mary-le-
Tower, Ipswich, on the 8th of that month. A certified copy of the
entry of his burial, in the parish register, is in my possession. On
a stone which was laid in his lifetime in the middle aisle of the
church, the following words (according to Clarke's History of
Ipswich) are still extant—

> 'Watch, Ward! yet a little while,
> And he that shall come will come.'

Under this stone it is supposed the bones of the good old Puritan
preacher were laid; and to this day he is spoken of by those who
know his name in Ipswich as

> 'Watch Ward.'

It only remains to add, that Ward married, in 1604, a widow
named Deborah Bolton, of Isleham in Cambridge, and had by her
a family.* It is an interesting fact, recorded in the town-books of
Ipswich, that after his death, as a mark of respect, his widow and
his eldest son Samuel were allowed for their lives the stipend
enjoyed by their father, viz., £100 annually. It is also worthy of
remark, that he had two brothers who were ministers, John and
Nathaniel. John Ward lived and died rector of St Clement's,
Ipswich; and there is a tablet and short inscription about him in
that church. Nathaniel Ward was minister of Stardon, Herts,
went to America in 1634, returned to England in 1646, and died at
Shenfield, in Essex, 1653.

There is an excellent portrait of Ward still extant in Ipswich,
in the possession of Mr Hunt, solicitor. He is represented with
an open book in his right hand, a ruff round his neck, a peaked
beard and moustaches. On one side is a coast beacon lighted; and
there is an inscription—

> 'Watche Ward. Ætatis suæ 43. 1620.'

The following extract, from a rare volume called 'The Tomb-
stone; or, a notice and imperfect monument of that worthy

---

* For this fact, and the facts about Ward's degrees at Cambridge, I am indebted to a well-informed writer in 'Notes and Queries' for October 1861.

man Mr John Carter, Pastor of Bramford and Belstead in Suffolk'
(1653), will probably be thought to deserve insertion as an in-
cidental evidence of the high esteem in which Ward was held in
the neighbourhood of Ipswich.   The work was written by Mr
Carter's son; and the extract describes what occurred at his
father's funeral. He says (at pages 26, 27), 'In the afternoon,
February 4. 1634, at my father's interring, there was a great con-
fluence of people from all parts thereabout, ministers and others
taking up the word of Joash King of Israel, "O my father!
my father! the chariots of Israel and the horsemen thereof!"
Old Mr Samuel Ward, *that famous divine, and the glory of Ipswich* came to the funeral, brought a mourning gown with him,
and offered very respectfully to preach the funeral sermon, seeing
that such a congregation was gathered together, and upon such an
occasion. But my sister and I durst not give way to it; for our
father had often charged us in his lifetime, and upon his blessing,
that no service should be at his burial. For, said he, "it will give
occasion to speak some good things of me that I deserve not, and
so false things will be uttered in this pulpit." Mr Ward rested
satisfied, and did forbear. But the next Friday, at Ipswich, he
turned his whole lecture into a funeral sermon for my father, in
which he did lament and honour him, to the great satisfaction of
the whole auditory.'

I have now brought together all that I can discover about Samuel
Ward's history. I heartily regret that the whole amount is so
small, and that the facts recorded about him are so few. But we
must not forget that the best part of Ward's life was spent in
Suffolk, and that he seldom left his own beloved pulpit in St
Mary-le-Tower, Ipswich.* That he was well known by reputation
beyond the borders of his own county, there can be no doubt.
His selection to be a preacher at St Paul's Cross, in 1616, is a
proof of this. But it is vain to suppose that the reputation of a
preacher, however eminent, who lives and dies in a provincial
town, will long survive him. In order to become the subject of
biographies, and have the facts of his life continually noted down,
a man must live in a metropolis. This was not Ward's lot; and,
consequently, at the end of two hundred years, we seem to know
little about him.

It only remains to say something about the Sermons and Treatises, which are now for the first time reprinted, and made access-
ible to the modern reader of theology. It must be distinctly un-

* It seems that he expounded half the Bible during his ministry in Ipswich!
See his preface to 'The Happiness of Practice.'

derstood that they do not comprise the whole of Ward's writings. Beside these Sermons and Treatises, he wrote, in conjunction with Yates, a reply to Montague's famous book, 'Appello Cæsarem.' There is also reason to think that he published one or two other detached sermons beside those which are now reprinted. I think, however, there can be little doubt that the nine Sermons and Treatises which are now republished are the only works of Samuel Ward which it would have been worth while to reprint, and in all probability the only works which he would have wished himself to be reproduced.

Of the merits of these sermons, the public will now be able to form an opinion. They were thought highly of in time past, and have received the commendation of very competent judges. Fuller testifies that Ward 'had a sanctified fancy, dexterous in designing expressive pictures, representing much matter in a little model.' Doddridge says that Ward's 'writings are worthy to be read through. His language is generally proper, elegant, and nervous. His thoughts are well digested, and happily illustrated. He has many remarkable veins of wit. Many of the boldest figures of speech are to be found in him, beyond any English writer, especially apostrophes, prosopopœias, dialogisms, and allegories.' * This praise may at first sight seem extravagant. I shall, however, be disappointed if those who take the trouble to read Ward's writings do not think it well deserved.

It is only fair to Samuel Ward to remind the readers of his works, that at least three of the nine Sermons and Treatises now reprinted, were not originally composed with a view to publication. The sermons entitled ' A Coal from the Altar,' 'Balm from Gilead to Recover Conscience,' and ' Jethro's Justice of the Peace,' would appear to have been carried through the press by friends and relatives. They have all the characteristics of compositions intended for ears rather than for eyes, for hearers rather than for readers. Yet I venture to say that they are three of the most striking examples of Ward's gifts and powers, out of the whole nine. The peroration of the sermon on Conscience, in particular, appears to me one of the most powerful and effective conclusions to a sermon which I have ever read in the English language.†

* How Doddridge could possibly have made the mistake of supposing that Ward died at the age of 28, is perfectly inexplicable !

† The engraved title-pages of two of the nine Sermons, in the edition of 1636, are great curiosities in their way. The one which is prefixed to the ' Woe to Drunkards,' is intended to be a hit at the degeneracy of the times in which Ward lived. If it was really designed by Ward himself, it supplies some foundation for the rumour that he had a genius for caricaturing.

The *doctrine* of Ward's sermons is always thoroughly evangelical. He never falls into the extravagant language about repentance, which disfigures the writings of some of the Puritans. He never wearies us with the long supra-scriptural, systematic statements of theology, which darken the pages of others. He is always to the point, always about the main things in divinity, and generally sticks to his text. To exalt the Lord Jesus Christ as high as possible, to cast down man's pride, to expose the sinfulness of sin, to spread out broadly and fully the remedy of the gospel, to awaken the unconverted sinner and alarm him, to build up the true Christian and comfort him,—these seem to have been objects which Ward proposed to himself in every sermon. And was he not right ? Well would it be for the Churches if we had more preachers like him!

The *style* of Ward's sermons is always eminently simple. Singularly rich in illustration,—bringing every day life to bear continually on his subject,—pressing into his Master's service the whole circle of human learning,—borrowing figures and similes from everything in creation,—not afraid to use familiar language such as all could understand,—framing his sentences in such a way that an ignorant man could easily follow him,—bold, direct, fiery, dramatic, and speaking as if he feared none but God, he was just the man to arrest attention, and to keep it when arrested, to set men thinking, and to make them anxious to hear him again. Quaint he is undoubtedly in many of his sayings. But he preached in an age when all were quaint, and his quaintness probably struck no one as remarkable. Faulty in taste he is no doubt. But there never was the popular preacher against whom the same charge was not laid. His faults, however, were as nothing compared to his excellencies. Once more I say, Well would it be for the churches if we had more preachers like him !

The *language* of Ward's sermons ought not to be passed over without remark. I venture to say that, in few writings of the seventeenth century, will there be found so many curious, old-fashioned, and forcible words as in Ward's sermons. Some of these words are unhappily obsolete and unintelligible to the multitude, to the grievous loss of English literature. Many of them will require explanatory foot-notes, in order to make them understood by the majority of readers.

I now conclude by expressing my earnest hope that the scheme of republication, which owes its existence to Mr Nichol, may meet with the success which it deserves, and that the writings of men like Samuel Ward may be read and circulated throughout the land.

I wish it for the sake of the Puritan divines. We owe them a debt, in Great Britain, which has never yet been fully paid. They are not valued as they deserve, I firmly believe, because they are so little known.*

I wish it for the sake of the Protestant Churches of my own country, of every name and denomination. It is vain to deny that we have fallen on trying times for Christianity. Heresies of the most appalling kind are broached in quarters where they might have been least expected. Principles in theology which were once regarded as thoroughly established are now spoken of as doubtful matters. In a time like this, I believe that the study of some of the great Puritan divines is eminently calculated, under God, to do good and stay the plague. I commend the study especially to all young ministers. If they want to know how powerful minds and mighty intellects can think out deep theological subjects, arrive at decided conclusions, and yet give implicit reverence to the Bible, let them read Puritan divinity.

I fear it is not a reading age. Large books, especially, have but little chance of a perusal. Hurry, superficiality, and bustle are the characteristics of our times. Meagreness, leanness, and shallowness are too often the main features of modern sermons. Nevertheless, something must be attempted in order to check existing evils. The churches must be reminded that there can be no really powerful preaching without deep thinking, and little deep thinking without hard reading. The republication of our best Puritan divines I regard as a positive boon to the Church and the world, and I heartily wish it God speed.

* To regard the Puritans of the seventeenth century, as some appear to do, as mere ranting enthusiasts, is nothing better than melancholy ignorance. Fellows and heads of colleges, as many of them were, they were equal, in point of learning, to any divines of their day. To say that they were mistaken in some of their opinions, is one thing; to speak of them as 'unlearned and ignorant men,' is simply absurd, and flatly contrary to facts.

CHRIST IS ALL IN ALL.

COLOSSIANS III. 11.

KING OF KINGS AND LORD OF LORDS,

JESUS CHRIST.

EVERY good name is as precious ointment; but unto thee, O Christ, hath God given a name above all names in heaven and earth, anointed thee with oil above all thy fellows. All thy garments smell of myrrh, aloes, and cassia; because of the scent of thy perfumes, thy name is a bundle of myrrh, cluster of camphor, and as the smell of Libanus. But we, the sons of men, have dull senses, stuffed with earthly savours. Oh, therefore, that thou whom my soul loveth wouldest shew thy servant where that fragrant spikenard is to be found which will cast a savour all over thine house; and help him so to pour some small portion thereof upon thine head, as might draw us, in the savour of thine ointment, to run after thee. Had he all the treasures and jewels of the world, would he not bestow them upon altars and crucifixes to thy honour, if thou likedst of any such services? But these vanities, he knoweth full well, thy jealousy abhorreth. This thou hast shewed him, that he that praiseth thee honoureth thee. Accept, therefore, and prosper the office of him that desireth not hereby to gain a name on earth; who wisheth all his thoughts and works may either honour thee or dishonour himself, feed thy flock or moths; who reckoneth himself unworthy to be as one of thy whelps, is willing to be of no name or number, so thou mayest be ALL IN ALL.

GUIDE THOU MY PEN, AND IT SHALL SHEW FORTH THY PRAISE!

CHRIST IS ALL IN ALL.

Christ is all, and in all.—Col. III. 11.

A MAGNIFICENT title, a most ample and stately style; too transcendent and comprehensive for any creature, man, or angel; due and fit only for Him, upon whose head it is here set by his elect vessel, chosen of purpose to be the ensign-bearer of his name among the nations; worthily honoured by Augustine for the best child of grace, and faithfulest servant of his Lord, because in all his writings he affects nothing more, nothing else, in a manner, than to advance his name, as here in the former part of the verse, to cry down and nullify all other excellencies whatsoever, that he might in the latter magnify, or rather, as you see, omnify his Lord and Master Christ: giving the Colossians to understand, that however there be many things with men, of great and different esteem, the advantage of a Jew being much above a Gentile, the dignity of a Grecian above a Scythian or Barbarian, many the privileges of a freeman above a bond-slave; yet all these with God are nothing set by, who hath so set all his love and good pleasure on his Son, that besides, or out of him, he regards no person, respecteth no circumstance, but slights all as cyphers of no value. Only look what there is of Christ in any man, either by imputation or infusion, so much is he in God's books, with whom Christ is all in all.

The extent of which praise, that we may the fuller comprehend, we may not measure Paul's phrase by our own ordinary language, in which by common abuse of speech, we lend it to everything we mean to commend a little above its fellows. As Solomon, speaking after the sense and fashion of worldlings, 'Bread (says he) nourisheth, wine refresheth, but money is all in all,' Eccles. x. It is not true of Christ only as a byword, or proverbial commendation, but in the fullest rack a proposition can be strained unto in our apprehension, and that in a twofold relation of God and man. Look what God can require for his satisfaction, or we desire for our perfection, is so completely to be found in Christ, that it need not be sought elsewhere.

With God, it is true that worthy patriarchs and saints have been somebodies: Abraham his friend; Israel a potent prince with him; Moses a faithful steward in his house; Noah, Samuel, and Daniel, prevailing favourites, that could do something with him; but all through, and for the sake of Messiah, the heir, the Son of his desires, and good pleasure, in whom he hath heaped up the fulness of grace and treasures of all perfection.

Unto us sundry things be of some stead and use in some cases, in their several times, places, and respects ; but unto all intents and effects of justification, sanctification, and salvation, in prosperity, in adversity, in life, and death, Christ only is all in all.

This all-sufficiency of Christ, as it cannot be easily conceived, nor possibly at once expressed, so hath not the Spirit of God thought fit in one or a few texts, after one or a few ways, but throughout the Bible, at sundry times and manifold manners, to set out the same unto us in types real, in types personal, in prophecies, in plain terms, in parables and similitudes, insomuch that Count Anhalt,* that princely preacher, was wont to say, that the whole Scriptures, what were they else but swaddling bands of the child Jesus ? he being to be found almost in every page, in every verse, and line.

Many renowned persons and things we read stories of; but the Spirit speaks not so much of them, as allegoriseth of another, meaneth them on the by and Christ on the main, who is the centre, at which all of them, as several lines, aim and directly point at.

The tree of life, the ark of Noah, the ladder of Jacob, and the rest of the like kind, what were they but Christ? whom because the world was not worthy so soon to see, nor God willing at once to shew so rich a jewel, he therefore enwrapped obscurely in these shadows, till in the fulness of time he saw fit to reveal him in open mirror ; directly by his forerunner pointing at him, ' Behold the Lamb of God,' &c.

And because these were but dead types, not resembling to the life him that was the Life of the world and Lord of life ; therefore all the prophets, kings, and priests of note, and the redeemers and benefactors of the Jews, what were they but pictures sent before of this Prince of glory, to follow after in his due time, and as stars extinguishing their borrowed light at the appearance of the Sun of righteousness, to whom Moses and Elias, in the persons and stead of the rest, did their homage on Mount Tabor, as unto the sum and accomplishment of the law and prophets ?†

To say nothing of the imaginary gods and proud monarchs of the world, all whose swelling titles, which they usurped in their coins, columns, and arches, of founders, preservers, repairers, dictators, consuls, &c., properly and of right belong to him, who alone is the Saviour of his people, ' King of kings, mighty Counsellor, Prince of peace, Righteousness, Immortality, only blessed for ever.'

In a word, this whole universe, this same great *all*, and all the things of mark and use in it, as they were made by, for, and through him, and but for him should not have been, could not continue ; so do they all willingly tender their services to illustrate his worth, as so many gems to adorn and embroider his apparel withal.   The glorious sun, the bright morning star, bread the most necessary, wine· the sweetest, waters the most refreshing, the rose of Sharon the fairest, all serving in Scripture to adumbrate pieces and parcels of his infinite perfection : and do not all jointly compounded make up an idea of him, that is light indeed, bread and water of life indeed, the only good, the chief good, the author and perfector, the root and branch, the Alpha and Omega, which two letters, as they are the principal, initial, and final of the alphabet, and comprehend in their compass all the

---

* Philip. Camerarius in vita Comitis Anhaldini Pastoris et Principis, &c.

† Glossa Hebr. in Isa. lii. vide Pelicanum in Deut. xxxii.

residue, so are they emblems of him that is eternity itself, perfection itself, first and last, ' all in all,' &c.*

Hear this, all you that worship the beast and his image, and tell me whether there can be two ' Alls in all ;' and if this be Christ's just and incommunicable title, what is to be thought of him that shall arrogate or assume it to himself ?   What else can he be but that ' man of pride, son of perdition, even that Antichrist ?'   The swelling titles, whereby your Gregory† foremarked out his successor, are but modest ones in comparison of this blasphemy.

Yea, but was there ever mouth so full of abomination, that durst belch out, or ears so Herodian, that durst put up such stuff ?   Search and peruse your own records, and tell us to whom these acclamations were used by your Lateran fathers, ' To thee is given all power in heaven and earth, thou art all in all.'‡   Was it not your lion at his entrance into the council ? And did that beast either rend his garment, or stop his ears ? at which it is wonder the earth opened not to swallow quick both speaker and hearer, as the chair of Hildebrand rent asunder on a less occasion.   Too little it was belike to be styled by ordinary parasites, the shepherd of shepherds, spouse and head of the church, œcumenical bishop, prince of priests ;§ unless he might be advanced above all Augusteity and Deity in this most hyperbolical manner.   What need we any further evidence of an antichrist ?∥ shall there ever come a prouder monster out the tribe of Dan ? or can Lucifer himself be more Luciferian ?   And yet forsooth this wretch, to blind the eyes of such as will be deluded, will be called the servant of servants, and all is made whole again, as if the Scriptures and ancient modern¶ writers had not forepainted out such an antichrist, as should by all fraud of unrighteousness climb into the chair of universal pestilence, under the colour and vizard of Christ, faith and piety (without which the world would have abhorred him, as the devil himself), undermine Christ, and subvert the faith, and overthrow all religion under the names of Christ's Vicar, and Vice-God, become in effect Antichrist, and Anti-God.

Somewhat more tolerable of the two, and yet blasphemously enough, do they give it to the blessed Virgin, in the closes of their rhyming Marials ;** of whom I doubt not with Calvin to say, that if one could spit in her face, drag her by the hair of her head, or trample her under feet, she would count it a less injury, than to have ascribed unto her the divine attributes of her Lord and Saviour, who alone is the eye by which we see the Father ; the mouth by whom we speak to him ; the hand by which he distributes all his treasures of grace unto us, from whom so much is sacrilegiously detracted, as is superstitiously given to saint, angel, man, work, merit, or creature whatever.   Mad and blind idolaters are they, wittingly ignorant that Christ of purpose trod the wine-press alone,†† shed his blood alone

---

* Vide Eglinum Iconium in Apocalypsin.
† Universalis Sacerdos, Epist. 30, ad Maurit, Regist. lib. 6.
‡ Vide orationem Gnathonicam Episcopi Patris Vacensis ad Leonem X. in ultimo Concil. Lateranensi.   § Bellar. de Pontif. Rom. lib. ii. cap. 31.
∥ August. lib. contra adversarios legis, cap. 12; Hilar. cont. Anxentium. Pareus in Apoc. Gratserus in regia plaga.   ¶ Qu. ' Moral ?'—ED.
            ** Tu spes certa miserorum.
                Verè mater orphanorum,
                Tu levamen oppressorum,
                Medicamen infirmorum,
                Omnibus es omnia.
                (Cal. in Deut.)

†† Fox in Apoc.

upon the cross, implying to us, that if we shall mingle therewithal, his mother's milk, the blood of any martyr else, it loseth its healing virtue, and turns into bane and poison to our souls. This eagle's feathers will not abide blending with others ; this sovereignty will not endure either party or priority ;* no Jupiter will Christ be, but a Jehovah ; no helper, but author and finisher of our salvation.† To all he-saints, and she-saints, merit and free-will-mongers, shall he not in his jealousy break out and say, What have I to do with you ? If you can do all, or aught at all without me, then let me alone, let me either be saviour alone, mediator alone, all in all, or none at all.

But to leave these self-cozened, and self-condemned idolaters, whose whole church and religion holds more of our lady than of our Lord, leaves Christ the least of all to do in matter of merit and salvation, well were it with many of us, who profess and hold the precious faith of Christ aright in judgment and doctrine, if in affection and practice he were, I say, not all in all, but somebody, and something.‡ In our tongue, terms, and countenance he may be heard and seen, but in our lives and deeds where is he to be found ?§ As a saviour and benefactor, many will own him, but as a lord and lawgiver few do know him; the prime of their loves, joys, services, their back and belly, their mammon, or anything shall have before him. He that should be both Alpha and Omega, it is well if he be the Omega of their thoughts and cares. May it not be justified of too, too many, that an hawk, or an hound, a die, or card, or flower in the garden, a new suit and fashion of apparel, and such other nifles and trifles are their all and all ; with most, and such as are of the wiser sort, of this generation, that which Solomon justly calls nothing (for so he peremptorily terms that, which miserable men of this world place all their confidence in), call their Pandora,‖ their Jupiter, worship as the great Diana, empress and goddess of the whole world, take away that from them, and take away all ; the having of it makes them, the losing of it undoes them. Great I confess is the power, and ample the command, that Mammon hath in this world, for many purposes, and in many cases. But in the hour of sickness let Nabal call and cry unto it, and see if it can deliver him in the evil day, and in distress of conscience. Let Judas see what comfort his money will afford- him ; in the day of death and judgment, what does a penny and a pound, an empty purse and a full full purse, differ ? Does not too, too late experience teach them to cry out, All is vanity, and force them with the Emperor Severus to say, I have been all things, and it avails nothing ; if I had a thousand worlds, I would give them to be found of God in Christ. Worthily therefore did Charles the Great change that old by-word of money into his Christian symbol, ' Christ reigns, Christ overcomes, Christ triumphs, Christ is all in all.'¶

All then let him be in all our desires and wishes. Who is that wise merchant that hath heart large enough to conceive and believe as to this ? Let him go sell all his nothing, that he may compass this pearl, barter his bugles for this diamond. Verily all the haberdash stuff the whole pack of the world hath, is not worthy to be valued with this jewel. Worthy of him thou canst not be, unless thou countest all dross and loss to gain him that is gain in life and death, unless thou canst, as the apostles, forsake all to

---

* Bern. in Cant.   † Lactantius.   ‡ Erasmus in Evangel.
‌ ? Sine Christo Christiani. Bern.   ‖ Aug. de Civit. Dei.
    Sic vetus illud ; ' Nummus regnat, nummus vincit, nummus imperat,' mutavit Carolus magnus. Apud Reusnerum.

follow him ; yea, as divers of the common sort of his followers, lay down all at the apostles' feet for him who laid down himself for us, emptying himself of his glory, to fill us with grace and glory ; yea, unless thou canst make nothing of thyself, and thine own righteousness, which is the hardest thing in practice that may be. Few or none, I think, there be in the sound of the gospel, but have some faint and languid wishes, Oh that Christ were mine! But would they know the reason why they attain not the sweet fruition and ravishing possession of him, ' I am his, and he is mine.' The reason is, because he will not be found and had of such as seek but lazily and coldly for him, that inquire not through the streets, as undone without him ; as had, rather than want him, want all the world besides, and crying as the spouse, ' Where art thou whom my soul loveth ? Whom have I in heaven like unto thee ? Men and brethren, what shall I do that I may enjoy him ? Give me Christ, or I die ; draw me, that I may run after thee.'

These are the affections that befit them that are like to be speeders. The sluggard lusteth, and wanteth. He that desires anything above him, equally with him, or without him, shall never obtain him ; he will be wooed in the first place with all thy soul, strength, and might, with all that is within thee, or not at all of thee.

All let him be in all thy loves, and above all other beloveds ; when thou hast gotten him, think not enough to make much of him, but remember he well deserves to be, and must be, all in all. Take him not by the hand, but embrace him with both thine arms of love, and hold him with all thy might ; love him till thou be sick of love for him ; such as will suffice any one ordinary object, wife, friend, health, or wealth, will not give him content, nay, not a compound of many, but a catholicon of all ; as he hath deserved, so he deservedly challengeth. All thy weak rivulets united will scarce make one current strong enough for him. He that did all suffered all, took all thine infirmities, finished all for thee ; is it not reason he should be all in all, without any corrival in thy affections ? Such as entertain princes can never think they shew love enough unto them, and shall anything be enough for this Prince of our peace and salvation ? I cannot but reverence the memory of that reverend divine,* who, being in a deep muse after some discourse that had passed of Christ, and tears trickling abundantly from his eyes before he was aware, being urged for the cause thereof, confessed ingenuously it was because he could not draw his dull heart to prize Christ aright. A rare mind in Christians, who think every little enough, and too much for him.

All let him be in all our references and respects to others ; yea, in all our elections and valuations of wife, friends, companions, servants, only to prize Christ and his image, his faith and graces , not kindred, not wealth, not greatness, not other parts, but only the whole of a man, which is his Christianity ; dare not to yoke thyself unequally with any untamed heifer that bears not his yoke. Spouse not but in the Lord, call none father, mother, or brother, but such as he did, that is, such as do his Father's will ; set not poor Lazarus at the footstool of thy heart, and Dives, with his gold ring and his purple, in the throne of esteem, lest Christ be offended for having his glorious gospel in respect of persons. Oh what a difficult virtue is this when it cometh to the practising, to oversee and neglect all glistering lures and stales of the flesh, and to know no man for any such carnal caparisons, but to consider him as a new creature in Christ, and delight thyself in them as the most excellent of the earth, the only true

* Mr Welsh,

gentle, noble worthies of the world. How royal and memorable was that practice of Ingo, an ancient king of the Draves and Veneds, who, making a stately feast, not as Ahasuerus, to shew the bounty of his own, but the glory of Christ's, kingdom, set all his nobles, which were at that time pagans and unconverted to the Christian faith, in his hall below, and certain poor Christians in his presence chamber with himself, with kingly cheer and attendance ; at which, they wondering, he told them this he did not as king of the Draves, but as king of another world, wherein these were his consorts and fellow-princes ; these he saw with a spiritual eye, clad in white robes, and worthy his company ; to them he would give civil due in the regiment of the commonwealth, but those he must love and honour in his heart as beloved and honoured of God. A rare and noble act, recorded by three historians,* worthy to be read to the shame of our times, wherein men of mean greatness know not how to shew the least respect to a Christian or a minister, in the name of Christ, to account them worthy their company, whom they ought to have in singular respect, and to account their very feet beautiful for their Lord's and embassage's sake, only with this proviso, that divine and nimious adoration be not given ; a fault, on the other hand, common in Popery to their spiritual fathers and founders of orders and rules, whom they obey and reverence above Christ, as Gualter† gives instance in a doating abbot of Germany, who snibbed a novice for talking of Christ and the gospel, and not of the rules of Saint Francis and his own order ; a common fault among sectaries, who hold, vaunt, and denominate themselves of this or that man, of this or that faction ; whereas with God, I dare boldly say, there is neither Calvinist nor Lutheran, Protestant nor Puritan, Conformitan or Non-Conformitan, but faith and love in Christ is all in all.

All let him be in all our joys, instead of all other contents unto us ; good reason is it that he should fill our hearts that filleth all in all things. If he be ours, Apollo is ours, Cephas is ours, life and death, things present and to come, the world and all is ours ; we Christ's, and Christ God's. In him let our souls rest and rejoice ; I say again, rejoice always in him. If he be our shepherd, what can we want ? If he be our host, shall not our table be furnished and cup overflow ? If we err, is not he our way ? If we doubt, is not he the truth ? If we faint, is not he the life ? What loss should disturb us, what want distemper us, so long as we lose not Christ ? What if God take away all and give us his Son ; how shall he not with him give us all things requisite ? What other mystery enabled Paul to want and abound, but the fruition of him, whose goodness and greatness is such, that all accessions add nothing, all defects detract nothing, to the happiness of him that enjoys him who is ' all in all.' ‡

Above all ; all let him be with us in the main of all, that is, in the point of justification ; there (be sure) we repose all our confidence in him alone, bewaring lest we share and part stakes with any act of our own ; yea, with any grace or work of his in us, lest he be in vain and of none effect unto us. This glory will he by no means endure should be divided with any

---

* Æneas Sylvius, cap. 20. Europ. Aventinus, i. 3. Annalium Bavar. Goul.

† Gualt. in 1 Cor.

‡ Paulinus, Nola capta à Barbaris, precabatur ad dominum ne excrucier ob aurum et argentum, tu enim es mihi omnia. August. de Civit. Dei, lib. i. ca 10. Fas tibi non est salvo Cæsare de fortuna queri. Hoc incolumi nihil perdidisti; non tantum siccos oculos, sed et lætos esse oportet. In hoc tibi omnia, hic pro omnibus est. Seneca in consolatione ad Polybium, quanto aptius de Christo ad Christianum, &c.

coadjutor, concause, or copartner whatsoever ; nay, he takes it ill and indignly at our hands, if having him we hold not ourselves completely righteous in God's sight, if for want of this or that grace we mourn overmuch, hang down our head, and will not be comforted, as if his grace were not sufficient for us, as if he were not better than ten, yea, than ten thousand graces unto us. If we stand upon this or that measure of grace, twenty to one if we had that we desire, we would be full and rich and stand in no need of him who is the giver of all grace, or that we would be prouder of the gift than of the author of every good gift, and not rest in him that is our wisdom, our righteousness, and redemption.

All let him be in all the graces of sanctification, who only, indeed, is the very life and soul of them all. What is knowledge but heathenish science, if he be not its object, whom to know is eternal life ? What is faith, and trust, and hope in God, if not in and through Christ, but a Jewish, wild, ungrounded confidence ? Patience, but a stoical blockishness ? Temperance, and all the whole bevy of virtues, but either natural qualities or moral habits unacceptable to God, unprofitable to ourselves, sour grapes, glistering vices, if Christ be not the form of them, without whom there is no quality that God relisheth in us, whereof Christ is not the root; wherefore, as apothecaries sweeten all their confections with sugar, and perfume their cordials with musk, so let us grace all our graces in Christ, without whom fools we are to pride ourselves in anything that nature, custom, or education hath done for us, in comparison of that influence we receive, and of those rays that come from this Sun of righteousness. Fools are we, when wanting grace, power, or strength to overcome ill, or do well, to seek supply anywhere else save of him, of whose fulness all the saints that ever were received grace for grace. Who would go to the pack, when he may go to the warehouse ? Who would fetch water at the cistern, when he may have it at the spring head better cheap?

All let him be in all our deeds. Whether we eat or drink, whether we pray, read, or meditate, give alms or work in our callings, let all be done in the name of our Lord Jesus ; begun with his leave, performed with his aid, and concluded to his glory, without whom we can do nothing, no more than the bird can fly without wings,* the ship sail without wind or tide, the body move without the soul. Whatever good works we do with an eye from his, and a skew† unto our own names, the more pain we take, the more penalty of pride belongs unto us ; the more cost, the more loss ; we and our moneys shall perish together ; whereas the least cup of cold water given for his sake, who knows our works and the intent of our works, shall not lose its reward. Verily, who would be so foolish as to do any work to any other paymaster, or who so ungrateful that would not do any work that he should require, that hath so well deserved to command more than all we are or can do ? Is he all in all with us, if we dare deny him anything ? I commend not the discretion, but admire the fidelity and zeal, of that renowned Fox, who never would deny beggar that asked in his name. Then are works good works, 'when the love of Christ constrains us to them,' and when Christ's eye is more than all the world besides ; especially if, when all is done, all the thanks and praise of the deed redound to him. That policy is remarkable in the apostles' cure of the cripple, and in St Paul, in that he would never suffer any part of the repute or honour of any of his acts or labours rest upon his own head, but repels it forcibly from himself, and reflects it carefully upon his Lord Christ : 'Not I, not I, but the grace

* Macarius,   † That is, a squint.—ED.

of Christ in me ; I live not, but Christ in me.' In which *not*, says Brad-wardine, there lies a great deal of subtilty, like that of Joab, that, when he had fought the field and gotten the upper hand, sent for David to carry away the credit of the victory. Oh, how difficult is this for us, not to lurch some part of the praise, and suffer pieces of the sacrifice to cleave to our own nets and yarn. Whereas, in truth, our deepest wisdom and strongest policy lay in this, not to glory in our wisdom or strength, but to glory in the Lord who worketh all in all things.

All let him be in all our thoughts and speeches. How happy were it if he were never out of our sight and minds, but that our souls were directed towards him and fixed on him, as the sunflower towards the sun, the iron to the loadstone, the loadstone to the polestar. Hath he not for that pur-pose resembled himself to all familiar and obvious objects : * to the light, that so often as we open our eyes we might behold him ; to bread, water, and wine, that in all our repasts we might feed on him ;† to the door, that in all our out and ingoing we might have him in remembrance ? How happy if our tongues would ever run upon that name, which is honey in the mouth, melody in the ear, jubilee in the heart. Let the mariner prate of the winds, the merchant of his gain, the husbandman of his oxen.‡ Be thou a Pythagorean to all the world, and a Peripatecian to Christ ; mute to all vanities, and eloquent only to Christ, that gave man his tongue and his speech. How doth Paul delight to record it, and harp upon it eleven times in ten verses, which Chrysostom § first took notice of, 1 Cor. i. 10. And how doth worthy Fox grieve to foresee and foretell that which we hear and see come to pass, that men's discourses would be taken up about trifles and nifles, as if all religion lay in the flight and pursuit of one circumstance or opinion ; how heartily doth he pray, and vehemently wish that men would leave jangling about ceremonies, and spend their talk upon him that is the substance ; that learned men would write of Christ, unlearned men study of him, preachers make him the scope and subject of all their preach-ing. || And what else, indeed, is our office but to elevate, not a piece of bread, as the Romish priests, but Christ in our doctrine ; to travail in birth till he be formed in a people, to crucify him in their eyes by lively preach-ing his death and passion. The old emblem of St Christopher, intending nothing else but a preacher wading through the sea of this world, staying on the staff of faith, and lifting up Christ aloft to be seen of men. What else gained John the name of the divine, and Paul of a wise master builder, but that he regarded not, as the fashion is now-a-days, to have his reading, memory, and elocution, but Christ known and him crucified, and to build the church skilfully, laying the foundation upon this Rock,¶ of which, if we hold our peace, the rocks themselves will cry. This being the sum of our art and task, by the help of Christ, to preach the gospel of Christ, to the praise of Christ, without whom a sermon is no sermon, preaching no preaching. **

The sum of the sum of all is, that the whole duty of all men is to give themselves wholly to Christ, to sacrifice not a leg, or an arm, or any other piece, but soul, spirit, and body, and all that is within us ;†† the fat, the inwards, the head and hoof, and all as a holocaust to him, dedicating, de-voting ourselves to his service all the days and hours of our lives, that all our days may be Lord's days. To whom, when we have so done, yet must

---

* Musculus et Brentius in Johannem.   † Bernard.   ‡ Nolanus.
§ In Præfat. ad Concionem de Christo crucifixo. || Philip Melanct. in Rhetor.
¶ Lutherus.   ** Perkin. in Prophetica.   †† Nazianzenus de Spiritu.

we know we have given him so much less than his due, as we worms and wretched sinners are less than the Son of God, who knew no sin. To him therefore let us live, to him therefore let us die. So let us live to him that we may die in him, and breathe out our souls most willingly into his hands, with the like affection that John of Alexandria, surnamed the Almoner for his bounty, is reported to have done, who, when he had distributed all he had to the poor, and made even with his revenues, as his fashion was yearly to do in his best health, thanked God he had now nothing left but his Lord and Master Christ, whom he longed to be with, and would now with un-limed and unentangled wings fly unto : or as, in fewer words, Peter of old and Lambert of later times, ' Nothing but Christ, nothing but Christ.'

A Concludiug Supplication to Christ.

THOU, O Lord Christ alone, that knowest how little account I make of this little honour and service I have done unto thee; how far it is from me to think I have said or written anything worthy of thee, and yet do nothing doubt but thou likest and acceptest well of what I have done, because I know it came of thee, that I should have the least will or skill to do it. Now, therefore, what is it I have to petition unto thee for, but that, as thou alone art worthy of that poor all that I am and can, so thou wouldest please to take posses-sion, not of any corner or limb, but of the whole temple of my soul, and tabernacle of my body. Thou who scourgedst out of thy Father's house buyers and sellers, who turnedst out the mourners out of Jairus's doors, chase out of my heart all carnal desires and delights, troublesome passions, root out all thorny cares, cause every proud thought and high imagination to fall as Dagon before thee, that thou mayest invest thyself in thine own throne, rule and reign as sole commander of my will and affections, dwell in thine own shrine, adorn it here with thy grace till thou replenish it with thy glory, even till thou thyself resignest up thy sceptre to thy Father, and God become All in All.

Luther's Prayer at his Death.

THEE, O Christ! have I known, thee have I loved, thee have I taught, thee have I trusted. Into thy hands do I commend my spirit.

AUGUSTINUS.

OMNIS MEA COPIA EXTRA CHRISTUM EGESTAS EST.

Paulinus Nolanus Augustini Cœtaneus et Familiaris.

VITA Deus noster ; ligno mea vita pependit,
Ut staret mea vita Deo : quid vita rependam
Pro vita tibi Christe mea ? nisi forte salutis
Accipiam calicem, quo me tua dextra propinat,

Ut sacro mortis preciosæ proluar haustu.
Sed quid agam ? neque si proprium dem corpus in ignes,
Vilescamque mihi, nec sanguine debita fuso
Justa tibi solvam, quia me reddam tibi pro me.

Quis tibi penset amor ?   Dominus mea forma fuisti,
Ut servus tua forma forem, sic semper ero impar, &c.
Hæc tibi Christe tamen tenui fragilique paratu
Pro nobis facimus, toto quem corpore mundus
Non capit, angustum* cui cœlum, terraque punctum est, &c.

Tu precor oh fons Christe meis innascere fibris,
Ut mihi viva tuæ vena resultet aquæ.
Qui te Christe bibent dulci torrente refecti,
Non sitient ultra; sed tamen et sitient.
Totus enim dulcedo Deus, dilectio Christe es,
Unde replere magis quam satiare potes.
Jugifeuus semper biberis, turbamque sitimque,
Potantum exhaustu largior exsuperas.
Te Domine ergo Deus panem fontemque salutis,
Semper et esurient et sitient animæ.†

> Quid enim tenere, vel bonum, aut verum queant,
>   Qui non tenent summæ caput,
> Veri bonique fomitem et fontem, Deum ?
>   Quem nemo nisi in Christo videt.
> Hic veritatis lumen est, vitæ via,
>   Vis, mens, manus, virtus patris,
> Sol æquitatis, fons bonorum, flos Dei,
>   Natus Deo, mundi sator ;
> Mortalitatis vita, nostræ mors necis,
>   Magister hic virtutis est.
> Deusque pro nobis, atque pro nobis homo
>   Nos induendo se exuit, &c.
> Totaque nostra jure Domini vendicat
>   Et corda, et ora, et tempora ;
> Se cogitari, intelligi, credi, legi,
>   Se vult timeri, et diligi, &c.‡

Cum multa sint quibus per vitam egemus, ære inquam, lumine, alimento, vestibus, ipsis naturæ facultatibus et membris, fit tamen ut nullius usum ex omnibus semper et ad omnia desideremus, sed nunc illud, nunc istud adhibeamus, alias alio ad præsentem inserviente necessitatem ; vestem quippe induimus quæ alimoniam non præbet, sed cibum appetentibus aliud quærendum est : contingere seu tractare cupientibus manus sufficit, sed cum auscultare oportet nihil commodat.   At Salvator in ipso viventibus sic semper et omnimodis adest, ut quibuscunque eorum necessitatibus consulat, et ipsis sit omnia, nec alio se vertere, nec aliunde quærere quidquam sinat, non enim egent aliquo sancti quod ipse non sit : generat nimirum ipsos, educat, alit, et lumen ipsis est et oculus idem, altor simul et alimentum, panis, aqua, unguentum, vestimentum, via, et viæ terminus.   Membra nos sumus, ipse caput.   Certandum est ?   Ipse certat unà ; præclare certamus ?

* Felicis Natalis, 9.   † Idem de Celso pucro.   ‡ Idem ad Ausonium.

præses et arbiter certaminis; vincimus? ipse mox corona est, sic unde-
cunque mentem nostram ad seipsum advertit, suavi tyrannide ad se solum
trahens, sibi soli copulans et astringens, nec ad aliud effundi, nec ullius rei
amore implicari patitur: ipse domum cordis implet qui cœlum et terram
implet, et omnia in omnibus.*

Quid obsecro summum bonum in omnibus et per omnia quæritis, eo uno
neglecto qui omnia est in omnibus? Quare requiem animabus vestris
quæritis, et non invenitis? nisi quia perperam ibi quæritis ubi non est;
extra Christum quod in eo solo est. Ideoque carbones pro thesauro, arcam
pro pretio, munusculum pro amica, gaudiola pro Amasio, vestigia pro cervo,
phantasmata pro rebus, nubeculam pro Junone, ancillulas pro Penelope,
umbram pro corpore, viam pro patria, media pro fine, stillas tenuissimas
pro suavitatis abysso, vanitatem pro veritate amplexamini.†

Vana salus, et nulla salus considere mundo,
Vera salus Christo credere, et una salus.

Christ all alone salvation brings,
All other are deceitful things.

---

* Nic. Cabasilas de vita in Christo, lib. i.   † Hugo de sancto victore in Ecclesiastem.

THE LIFE OF FAITH.

TO THE

HONOUR AND USE OF THE RIGHT HONOURABLE

THOMAS EARL OF SUFFOLK,

LORD OF WALDEN,

KNIGHT OF THE HONOURABLE ORDER OF THE GARTER,

ONE OF HIS MAJESTY'S MOST HONOURABLE PRIVY COUNCIL.

THIS manual I first consecrate to your Honour. The greatest greatness hath no greater honour belonging to it, than to be an *Abrech* to persons, books, and causes of this nature. Such cedars have their spreadth and tallness to shelter such fowls of the heaven under their shadow ; and faith is content in this valley of unbelief to receive defence and countenance, where it rather giveth both. As Christ, in that old allegory of Christopher,* seems to be supported by him, whom in truth he supporteth ; and verily, such books as have life in them, give a longer life to their patrons, than the stateliest buildings and largest monuments.

Principally, I dedicate and devote it to your use ; charity began at home. I first meditated, collected, and scribbled them for mine own benefit, carried them about me with Antoninus' title, τα εἰς ἐμάυτον, Notes for myself. That which, with all my might in seeking, I have sought to attain, is the truth and effect of that which many things promise, but faith is only able to perform. Fulness of joy and constancy of content, in the midst of the changes, wanes, eclipses, and fulls of all external things, and that one day, as well as another, throughout the course of a man's life, in that latitude and extent whereof this life is capable. To cry out, ' I have found it, I have found it,' might savour of vanity and arrogancy. Altogether to deny it, were an injury to the truth of God's Spirit, word, and grace. Such as have found out sailing by the compass, the art of printing, or should one man discover a speedier passage to the Indies, or meet with a special cordial in physic,

* Melancth. in Rhetoricis.

or any less profitable secret, should he not justly be censured as envious and injurious to let such an one die with himself? What a sacrilege were it, then, to engross such a true elixir of spiritual life, as upon some proof I am sure these prescripts contain. The substance, therefore, of them I imparted first to my flock in sermons; nextly, considering how much I stood obliged to your Lordship, and what special use you might have of them, I translated and copied them out in the form wherein now I humbly commend and earnestly recommend them to your serious perusal and thorough trial.

If, upon both, good shall be thought the better, the more communicated, others shall account themselves beholden to your Honour as the principal occasion of publication.

More I would say, but I fear to spoil the elegancy of Augustine's preface to Romanian, by Englishing of it; wherein is the sum of what I would say. Whither referring your Lordship, I rest, and continue as ever I have done since my reference, without intermission, publicly and privately to pray to the Lord of lords, that you may find all favour in the eyes of God and man, and that all true happiness may be multiplied upon you and yours in this life and a better.

Your Lordship's in the Lord,

SAMUEL WARD.

THE LIFE OF FAITH.

CHAPTER I.

The Just shall live by his Faith.

THE basest life excels the best mere being, as much as Adam the red lump of earth whereof he was made. The living dog, the dead lion. Between life and life, what a breadth of difference is there! from the mushroom to the angels, how many kinds of life! Yea, in one and the same kind, how many degrees! The bond-slave hath a life as well as the king, the sick man as the whole, but such as in comparison may rather be termed a death. One best there is in every kind, as it approacheth nearest to that fountain of life and being, with whom to be, and to be most happy, is all one. Poor man hath, or rather had, a certain pitch and period of happy life, consisting in the image and favour of his Creator, from which having once fallen, it would pity one to see how lamely and blindly he re-aspires thereunto. The most part groping as the Sodomites after Lot's door, the blind misguiding the blind in the common labyrinth of error, each one imagining he hath found the way, and so tells his dream to his neighbour for a truth. The covetous, when he hath gotten goods, as if he had gotten the true good, applauds his soul, as if it were the soul of some swine, ' Soul, thou hast many goods, now,' &c. The voluptuous, when he hath satiated himself with the husk of pleasure, cries out, he hath lived the only royal and jovial life. The ambitious, when he hath climbed the pitch and slippery hill of honour, builds his nest in the stars, thinks himself in the sky, and highest sphere of happiness. Alas, alas! do not all these know they are in the chambers of death? Dead whilst they are alive; no better than walking ghosts in the shapes of living men; seeking and placing a spiritual and heavenly jewel in earthly pelf, in watery pleasures, in airy honours, which, being all dead, cannot afford that life which they have not themselves. Verily, if one live an hundred years, beget children, plant and build, and see no other good but such as these, the untimely birth is better than he. What then? Is this tree of life not to be recovered, nowhere to be found again? Yes, doubtless; though there be many by-paths, there is a way; though many errors, there is a truth; though many deaths, there is a life. And behold, O man, that standest upon the ways, inquiring after life, he that is ' the Way, Truth, and Life,' that came to heaven to vanquish death, and by his death hath brought thee to life again, who only hath the words of life, he hath shewed thee the true way to life. Hath he not twice or thrice shewed thee in this lively oracle of his, The just shall live by faith? Hab. ii. 4, Rom. i. 17, Gal. iii. 11, Heb. x. 13. Yea, but if a man like to ourselves might come from the dead, that hath made proof of this way and life, and would speak of his own experience, would we hear? Behold Paul slain by the law, revived by the gospel; what do we think of him? Did he not, from the time of his conversion to the time of his dissolution, enjoy a constant tenor of joy? live, if ever any, comfortably, happily? and doth not he tell us, even while he lived in the flesh, that he lived by the faith of our Lord Jesus Christ? Gal. ii. 20. Surely he must needs be blessed that liveth by the same faith with blessed Paul. Come, therefore, you which desire to see good days, and lay hold on the ways of life; 'believe and live.'

CHAPTER II.

Christ the Fountain, and Faith the Mean of Life.

WHAT then? Commit we sacrilege against Christ in deifying of faith? Rob we the Lord to adorn the servant with his divine honours? God forbid. Let that be given to Christ which is Christ's, and that to faith which is faith's. Let the power of life and death be entirely reserved, ever ascribed to the Lord of life, the well of life, the light and life of the world, the breath of our nostrils, the life of our lives. Thy body, O man! hath its soul, which enlives it, and so hath thy soul its soul whereby it lives, and that is Christ, the quickening Spirit. Take away the soul from the body, and earth becomes earth; sever Christ and the soul, what is it but a dead carrion? Elementary bodies lighten and darken, cool and warm, die and revive, as the sun presents or absents itself from them. Christ is to our souls the Sun of righteousness. Sin parts us, faith re-unites us; and so we live, primarily and properly, by Christ as by the soul; by faith, secondarily, as by the spirits, the bond of soul and body; by a personal and special faith appropriating Christ to the believer, as the leg or arm lives by proper sinews, arteries, and nerves, uniting it to the liver, heart, and head; such an one as Paul had in Christ that died for him, whereby he engrosseth the common God to himself, as if his and nobody's else.*

Thus saith he himself that is the Truth and the Life, 'I am the life and resurrection of the world; he that believeth in me, though he be dead, yet shall he live and not die,' John xi. 25. And this is the testimony of those three heavenly and earthly witnesses, 1 John v. : God gave life to the Son; and he that hath the Son, hath life; and he that hath faith, hath the Son. So that whatever we lend to faith, it redounds to the honour of Christ; neither have we any sinister intent to praise the womb or the paps of faith, but to cast all upon Christ, who gives and works this faith in us, vivifies and nourishes it, yea, justifies the imperfection thereof by the perfection of his merit. Nay, let faith know, that if she should wax arrogant towards her Lord, or insolent over her fellow-servants, she should, Lucifer-like, fall from her dignity; and in so doing, of the best of graces, become the worst of vices. Verily, what hath the habit of faith, in itself considered, better

---

* Chrysost. in 1 Cor. i. 10, Ευχαρισῶ τῷ Θεῷ μου, ἁρπαζει και ἰδιοποιειται τὸν χοίνον Θέον.

or equal with love? Is it not a poorer and meaner act to believe, than to love? more like a beggarly receiving, than a working and deserving hand? Hail, then, O faith, freely graced, graciously exalted above all Christ's handmaids. Thy Lord hath looked upon thy mean estate, because that, having nothing of thine own, as other virtues have, whence thou mightst take occasion to rejoice, thou mightst the better exclude that hateful law of boasting, the more humbly and frankly reflect all upon thy Lord, who willingly emptied himself, that he might fill thee with honour; whiles he says to the cured of the palsy, ' Go thy way, thy faith hath saved thee.' Henceforth calls he thee no more servant, or friend, but styles thee as Adam, his spouse, *chavah*, the mother of all living; counts it no injury to divide his praises with thee, likes it well that thou which dost nothing but by him, shouldst be said to do all things which he doth; ' to purify the heart, to overcome the world, to save men,' &c. And *è contra*, he to do nothing without thee, which yet does all of himself. He could work no miracles in Capernaum, because they had no faith. So glorious and wonderful things are spoken of thee (I had almost said), so omnipotent is thy strength, which hast said to the sun and moon, ' Stand ye still;' yea, if but as big as the least grain, canst say to the greatest mountains, ' Remove.' What can God do which faith cannot do, if requisite to be done? Questionless, justifying faith is not beneath miraculous in the sphere of its own activity, and where it hath the warrant of God's word. It is not a lesser power than these to say, ' Thy sins are forgiven thee, thy person is accepted of God; whatever thou askest, thou shalt have,' &c. Wherefore, we need not doubt under Christ, without fear of *præmunire*, or offence to his crown and dignity, to affirm of faith, that it is God's arm and power to the enliving and saving of every believer, as it is written, ' The just shall live by faith.'

CHAPTER III.

The third kind of the Life of Faith.

But lest we seem to speak swelling things, whiles we soar in the cloud of generalities, let us descend to some solid particulars. Three things there are, whence cometh death to the soul of man. Sin, with the guilt thereof, gives the first deadly blow, exposing it to the wrath of God, who is a consuming fire, whose anger is the messenger of death, whence came the first thunderbolt, striking through the soul that sentence of God to Adam, ' Thou shalt die;' and such as Nathan's to David, ' Thou hast sinned, and art the child of death.'

The second is the spot and corruption of sin depraving, yea, deading all the faculties of man to spiritual actions, which made Paul cry out, 'That which I would do, I do not; and, wretched man that I am, who shall deliver me from this body of death?'

Thirdly, that swarm of plagues, and army of punishments, in the rearward whereof comes first a second death. All which made Job cry out, ' Why is light given to him that is in misery, which longs for death more than for treasures, and joy when they can find the grave?' Job iii. 20.

Were it not for these three, man might live, fare, and do well; but sin having entered into the world, brought in death with it, which reigneth and triumpheth over the sons of Adam, with this three-forked sceptre, of guilt, of corruption, of punishment.

Here comes in faith with a threefold antidote, brings us to the tree of life, whose fruit and whose leaves heal us of the sting and deadly poison of sin, working in us a threefold life, opposite to the forenamed deaths.

The first is the life of righteousness, discharging us from the sentence of death, restoring the light of God's countenance, appeased in Christ our Surety, which made David cry out, 'Blessed is the man whose sin is covered,' Ps. xxxii.

The second is the life of the Spirit, or new life, regenerating and reviving every faculty, and quickening us to every good work, which makes Paul glory that ' he is able to do all things, through Christ enabling him,' Phil. iii.

The third is the life of joy and comfort, cheering the soul in the midst of all trials and tribulations, which made Job, in the valley of death, exult and trust in his living Redeemer, and Paul insult over all kind of calamities as more than conqueror, Rom. viii.

In these three, being contained whatever accomplisheth the life of the soul, may not faith well be said to supply abundantly all things pertaining to life and godliness ? But what do I treating of the kinds of life ? What should I blot paper, and tire my reader, in writing of the kinds of faith, the degrees of faith, or any other motions of faith, things so well known of those that know anything of Christ ? That nothing so much vexeth me to see so much spoken and written of faith, so little done by it, the theory of it so thoroughly canvassed and cleared in controversies and sermons, and the practice of it so obscured and disgraced in the lives of Christians.

CHAPTER IV.

The Use of Faith.

OH FAITH ! when I read of thee, when I meditate of thee, when I feel any part of thy virtue, I find thee to be a wonder-worker, I conceive nothing but high and stately things of thee. When I look into the world, and upon the lives even of such as call themselves believers, especially of the common sort, I begin to question my thoughts for dreams, and to say, Faith, thou art but a name, a sound, a mere word, no powerful thing. Why are many of thy followers so dead, so mopish, so melancholy? Why are worldly men as merry, as jocund as they ? Yea, why are many civil men as right-eous as they ? Whence should this wrong and disparagement proceed ? Is thy virtue exhausted, thy strength decayed, in this old age of the world ? or is it because men know thee not ? Verily, neither of these. No drug, no herb, so commonly extolled, so famously known.

Paul of old, Luther of late, with infinite more, every catechism have blazoned its name, described its nature, set out its properties and effects to the full. Only the misery is, the world either knows not the use, or forgets the practice of it. There wants a practical Luther, which should deal by faith as Socrates by philosophy, who brought it out of the skies and books into cities and houses, taught and urged the familiar and quo-tidian use of it.

Doth not all the praise, beauty, and lustre of faith, as well, or more than of other virtues, consist in action, and not in notion? Is not the gain and benefit of it in sense and feeling, not in knowledge or discourse? Is not the throne and seat of it rather in the heart than in the head? Who knows not there is a doctrinal speculation and discourse of faith easily by reading and hearing attained? Such an one as scholars, that never went out of their studies and schools, have of remote countries, of their commodious situations, pleasant rivers, high mountains, costly buildings, rich mines, jewels, and other commodities; with what a frigid and jejune contemplation is it, in comparison of that delight and benefit which the merchant and traveller enjoyeth by a real sight and fruition of them? What is the notional sweetness of honey or sugar to the experimental taste of them? And yet this airy, windy stuff is all the world, at this day, cares for and hunts after. The schoolmen and casuists, what do they but languish into useless, needless, and endless questions, spending their thoughts about this magnificent virtue, in cold and bloodless subtleties of the subject, object, kinds, &c.?

Preachers for the most part inuring themselves to declaim in praise of some moral virtue, and to inveigh against some vices of the times, happily sometimes find leisure to weave a curious spider's web in commendation of faith, rarely shewing or pressing the use of it.

In a word, will you see the fashion of the world? The schools dispute of it, the pulpit preacheth of it, profession talketh of it, profane men swear by it, two or three, few or none, live by it. I met with a story of an ancient Hebrew, a reverend Rabbi, who, that he might the more lively convince the people in his time of their neglect of practice of this excellent grace, put himself into the habit of a mountebank or travelling aquavitæ-man, and made proclamation of a sovereign cordial water of life he had to sell. Being called in, and demanded the show of it, he turned them to the Bible, the fountain of life, and to several places of it, as the 34th psalm, &c., intimating that if they would make use, and daily drink of the water they had, they might (as it should seem he did) live far better, and more comfortably than usually they did.

And, indeed, why is there such a price put into the hands of fools, that know not the worth and improvement of it? As secrets and mysteries in good artizans, that have sometimes a faculty whereby they can earn ten or twenty shillings the day, and might live as well as landed men; but then they have another boon withal, they love idleness, pastime, and good-fellowship, and so live like beggars; or as land and money in the hands of those (whom we therefore aptly call misers) to have and to hold, but never make good use of it. Who may well be said to use the world as if they used it not, for they put it forth to use, or lock it from themselves and others, go basely, fare hardly, live in debt to back and belly, as if they knew not it would buy them good meat and good clothes, and other necessaries and conveniences for their lives. It is possible a man may have a tool, a medicine, or an engine, and not the skill or strength to use it. It is possible a man may have a gift of God, and not the gift to use it thoroughly, else needed not Paul call on Timothy to stir up the gift that was in him. Among all the gifts of God there is none more useful than faith. Others are profitable for some few things; this is for this life, and the life to come, for all parts and purposes of our lives; in the use of it manifold and rich every manner of way.

CHAPTER V.

The first use of Faith to new-born Babes.

AND first, let me begin with thee that art beginning to live this life, thou embryo that art in hatching, that hast so much life as to know thyself dead in sin, and to desire to live in Christ (for what should I cast away speech upon skelets* and skulls, carnal men I mean, mere strangers to this life of faith? I expect not reading should put life and spirit into them, only I pray for such, that they may hear God's voice in the ministry, and live). But as for thee whom the law hath wounded, and the gospel is healing, who art even at the birth, and stickest between the knees, only wantest power to come into the light, who livest, but feelest not thy life, holdest Christ but with benumbed hands, believest, but canst not yet believe thou hast faith, what is the matter thou art still ensnared in the cords of death? Why loosest thou not the handkerchiefs, and comest out of thy grave, and walkest cheerfully in the land of the living? Suffer faith to do her perfect work in thee, to form Christ in thee. Suffer not thyself always to be detained in the throes and throbs of fear and doubt.

The common causes of this slowness of belief and snares of death, I observe in most to be one of these three :

First, Immoderate aggravation of sin.

Secondly, Foolish and proud humility.

Thirdly, Preposterous desire of sanctification before justification.

First, Thou wouldest believe, but thou hast been a sinner. Whom came Christ to save but sinners? And whom doth he justify but the ungodly? O, but thy sins are scarlet, crying, scandalous sins! Said I not all things are possible to faith, only if thou canst believe? Are not all faults easily pardonable to an infinite mercy, which exceeds man's as heaven doth earth, which can readilier forgive seventy than man seven offences? Well did Martinus answer the devil, himself objecting his former life to him, that even he might be pardoned if he could believe. Did not Christ take the flesh of Rahab and Bathsheba, and did he refuse to take their sins upon him? Did not his blood wash David's bloody sin as white as snow? Doth not he delight to forgive much, that he may bind to love much? Shall not his favour abound to the sense of thy faith, where sin hath abounded to the wounding of thy heart? But thou art an old habituate sinner. As if Christ came from heaven to cure only small scars, green cuts, and not deep inveterate wounds, diseases of eight, of twelve, of eight and thirty years old, to cast out single devils, and not legions also. O, then, take heed thou add not to thy great and many sins a greater than all, Cain's sin, which was greater in infidelity than in fratricide. All thy help is to look off thyself, an object of confusion, and to look upon Christ, an object of consolation ; and then, how fiery and deadly soever thy sting be, by mere looking (a strange cure, I confess, yet most approved), that is, by sole believing, thou shalt be cured, and live.

Secondly, But, forsooth, thou wilt be more mannerly than so. With Peter, thou wilt not suffer Christ's precious hands to wash thy foul feet. Take heed thy modesty turn not into pertinacy, lest he swear in his anger thou shalt have no part in him, if thou stubbornly refuse his gracious offer. He liked well the humility of that Canaanitish that bore the term of dog, but better her confidence that would not be said nay of the crumbs of his

* That is, 'Skeletons.'—ED.

table. And shalt thou not ten times more honour him and please him in trusting his mercy, and sealing to his truth, than in fearing his justice, and dreading his power? Take heed of pride in the clothes of humility. Be not deceived; it is pride, and high pride, not to come when thou art called. Faith is obedience, and obedience is more acceptable than courtesy and compliment. The sooner thou comest the better welcome. It is rudeness, and not good manners, not to do as thou art bidden to do, yea, so often and earnestly charged to do. To do the work of God is to believe in him (John vi.) whom he hath sealed and sent to be thy Saviour.

Thirdly, Oh! but thou wouldst fain first repent, amend, and do some good works, and then thou wouldst be bold to come. That is, thou thinkest thou shalt not be welcome unless thou come with thy cost. Thou wouldst accept of a pardon if thou mightst pay for it; but his are free, and he bids thee come and buy without silver, or else he says, thou and thy money perish. Thou wouldst go the old and natural way to work. 'What shall I do to inherit everlasting life?' but that is now for-done and impassable through our infirmity. Besides, before thou canst walk or work, thou must be alive. Did Christ indent with Zaccheus for restitution and alms? Or Paul bid the jailor first repent, become a new man, and then believe? No, they knew that the one would voluntarily, necessarily, together and immediately follow, or rather accompany the other. Wherefore swim out of these weeds, lay hold on the rock, and to facilitate thy birth by the act of believing, set before thy eyes Christ's freedom to all suitors in the time of his flesh, repelling none that truly desired the price of his blood. And especially, God's esteem of faith above all other graces, deeds, or acts of thine.

Study, strive, endeavour to believe, as thou dost in a difficult point to conceive. Pray for a faculty, and for the act of believing. Be not ever believing, and never a believer; ever beginning to live, and never living. Live to-day, to-day is salvation offered, step from death to life, and write this day thy birthday, and number from hence the days of thy life, in which, of a child of perdition, thou art made the son of God through faith, and so made for ever. Dost thou believe this with thy whole heart? Drive on the chariot of thy life with joy and rejoicing till thou come to the mark.

But what sign shall I have of the truth of my faith? May it not be presumption, if without repentance and sanctity? How shall I be sure it is not that vain and dead faith St James speaketh of!

At the first it shall suffice to find and feel a change of the mind, an unfeigned purpose, desire, and resolution of new universal obedience, which is contemporary with faith, though the younger and a second brother in order of nature; which, where it is, sufficeth to warrant faith, and to embolden the conscience in the first act of conversion. Zaccheus the jailor, and all new converts, had not any more, could have no experience of amendment of life, and yet relied upon the word, 'Believe, and thou shalt be saved.'

CHAPTER VI.

The use of Faith to Young Men in Christianity.

Put off now thy sackcloth and ashes; put on the garments of joy and gladness. Let not white raiment be wanting, nor oil to thy head. Live,

I say, live to-day, live to-morrow, live, O Christian, for ever. Not for one or a few days, but all the days of thy life.

This thou mayest do, if thou wilt learn to use thy faith, not as men use wedding apparel, for a week or two after marriage, and then lay it up for high and solemn days only. This indeed is the fashion of believers at their first conversion, being justified, to have peace and joy in believing the remission of their sins, and for a while to be glad of their estate, but then to neglect and terminate the use of faith, as if it had now done all it should or could do ; except till they relapse again into some foul sin, then to recover life again, using it as usquebagh and strong waters for swoons and heart qualms only, not being acquainted with a daily and quotidian improvement of it ; which ought to be as constant and continuate as is the use of fire and water, of salt, of bread, or wine, or whatever is more ordinary and necessary than other: such as no part of our lives may well be without. Serves faith for entrance and beginnings, and not for proceedings and increasings ? Are we not nourished by the same elements of which we consist ?

Is faith the midwife, and breeder of joy and peace, and not the nurse and foster-mother of them ; cherishing and feeding thee till thou come to a full and perfect age in Christ ? Is not the fruit of it sweeter in the ear than in the blade ?

Hearken therefore to me, O thou of little faith, and less use of it. Dost thou desire to have a continual feast, to rejoice always in the Lord ? I know thou desirest it with all thy soul.

Let me prescribe a diet, a daily diet without omission, strictly to be kept (the Lord give thee and me grace to observe it). Look how duly thou refreshest thy bodily spirits, by use of repast or recreations ; so often at the least be sure to cheer up thy soul by the use of thy faith.

Let thy soul have two or three walks a day up to Mount Tabor, that is, into some retired place of meditation and prayer, such as Isaac's field, Cornelius's leads, David's closet, &c.

But what is there to be done? I answer, still make use of thy faith.

But what is that you call using of faith ? I now come to the point, to the chief mystery of spiritual life. Stir up thy soul in this mount to converse with Christ. Look what promises and privileges thou dost habitually believe, now actually think of them, roll them under thy tongue, chew on them till thou feel some sweetness in the palate of thy soul. View them jointly, severally. Sometimes muse of one, sometimes of another more deeply, and lest (as patients oft do in physicians' bills) thou still complain of obscurity, thus do : think with thyself how excellent a thing it is to have all thy debts cancelled, how sweet a thing to have God appeased, how glorious a thing to be the son of God, how happy and safe a condition for thee to be sure of thy perseverance and salvation, how pleasant a state to be void of the fear of death and hell, how richly and stately a thing to be heir of glory.

Feast-makers in ancient time had special officers that cheered up their guests ; they thought it not enough to set store of meat before them, but one must come in and say, Fall to and be merry, Let us eat and drink, It is a good time, &c.

Thus say to thyself, as Paul to the Corinths (ἑορτάζωμεν), Let us feast and be merry. Christ hath made holidays, our paschal lamb is slain. Have any more cause to be merry ? With these soliloquies mingle some ejaculations to heaven, for grace and aid. And leave not, descend not this mount till thou findest and feelest thy soul in some cheerly plight, revived and warmed with these spiritual flagons of wine, in the strength whereof thou mayest walk all the day following.

This is that which the Spouse calls 'walking into the gardens and eating of the fruits,' &c. Which, in plain terms, I call using of faith, and living by faith. Which, if thou wilt duly inure thyself unto, thou wilt not marvel why I called it ' ascending Mount Tabor.' Thou wilt say thyself, upon good proof, ' It is good to be here,' daily to be here, often to come hither. This is that exercise of faith which Paul enjoins Timothy, and calls stirring up, or enkindling.

Fire in the embers unstirred glows not, heats not the house ; sugar in the cup unstirred sweetens not the wine. And in such it is all one not to have faith, and not to use it. It may well be said of money-hoarders, They have no quicksilver, no current money; they have no more that which they have than that which they have not. And so of such believers as do not thus use their faith, they have no lively faith. They were almost as good (for matter of feeling, and for present comfort) be without faith. A man is little the better for a sleeping habit. It is a rare portion, saith Solomon, and that which God gives only to such as are good in his eyes, to make use of wealth, to eat, to drink, and be merry : it is a much rarer to use faith. What is a man the better for a lock, if he have not the key to use it withal? It is not a trade, but a trade well followed ; it is not land, but land well tilled ; that maintains men.

O that this did as clearly appear to the world in the matter of faith, as it doth in all other habits, graces, gifts, virtues, and good things whatsoever, that the principal beauty and benefit of them consists in use, fruition, and action ; not the bare possession ; yea, the very increase and perfection of them ! Use limbs, and have limbs ; the more thou dost, the more thou mayest. The oftener the liberal man gives alms, and does good turns, the more his liberality grows and shines. Use will breed perfectness, and through disuse things perish and come to nothing ; as the ploughshare, laid up, rusts and consumes ; employed, glisters, doth good, and lasts the longer. Let any man diligently and thoroughly improve, and great will be his faith, and great the joy it will bring in.

CHAPTER VII.

An Enforcement of the former Use, with a Reproof of the Neglect and Disuse of Faith.

WHEREFORE I say again, ' Live by faith;' again I say, always live by it, rejoice always through faith in the Lord. I dare boldly say, It is thy fault and neglect of this exercise if thou suffer either thy own melancholy humour or Satan to interrupt thy mirth and spiritual alacrity, and to detain thee in dumps and pensiveness at any time. What if thou beest of a sad constitution, of a dark complexion? Is not faith able to rectify nature ? is it not stronger than any hellebore ? Doth not an experienced both divine and physician ⁕ worthily prefer one dram of it before all the drugs in the apothecary's shop for this effect ? Hath it not sovereign virtue in it to excerebrate† all cares, expectorate all fears and griefs, evacuate the mind of all ill thoughts and passions, to exhilarate the whole man ? But what

⁕ Dr Bright of Melancholy.　　　　† That is, ' clear the brain of them.'—ED.

good doth it to any to have a cordial by him if he use it not? to wear a sword soldier-like by the side, and not to draw it forth upon an assault? When a dump overtakes thee, if thou wouldst say to thy soul in a word or two, 'Soul, why art thou disquieted? Know and consider in whom thou believest.' Would it not presently return to its rest again? Would not the Master rebuke the winds and storms, and calm thy mind presently? Hath not every man something or other wherewithal he useth to put away dumps, to drive away the ill spirit, as David with his harp: some with merry company, some with a cup of sack, most with a pipe of tobacco, without which they scarce ride or go. If they miss it a day together, they are troubled with rheums, dulness of spirits. They that live in fens and ill airs, dare not stir out without a morning draught of some strong liquor. Poor, silly, smoky helps in comparison of the least taste (but for dishonouring of faith I would say whiff), or draught of faith.

O that wise Christians would as often take the one side as idle gulls do the other! Would not the drawing in of sweet air from the precious promises breed excellent blood and cheerly spirits? It is a mystery in bodily health that to keep the arteries and the nostrils, veins and other passages to head, heart, and liver clear and free from colds and obstructions, maintains a healthful and cheerful temper. The pipe of faith is the same to the soul. He that is asthmatical, narrow-breathed, or strait-breasted in his faith, cannot be but lumpish and melancholy. Wherefore as thou lovest thy mirth above all other, tend this vital artery; above all keepings keep thy faith, and it will keep thy joy. It will keep it in an even, everflowing current, without ebb and flow, clouds and eclipses, turning ever upon the hinges of heavenly and solid mirth. And, indeed, how or why should it be otherwise? Do not Christians consider how unseemly it is for them to go drooping, hanging the head? Is any so simple to think, because he is a Christian, that he should affect a sad carriage, a dejected look, a demure countenance like an image? Away with such monkish hypocrisy! How doth it become the righteous to rejoice? Do they not consider how they wrong themselves of the main benefit of their justification? What is a Christian but his mirth? Wherein doth the kingdom of heaven consist but in joy? Do they not see how they offend standers-by and beholders? Is not heaviness a check that drives away, and mirth as a lure that wins, to the liking of their profession? Men wonder to see a rich man, that hath the world at will, all things at heart's desire, to be but in a fit of heaviness. What, say they, should he ail? The Irish ask such what they mean to die. But I wonder a thousand times more to see one that hath Christ his friend, that believes God to be his shepherd, that knows all must work for the best, to be at any time out of tune, or out of sorts. For a Nabal to be all amort like a stone, it is no news to me; but to see Nehemiah's countenance changed, there must needs be some extraordinary cause. Should such a man as he fear, or cark, or grieve? What if it do not yet appear what thou shalt be? Is a young ward prouder and gladder (in his minority) of an uncertain reversion, than a yeoman of his present estate? And is not faith an hypostasis and evidence to thee of an infallible inheritance? Canst thou be sad, which mayest say, not to thy belly, but to thy soul, Thou hast, not many goods, but fulness of all treasures, laid up, not in the earth, where moth and canker and thieves may come; but in heavenly places, out of the devil's reach, and that not for many years, but for ever and ever, never to be taken from thy soul, nor thy soul from them? O thou vain man! shew me thy faith by thy joy.

If thou livest dumpishly, and yet say thou livest by faith, I will as soon believe thee as him that shall say he hath the philosopher's stone and lives like a beggar. If it were ever well with thy faith, could it ever be amiss with thee? Should not the temper of thy body follow the temper of thy soul, and the temper of thy soul the temper of thy faith? The body may incline the soul, but the soul commands the body, and faith is the lord of them both. According to thy faith so be it unto thee, so will it be with thee. Use thy faith, and have joy; increase thy faith, and increase thy joy.

CHAPTER VIII.

The Use of Faith to a grown Christian.

NAY, Christian, now I have gotten thee hither, I must draw thee yet a peg higher, and tell thee, it is a small thing for thee to come to an ordinary pitch of cheerfulness, except thy joy exceeds the mirth of a worldling, yea, of a professed epicure, in the quality and quantity of it. If thy mirth be not a sweeter and more ravishing mirth, of an higher kind, of a more pure defecate* nature, of a more constant tenure, than any carnal man whatever, thou disparagest faith, thou art very little and young in the kingdom of heaven, which consists not in meats and drinks, but in joy unspeakable and glorious, in the joy of the Holy Ghost. And must not that needs be another manner of joy than ever entered into the heart of a natural man, than ever a Sardanapalus tasted of? Yes, undoubtedly. So must be construed that text, 1 Cor. ii., not of the joys of heaven, which here the spiritual man himself cannot tell what they shall be, but of the gospel's joy, of the wine and fatlings already prepared, and now revealed to the believer by the Spirit; which if the carnal man scorn and scoff at, thou canst no more help him, or prove to him, than a seeing man to a blind man, that he sees orient rich colours. It is enough for thee secretly to feel and enjoy it. Only it ought in thy life to be expressed; yea, so to shine in thy forehead, so to be read in the very face of thee, that their teeth may be set on edge, and that they may inquire, what is thy beloved above other beloveds? what is that makes this man thus merry in all estates? Thus let them envy at thine, let not thy soul descend to theirs.

Are not the gleanings of Ephraim better than the vintage of Abiezer? Shouldst thou that hast tasted of the grapes of Canaan, long after the onions and garlic of Egypt? Is Pharphar like unto Jordan? hast not thou rivers of water ever flowing out of thy belly? and wilt thou stoop to their puddle waters, to their stolen waters, bousing, carding, dicing, whoring, &c., which should not thy soul altogether loathe and abhor, after the taste of faith's nectar and ambrosia? But even their ordinary and lawful delights, the wine and oil, music, hunting, hawking, &c. To these God allows thee to stoop for thy body's sake, as the eagle to the prey, or as Gideon's soldiers to sup thy handful, not'to swill thy bellyful. If Plato could tell the musicians, that philosophers could dine and sup without them, how much more easy is it for St Augustine to wean himself from the childish rattles and May-games of carnal delights, to be merry without the fiddle? Good leave hast thou, yea, right and title to use all external recreations, whereof before thou wert

* That is, without sediment or alloy.—ED.

but an usurper, but use them aright as if thou usedst them not, knowing how to put thy knife to thy throat, and how to be without them, to be as one that liveth not by them, but by faith.

Were it not odious to see a man that hath a spouse peerless for beauty, to live with a deformed blouse? to see one professing some liberal science, to live by some base manual trade? No better sight is it to see a Christian upholding his joy by coarse and earthly pleasures, that hath more noble and generous, yea, angelical delights; than which, what hath heaven better but in degree only, and manner of fruition? what hath this world comparable? Alas! poor philosophers, when I read your treatises of tranquillity of mind, of consolation, of remedies against both fortunes, though in some things you come near the kingdom of heaven, yet how dull are your comforts to one of ours? the highest of yours to the lowest of ours? Had you but through a crevice, or lattice seen the things which the eye of faith seeth with open face, how would you, in comparison of Christianism, have loathed your stoicism and epicurism? Had you but with the tip of your tongue tasted of faith's dainties, how would you have magnified faith above all your cardinal virtues! You that so composed your lives by jejune and empty contemplations of an antarchy in virtue by the rules of nature; what stately lives would you have led and lived, if the grace and hopes of the gospel had appeared to you by the rules of faith! As for you, poets of the lighter and pleasanter vein, when I read your odes and sonnets, chanting out your choice joys and loves, your wishes and vows, framing a conceited happiness to yourselves, as the highest you could imagine or desire, what low strains and mean air do I reckon them, in comparison of our Christian and divine hymns! what pitiful subjects for such sublimated wits! What difference between your oaten pipes, and our heavenly harps! Solomon, that loved both these loves, lived both lives, and sung songs of both sorts; when God raised his muse to a higher tune, and taught it to sing the *Song of Songs*, how despised he his former windy vanities, in comparison of his new spiritual delicacies!

Wherefore, O Christian, that hast such transcendent objects of thy thoughts above all other men, why shouldst thou not ever keep thy soul upon the wing, ever in a manner be in the third heavens, rolling and tumbling thy soul in these beds of roses: I mean these meditations of thy justification, sanctification, and salvation through Christ, without which why should one day pass thee? why any one part of a day? Why should not thy soul have her due drinks, breakfasts, meals, undermeals, bevers,* and aftermeals, as well as thy body? Thus to redeem time, thus to task and tie thy soul to such a heavenly round of work, would it not make the mill of time pleasant, the yoke of business easy? would not precious time glide swiftly and easily away, like a boat with full wind and tide, needing no oars; or a free mettled horse needing no spurs, needing no idle pastime to drive it before thee? Shall it not be a pleasure to thee to want other pleasures? Thus mayest thou make all thy days, Christ-tides, Easters, Whitsundays, birthdays and holidays; not envying Felix his felicity, Festus his festivity, not Dives his daily purple and delicious fare, but living a life kingly and angelical in comparison of the vulgar sort.

That is, 'draughts.'—ED.

CHAPTER IX.

An Objection Answered, and Passage made to the Life of Sanctification.

HAPPILY thou repliest, all this were possible and easy, were it not for that even amidst this diligent practice of faith, even in the strictest watch, in many things the best fail, many known frailties will escape, and more escape unknown; and how can mirth choose but be damped with frequent slips?

The answer is, such an one as keeps the watch of his God, and pretermits no day without the forementioned duties, shall seldom or never fall into any foul slough, and dash the ship of his faith against any dangerous rock; and if he do, long he cannot lie, but his faith will set him on work to go out, weep bitterly, and make his peace presently with his Lord and conscience, that he may enjoy his wonted repasts. And for his ordinary infirmities it will daily fetch him out a pardon of course, washing and scouring his soul every morning and evening, more duly than any pharisee his face or hands; and set him on work every day as he runs into arrearages, to draw the red lines of Christ's cross over the black lines of God's debt-book. And what if, as an all-seeing God, he sees our violation of his law, and knows better than our own consciences every peccant act of ours, in thought, word, or deed; what if God look upon the handwriting against us; doth he not see the bills cancelled with the precious blood of his Son and our Surety? which, for matter of guilt, defilement, and punishment, is all sufficient to expunge, cover, nullify, abolish, and wholly to take away our sins, in such sort, that he neither sees, will see, nor can see, them as sins and debts bearing action against us, obliging us to any penalty, no more than the creditor who, though he sees the items in his book, and knows what debts have been, yet sees them crossed, cleared. And what thought then need the debtor take for such debts? Why, but is not this to make faith a pander to sin? And to make good the papists' and worldlings' slander of Solifidians, that make no more of it but drink and take tobacco; sin, and believe; get a pardon of the old and a license for the new.

Oh! peevish and froward generation, to whom it is not given to know the mystery of faith, which is of the nature of sovereign, mundifying* waters, which so wash off the corruption of the ulcer, that they cool the heat and stay the spread of infection, and by degrees heal the same; and of cordials, which so comfort and ease the heart, as also they expel the noxious humours and strengthen nature against them.

These are ministered only to prepared bodies, these pearls are not for swine, this divinity we preach not in Gath and Askelon to uncircumcised profane ones, that will turn every good thing to their own destruction. But this belongs to the sealed fountain, to the spouse of Christ alone, which, when she hath washed her feet, how loath is she to foul them again? When she hath appeased her beloved, how doth she adjure herself and others, by the hinds and roes, not to awaken and offend him again?

The text saith not, Every hypocrite, every profligate professor of faith, that lives as he lists, shall live by his faith, but the 'just,' or 'righteous.' Which golden sentence is, indeed, ambiguously enunciated of purpose by the Holy Ghost, that it may either way be taken, 'The just by his faith shall live;' or, 'The just shall live by his faith;' yet so, as it hath but one right ear

* That is, cleansing.—ED.

to be holden by, and that is only for the hand of the righteous man ; implying that whosoever believes or lives by his faith, is also, and must of necessity be, a righteous man, a just man, not only imputatively, but inherently
in part; such an one as unfeignedly loveth righteousness, studieth the
practice of it, denieth and hateth all unrighteousness, endeavoureth every
day to be more and more righteous, and so deserveth the denomination of
righteous.

So that, look how the rational soul includeth and implieth the animal, so
doth justification sanctification, being individual.*

CHAPTER X.

How Faith Sanctifies and Mortifies.

So I slide into the second part or kind of Christian life, consisting in holiness and righteousness, which I shall easily demonstrate not only to be an
individual companion, but a natural and necessary effect of faith.

For look how the strength of the heart breeds not only cheerfulness but
activeness ; motion as well as health (whence it is that life is put for liveli-
ness and agility) drives away all lassitude, hebetude, and indisposition,
brings in aptness and delight to stir; the like doth faith in the soul, which
may, as the former in the body, for a time stand with some slight distempers, spots of the skin, ache of limbs, but not long with deadly diseases,
either vanquishing them or vanquished by them. This noble use of faith will
excellently appear in both the parts of this new life, mortification and vivifi-
cation ; and in each of these two manner of ways faith doth produce this
effect : partly as a moving, partly as a procreant cause. In the first kind,
admirable is the Peitho and Suadeo† of faith above all the oratory in the
world. All the common incentives taken from profit, pleasure, and honour,
all the topic places of logic, figures of rhetoric ; what poor and weak engines
are they to the irresistible petarre of faith, which sayeth but Ephphatha,
and presently our everlasting gates yield and stand open.

For thus it goes to work with us; Hath Christ given himself for thee, forgiven thee so many debts, conferred favours of all kinds upon thee; and
what hast thou to retribute ? If thou give all thy goods to the poor, thy
body to the fire, thy soul to his service, yea, were every hair of thine head
a man or angel, were not all short of recompense ? Lovest thou, lovest thou
this Saviour of thine ? and darest thou, or wilt thou dare, venture upon anything displeasing him ? is there anything too good, too hard or dear for him ?
Mary, if thy tears will wash his feet, wilt thou not pour them out ? Is
thine hair too good to be the towel ? Is there any spikenard too costly for
his head ? Joseph, the Lord requireth the handsel of thy tomb, and wilt
thou deny him ? Zaccheus, lovest thou thy wealth above his honour that
hath saved thee ? Stephen, lovest thou thy life above thy Master ? Can,
or did, any believer give the nay to these melting commands, or commanding entreaties of faith ? Will it take the repulse ? Doth it not constrain
and extort more than all racks and strappadoes ? allure more than all wages
and prizes ? Doth not this magnet as easily draw weighty iron as other jet
doth straws ? So that when thou wouldst be sure to speed and obtain any-

* That is, indivisible or inseparable.—ED.

† That is, ' the πειθω and *Suader*,' the persuasive power of faith.—ED.

thing of thine untoward heart, set faith a-work to make the motion, and that will be sure to speed; not only by this persuading faculty, but also by a divine power secretly effecting what it requires, conveying into the heart will, and ability unto the deed. It stands not without doors as a mendicant, flexaminous * persuader, but enters into the closets of the heart, shoots the bars, unlocks the bolts, takes away all reluctation and redaction, infuseth a pliable willingness; of wolfish and dogged, makes the will lamb-like and dove-like; of wild and haggard, morigerous and mansuete.

No otherwise than the medicine curing the vicious stomach, and restoring it to health, makes it long for wholesome meat, as before for coals and ashes.

All this it doth by fetching supernatural efficacy from the death and life of Christ; yea, part of that mighty power whereby Christ raised himself from the dead, cured all diseases, and wrought all his miracles; by the virtue whereof it metamorphoseth the heart of man, creates and infuseth new principles of action. Make trial of this in mortifying thy flesh to sin, and quickening thy spirit to holiness.

For example, complainest thou of some prevalent corruption, some violent passion that oft carries thee headlong against thy desire and resolution, as Castrusius to Jerome, Who shall help me subdue Nebuzaradan, Goliah, Holofernes, my raging lusts that are too mighty for me? Answer thyself as David himself to the like, ' Through thee, O Lord, shall we do valiantly; over Edom shall I cast my shoe,' &c. Yea, when thou hast spent all thou hast upon other physicians, tried all moral conclusions of purposing, promising, resolving, vowing, fasting, watching, self-revenging, yet get thee to Christ, and with a finger of faith touch but a hem of his garment, and thou shall feel virtue come from him to the curing of thy disease. What if thou hast often encountered thine enemy and received the foil, relapsed after victory? Yet cast not away the shield of faith; but, with the Israelites against the Benjamites the second and third time, set afresh in the name of the Lord, and they shall fly before thee.

Complainest thou with Augustine of his inbred, hereditary, habitual, inveterate vices, holding thee in the adamantine chains of custom, against which thou hast often resolved and resolved, *modo et modo*, now I will leave them, and now I will forsake them. Why should I not, as well as such and such, as Potitian and Victorinus? And yet they keep thee prisoner still, full against thy will and endeavours. Find out the cause which he had revealed to him, *In te stas et non stas*, Thou standest upon thine own feet, and therefore fallest so foully; thou wilt, like a child, go alone and of thyself, and therefore gettest so many knocks. Die to thyself, renounce the broken reed of thine own free will, which hath so often deceived thee, and put all thy trust in the grace of Christ, and it will crucify the old man, and give him his *hoc habet*, his death's wound, pierce his sides, and break his knees in pieces. Be weak in thyself and strong in the Lord, and through faith thou shalt be more than conqueror. Leave tugging and struggling with thy sin, and fall, with Jacob, to wrestle with Christ for a blessing; and though thyself go limping away, yet shalt thou be a prince with God, and be delivered from Esau's bondage. Yea, what if Satan, what if legions of principalities and powers, have long held possession in some strong fort of thy heart, begin to plead prescription, scorning, as the Jebusites, to be ejected out of their impregnable tower? Hast thou faith, and canst thou believe? Persist in resisting, and he shall fly, and thou shalt see him fall like lightning before thee. Christ raised from the dead

† That is, ' bowing or cringing.'—ED.

not only the daughter of Jairus, which was yet within bed, not laid forth; nor the son of the widow, newly carrying out of the gate to burial; but Lazarus, that had four days lain in the grave; to that end, saith Augustine, that such as have long been dead in sin, yea, such as upon whom Satan hath rolled the stone of custom, and such as stink in the nostrils of the world through putrefied sores of sins, should not yet despair, but know that (which falls out in frequent experience), faith can cure diseases past all other cures and hopes.   Through faith thou shalt roll away the stone from the cave of Machpelah,* and take out the five kings that have domineered and tyrannised over thee, set thy feet in the necks of them, and triumph over them.

CHAPTER XI.

How Faith Vivifies.

AND what is there yet further thou wouldst have faith do for thee?   Oh, sayest thou, it is not enough to be healed of the disease, unless thou mayest take up thy bed and walk, yea, and leap and skip as the lame restored to his limbs.   Oh, that I could find that life of grace which I see in some that can make it meat and drink to do the will of God!

Though I be not pestered and mastered with any reigning corruption, yet I find myself so dull and untoward, that I take no pleasure in my life. Know also that this quickening power, faith, only can help thee withal.   To pray, to meditate, to have thy conversation in heaven, to keep a Sabbath cheerily, is as easy to thee as to iron to swim, and stones to ascend upward; but nothing is impossible to faith.   It can naturalise these things unto thee, metamorphose thee, make thee a new creature, of a mole of the earth a fowl of heaven, of a snail a dromedary; such a change as the sun works in the vapour, when of an earthly, heavy substance it makes it light and airy, apt to ascend into the middle region.   Such a change Cyprian saith he felt in his conversion.   And how else came David to that high delight in God's service, that he loved the commandments of God more than thousands of gold and silver, the honey, and the honeycomb, that he rose at midnight to meditate in them.   The selfsame duties may be done by the civil man and by the believer, for the outside and deed done.   Both may go to church, hear a sermon, read a chapter; but the one goes as the bear to the stake, as a slave to the mill, and the dullard to school, in comparison of the other, who hath a different internal principle, which is as a spring and oil to the wheels, that makes them go smoothly and currently, makes the yoke light and easy.   ' They that trust in the Lord shall renew their strength, lift up the wing as the eagle, run and not be weary, walk and not faint,' Isa. xl. 31.

Faith it is that fetcheth sap from the root Christ, that makes every tree bring forth fruit in its kind, every Christian in his own calling.   What else made David so worthy a soldier?   What taught his fingers to fight, so that a bow of steel was broken in his hand?   What made Paul an able minister of the gospel, gave him the door of utterance, made his tongue as the pen of a ready writer?   *He believed,* therefore he spake.   What made Onesimus, of a false eye-servant, trusty to his master as to the Lord?   The like might be said of all trades and sciences.

Look what a full treasury of all sorts of graces Christ hath stored up in

* Evidently a misprint for ' Makkedah,' see Josh. x. 16.—ED.

him. Faith draineth and deriveth them out of his fulness to the use of every several Christian, even ' grace for grace.'

Faith is the conduit cock that watereth all the herbs and flowers in the garden. All which the more I consider, the more I pity the preposterous care and unhappy travail of many well affected, who study the practice of this and that virtue, neglecting this cardinal and radical virtue, as if men should water all the branches of a tree, and not the root. Fain would they abound and shine in patience, meekness, zeal, yet establish and root not themselves in faith, that should maintain all the rest; are ambitious to do good works, build hospitals, give alms, but study not to do the work of the Father. And what is the work of the Father but to believe in the Son whom he hath sealed and sent into the world to be relied on for salvation? which work is the gratefulest work that we can perform, and which will make grateful all that we do besides, without which all that we can do will not please him. What cares he for thy thousand of rams, thy rivers of oil? Hath he not shewed thee, O man, that he that trusteth in his Son honoureth him most of all, in putting to his seal that he is true? This honour, if thou wouldest do unto him, he would honour thee with all other graces, and withhold no ornament, no good thing from thee, if it be fit for thee. Meek thou shalt be as Moses, patient as Job, zealous as David, thy soul and life embroidered with all kind of shining graces, as the high priest's apparel with jewels. Wherefore, add this prescript to the former when thou art on the top of mount Tabor, solacing thy soul in thy Lord, and his favour through faith, feasting and banqueting with him as Esther with Ahasuerus. Bethink thyself what suit thou hast to him, what troublesome enemy thou wouldst be rid of. Suppose it to be some potent Haman of pride, make but thy complaint, and it shall be executed and crucified before thine eyes. Consider what grace thou standest in need of, and make thy petition as Achsah to Caleb, Judges i. 14, and he shall give thee the springs above and the springs beneath.

This prescript, if thou wilt daily observe, some days more largely and fervently, as the Spirit that blows how and where it lists shall assist, and as occasion shall require, but every day more or less, though I will not promise thee thou shalt attain to perfection of degrees, such as the perfected spirits of the just enjoy in glory, because here thou shalt ever believe but in part, and therefore be holy but in part, yet this I dare promise, as thou growest from faith to faith, so shalt thou grow from strength to strength in all other graces, till by degrees thou attain to the fulness and maturity of age in Christ, which shall make thee a saint in the earth, a light in this dark world, and make thee able to live in holiness and righteousness all the days of thy life, with much more comfort to thyself, and credit to the gospel, than strangers to this life of faith either do or imagine may be done.

CHAPTER XII.

How Faith upholds Life in Affliction.

SAY then, O Christian, is there anything yet behind that may impeach the complete happiness of a believer's life? Speak now, if there be anything that hinders it, which faith cannot help?

O yes, says the flesh (which ever is cowardly and loves ease), though a man be never so justified and sanctified, yet may he live in poverty, in crosses, yea, in great and manifold pressures; and what a life can there be in such extremities? Oh, how doth faith here lift up the crest, shine and triumph above nature, reason, and all moral virtues in her incomparable valour? Being in all these not as they, only a patient perforce, or a mere bearer, but more than conqueror, not only not daunted, but rejoicing to fall into manifold trials and tentations, knowing itself to be the adamant that nothing will break, the palm that sinks not under the weightiest of burdens, the oil that ever overswims the greatest quantity of water you can pour upon it, the sheet anchor that holds when all other tackling breaks. Here is the crown and garland of faith. Were it not for conflicts, what superexcellent use were there of faith? Every cock-boat can swim in a river, every sculler sail in a calm, in daily and ordinary gusts every man of a patient temper or cheerly disposition can hold up the head; but when a black tempest comes, a tenth wave flows, and one deep calls another, nature yields, spirit faints, heart fails, then to stand erect, then to live and reign, that only can faith do, which hath the word for its compass, and Christ at the helm. The greatest adversities that are, are but the exercise, yea, the foil and lustre of faith. Man glories when he can tame tigers and lions, thinks himself a stately king when he can make an elephant bow and stoop to him, when he leads a bear on the ring, or can handle a serpent without hurt; but what a small conquest is this to that of faith, when it makes shame, poverty, sickness, persecutions, banishment, yea, death itself, not only not dreadful and harmful, but tractable and serviceable. Questionless, great and sundry advantages hath a Christian, by virtue of his faith, above any naturian or politic, by all his reason; only, here is the defect of Christians, that they want skill, or else forget to hold up their shield when a dart comes suddenly upon them. Like him that was robbed by a thief with a staff only in his hand, having himself a pistol at his back, ready charged, but surprised upon the sudden, altogether unmindful, or unable to use it. And if a man hath a target that is impenetrable, what is he the better if his heart or art fail him when he should defend himself by it? This makes Christians, when they ail anything, with Saul to run to Endor, 1 Sam. xxviii. 7, with Asa to send out to the physicians, 2 Chron. xvi. 12, as if faith could stand them in no stead. When, therefore, a storm rises, presently run and awaken thy sleeping faith, knock at faith's door, Ho! faith, help at a pinch, now do thy office! and faith will presently relieve thee with one of these special cordials.

First, Whereas sense and reason did but dimly and cloudily suggest to their followers certain broken and confused opinions, little better than dreams of destiny and providence, faith will confidently and evidently assure thee of this ground of comfort, that the least tick befalls thee not, without the overruling eye and hand, not only of a wise God, but of a tender Father and fellow-feeling elder Brother, who, knowing thy mould, do more exactly measure out every cross unto thee than the carefulest apothecaries do their scruples and drams of dangerous physic.

Secondly, Out of this principle faith will extract these infallible conclusions; this estate is not the axe of perdition, but the pruning-knife of affliction; this cup is not a potion baneful, but medicinable, how bitter and wringing soever. Whatever befalls, being in Christ, it cannot bend to thy confusion, condemnation, or utter undoing, but an issue shall be given out of it. What terrible noise soever the storm shall make over thine head, it shall be but as hailstones upon the tiled or leaded house, that rattle more than hurt. Thou art kept by the power of his might, the evil one shall not touch thee, thou art in safe harbour under the rock Christ, and mayest know in whom thou hast trusted, and art sure never to be confounded. If it be sickness or poverty, it is in thy Father's own hand. If the rod be in some malicious enemy's hand, if he turn thee over to a servant to scourge thee, and dress him in the devil's habit to scare thee, yea, though Satan himself buffet thee, yet he stands by, looks on, will moderate and number the stripes. The devils could not go one inch beyond commission in the swine. He knows thy strength is not the strength of whales or stones, and therefore will not permit them to lay on more than thou shalt well bear. His wisdom and grace shall be sufficient for thee. He that is in good terms with a prince fears not the approach of heralds or pursuivants, he that is out of debt fears not bailiffs or sergeants, but imagines they come upon some good messages.

Afflictions are scarebugs * to wicked men, as bushes to thieves ; but if thou be a believer, at peace with God in Christ, they lay off their terrible vizard, and come with an amiable countenance. God thy Father hath given the whole host and army of afflictions more inviolable charge than David's, ' Do the young man, my son Absalom, no harm ;' do my anointed no harm.

Thirdly ; Faith will further assure that he hath not only given them a prohibition, or negative commission, but an affirmative injunction to do thee all good that may be. He hath said unto them, purge, refine, try, exercise, breed the quiet fruit of righteousness, give him experience of his faith, make him bring forth more fruit ; so that, though there be in thy physic some malign or poisonful ingredients, yet, being administered by him that knows thy temper and disease, and entirely affects thy health, it shall be so mingled with allays and correctors, that the confection shall be good, and altogether shall and must work for the best. When thou feelest thy bowels wring, or (as in a sea-sickness) art dead sick for the present, remember thou shalt be the better many days after. And though, with Job and David, thy querulous flesh complain, and grunt and groan, yet when it is over a little, thou shalt be able to say, ' Oh, this was good for me !' I would not for anything but I had borne the yoke in my youth, that I may live the more comfortably in age. Considering that sick thou art, and that of many humours, thy Father should not love thee, if he should feed thee with sweetmeats, and mingle no aloes with them ; much folly is bound up in thy back ;† and if thy indulgent Father should forbear the rod, he should hate, and not love thee.

Fourthly ; Moreover, faith will remind thee of Christ's partnership in thy affliction, and of thy conformity with him, ' the firstborn, only begotten, and entirely beloved Son of God.' If he that was without sin, yet was not without stripes, wilt thou look to be a cockered Adonijah ? And what if the cross be heavy, and thou a weak child, yet Christ, a giant at one end, bears part of it, and makes it light and easy ? He is quick of feeling ; when Stephen is stoned, he saith, ' Saul, why persecutest thou me ?' Besides, what more honourable badge and cognisance canst thou have of thy sonship, than this resemblance of him, not as now glorified in the heavens, which thou must stay for till thou come there, but as in the way to glory, when he despised the shame, suffered the crown of thorns, the sceptre of reed, the spittings, buffetings, mocks and mows, and all reproaches of vile sinners, the piercing of the spear, and shewed himself to be the Son of God,

* That is, ' scarecrows.'—Ed.   † Qu. ' heart ?'—Ed.

not by descending from the cross, but by enduring the cross ? 'And shall I not (saith he) drink the cup which my Father hath tempered ?' And if thou wilt be his disciple, the first lesson in his school is, Christ's cross. Deny thyself; take it up and follow him, and glory with the martyrs, Now am I like my Lord and Master.

Lastly; Faith will set before thee, as before him, the infinite recompence of reward, not only renown in this world, which yet by faith the patience not only of Job, but of all martyrs have obtained, but that far most excellent hyperbolical weight of glory; which Paul, eyeing, counted his afflictions (which to us would have been intolerable) light and momentary, not worthy the naming in comparison; which made him not only not weep and howl, but sing in the dungeon, and reckon it a special favour and honour to be counted not only a believer, but a sufferer for Christ. And God forbid that a believer should glory in anything so much as in the cross of Christ, in his wounds and scars for his Lord and Master. As that worthy Vincentinus said to the tyrant, 'Threaten these things to your courtiers and carpet knights; racks, strappadoes, torments, are but a play to us; we soldiers choose to be in Christ's garrison, rather than in the court; in the field and fore-front of the battle, than in the palaces of princes.' The more hazard and peril, the more glory and honour. And what else desire we but to die daily, that the life in Christ may be manifested in us ? Yea, in the very instant of death, faith helps the believer to live, so as he may be said not to see death, and never to die (but that requires a just treatise by itself). Let all the complaints, grievances, wants, and miseries of the world be searched and guaged, the bottom will be found either to be want of faith, or of the use and practice of faith; so that we may well say with Augustine, to any Christian sinking under his cross, or shrinking at his enemy, 'Hast thou lost thy faith ?' and conclude with that worthy ensign-bearer of Christ,* 'Many are the troubles of the righteous, but by faith we stand, by faith we fight, by faith we overcome.'

CHAPTER XIII.

An Epistle to the Reader, pressing the Use of Faith.

Now reader, for so I choose to call thee in a postscript, when thou hast read the book, rather than in a preface, when thou mayest there leave, as many do; give me now leave to grapple with thee, and minister to thee an interrogatory or two.

How many dost thou know, within thy conscience, live this life of faith ? Many thou seest live by their lands, by their wits, by their shifts; but how many by their faith ? For the want of this use of faith, do not many poor Christians think and say of it, as a poor labouring countryman said to his neighbour in serious private talk, that he never believed there was any such sum as a thousand pounds of money, but that only rich men gave it out so, in boasting, or policy, to excite others to labour. So saith the common protestant, out of doubt there is no such sweetness in the life of faith; for we see not believers so cheerful and contented above other men. If artists

* Fox in 14. Apoc.

and tradesmen did no more daily and duly follow their work, than most Christians do practise their faith, would they not be stark beggars ? But to ask thee a more profitable question. Leave judging of others, and answer me in good serious sooth, between God and thy soul, Hast, and dost thou thyself live by thy faith ? Let me a little put thee to it ; prove and examine thyself, and take, for instance, this present week, or day past, wherein thou readest this little manual. How hast thou, and usually dost thou spend the day ? What thought didst thou awake withal ? What was thy morning draught for thy soul next thy heart ? What hath cheered and made thee merry in private and in company? Whether thy sports and meals, more than thy heavenly ejaculations ? Deal plainly, not with me and this book (which yet shall witness against thee, if thou refuse to practise it when thou hast read it), but with thyself. Hast thou, or hast thou not, challenged some time, more or less, half or quarter of an hour, at the least, for this exercise of thy faith ? Hast thou not troubled thyself about the many things, that this one only needful hath been forgotten, that which only should be called work and business ? Hast thou not melted the day, yea, it may be the week, or month past, and made thy soul wholly to fast and pine for want of these refreshings ? If so, as I justly fear it in most of my readers, how much more in such as are usually no readers ? Why, then, let thy heart smite thee for thy folly ; smite thou thyself upon the thigh, and say, How have I lived, or rather not lived, but consumed precious days in time-eating vanities ? How comes it about, that the greatest part of my life is the least part wherein I have lived ?

Oh, then, recover and recollect thyself before thou go hence and be no more. Wilt thou die before thou hast lived, as boys slubber out books before they learn their lesson ? Oh, learn to live this life; it is never too late ; it is never, I am sure, too soon; it is no shame to learn it what age or condition soever thou be of; be thou prince, potentate, nobleman, or gentleman, though few such readers I look for : remembering well what Bradford tells the Earl of Bedford, and Augustine tells Romanian, whiles he was in the mouths of all men, most honourable, most munificent, most fortunate, in the full of his prosperity, in the source of pleasures, in the top of greatness, &c. Who durst lisp a word of a better life, of true happiness? or what boot was it for any man to make mention of any such matter ? Yet if any such God will persuade to make trial of this life, thou which sayest, What is a gentleman but* his pleasure ? shalt then tell me, as Solomon of his youth, such gentry is but vanity, true pleasure there is none but in this life. What is a Christian but* his faith, and what is his life but* the use of his faith ? Beest thou a scholar, a prophet, or a son of the prophets, what is thy work, what is thy scope, or what should it be in thyself and others, but this life of faith? What is Paul or Apollos 1 Cor. iii., but such as by whom you have believed ? Whatever you teach, before you have taught this, you were as good preach to the stools and stones of your churches. What are your auditors but dead bones, and skulls, till they believe, and till Christ be formed in them ? Get first an hold whereon you may fasten your engines to draw them to virtues and good works. You which do that in souls which Elisha did in bodies, raise them from their graves—interpreters one of a thousand get the tongue of the learned to declare their righteousness unto them, the righteousness I say of faith—shew yourselves skilful workmen, such as have been brought up not only in morals of the heathen, subtilties of schoolmen, sentences and

* That is, ' without.'

conceits of postillers, rosaries, destructories, anthologies, but in the wholesome
word of faith, which is the arm and power of God to the salvation of every
believer.   Above all, let it be our wisdom to live ourselves by that which
we teach others to live by; we that have, or might, or should have more
faith than common Chistians, is it not a shame if we live not more happily,
and carefully than private Christians? not by our livings, wherein the laity
have gotten the start of us for the most part, but by our faith, wherein we
have the advantage of them, or else shame be it to us.

Is it not a shame to see an owner of a thousand pounds a year live as
meanly as a poor farmer? a master and professor of an art, as a mean
practitioner?   Yet this must I say even to the meanest tradesmen and
poorest people, this life belongs not to such only that are book-learned, but
is equally obvious and open (as the king's highway) to all sorts of travellers
to heaven.   Honourable lives, pompous lives, voluptuous lives, poor folks
have small hope to attain unto; but a true happy life they may and do live,
as well as the learnedst clerks and greatest princes, if they get the gift
to practise that which such for the most part do but study and talk of.
To conclude, whatever thou art, or whoever, that desirest to mend thy
condition, to better thine estate, to multiply thy life, to change thy few
and evil days of thy pilgrimage, into good and many, behold, here is
the art of living well-and living long.   Life is not to be numbered by its
hours, but measured by cheerfulness, as moneys not by tale but value.
A little piece of gold contains a great many pieces of silver.   Manhood
consists not in the bulk of bones, but in the mettle and spirits.   Is not one
week of an healthy man, better than a year of a crazy; one sunshine
hour, than a gloomy day?   I have often mused how a man might come
nearest to that life which Adam lost, and recompense in this latter age of
the world (wherein the lives of men are so contracted) the longevity of those
that lived before the flood.   And this is the best help I find: to live well is
to live twice.   A good man doubles and amplifies his days; one may speak
as much in few words as another in many.   Persius wrote more in a few
leaves than Marsus in large volumes.   One day led by the rules of faith, is
better than an immortality of vanity.   A man may live to as good content
to himself and others in a short space, as others in a long life; some are
old in years tediously drawn out, others in hours cheerfully spent; some have
been long, and others have lived long: and they only are such as have lived
this life, of whom I conclude, as doth the story of the Kings, and Jeremiah's
prophecy touching Zedekiah* upon his advancement by the king of Babel,
his portion was a continual portion, a kingly portion, every day a certain
all the days of his life; such I say it is, or might be, if Christians might be
persuaded not to content themselves to profess or think they have faith,
but to live by their faith; only before I part with thee, take from me one
caveat, one advice, one request, and so an end.

First, Take heed thou mistakest me not in all this, as if I had spoken of
an absolute perfection in this life, equal to vision and fruition in the life to
come, confounded heaven with earth, as if I thought myself, or any other
to have comprehended.   If any man thinks he believes anything, he believes
nothing yet as he ought to believe, but all things in part, and imperfectly.
We cannot by all our assiduousness in reading, prayer, and meditation
have God's Spirit at an absolute command, no more than mariners the
wind, or husbandmen the showers; so as the most observant believer hath
his *turbida intervalla*, his buffetings, lest he be too much exalted, his deser-

* Qu. 'Jehoiachim?'—See 2 Kings xxv. 27; Jer. lii. 31.

tions, wherein his beloved will hide himself behind the grates, not to be found of him for a while, that he seek him more eagerly, and prize his presence more thankfully, more heedfully keep him when he hath him, and be wholly dependent on his grace; yet so, as this remains most sure and certain, that the constant and daily practiser of his faith shall constantly and congruously be seconded with the gusts and gales of his Spirit, the only true *Zephyrus* and *Favonius;* shall have Satan tied up from long and frequent molesting him; shall not have such tedious absences of the Spirit, such uncertain fits and moods of his joy and comfort, as the negligent and loose believer, but a more stedfast frame and tenor of joy than any other kind of man in the world that takes not this course.

Provided that thou take this advice, that for the better and stronger use of this faith, thou seal up thy senses, and chain up thy reason. Walking by sight, and walking by faith, are opposite things; and, therefore, as men fortify the visual beams of one eye by closing the other, so must thou wink and close up the eye of thy soul to all worldly things, that thou mayest, by the prospective of faith, fix thy spiritual eye upon heavenly delights; not that thou needest go out of this world, and sequester thyself like an eremite into dens and caves, retired from all society, but even in the midst of all glittering objects, see them as if thou sawest them not; that is, without being deeply affected with them. So looked Paul from off the things that are seen even in the midst of Rome, and looked upon things which were not seen; and Moses in Pharaoh's court saw him that was invisible.

A right believer goes through the world, as a man whose mind is in a deep study, or as one that hath special haste of some weighty business, goes through a street, that gazeth on nothing, hears nothing, minds nothing that is in the way, but only that which his head is taken up withal. Our conversation is in heaven, our treasure is in heaven. O that all our thoughts were there, so as no earthly object might detain or distract them, no more than needs must be in our calling, so that the main bent and intention of all that is within us might be set upon the daily nourishing of our faith!

For which purpose, I make this parting and farewell suit unto thee, as thou meanest to receive any good by this book. That thou wouldst, even from this very hour wherein thou endest the reading of it, determine and covenant betwixt God and thy soul, never whilst thou livest on the face of the earth to omit one day (God enabling thee by his Spirit) wherein thou wilt not vindicate and redeem, at the least, one half or quarter of an hour, either twice or once in the day, at the least; wherein all other affairs laid aside, thou mayest withdraw thyself apart from all company and occasions, with a *non obstante*, to practise the exercise formerly prescribed. That is, by prayer, reading, and meditation, to put some strength and life into thy faith, till thou hast cheered, and revived, and warmed thy soul therewithal. This, if thou shalt inviolably observe, the strength, the feeling, the comfort, and the fruits of thy faith will, by little and little insensibly, and in a little while most sensibly, thrive and grow, till thou comest to the ripeness of age in Christ.

What hurt can it be to thee if thou shouldst bind thyself by vow hereunto, or, if thou fearest thy strength, yet by full purpose thus to do all and every day of thy life? that so in these lees and dregs of time, whilst fleshly protestants are raising contentions about matters of faith, or making sects and schisms in the church about needless trifles, thou mayest edify thyself in thy most holy faith; and whilst thou livest in the dark womb of this world, live by the navel of faith, till thou comest to have thy mouth satiate with fulness of all good things at the right hand of God. When, as Eliza-beth Folk said, 'faith shall cease to be faith, and be turned into fruition, and we receive the end of our faith, the salvation of our souls.'

These things I have written, that your joy may be full. 'The just shall live by his faith.' 'According to thy faith, so be it to thee.' 'Lord, increase our faith.'

THE LIFE OF FAITH IN DEATH.

EXEMPLIFIED IN THE LIVING SPEECHES OF DYING CHRISTIANS.

TO HIS DEAR AND LOVING

MOTHER.

I HONOUR Augustine much for honouring his mother so much after her death, whose name and example had otherwise lain in obscurity. But I like better, and wish rather, to follow the piety of Nazianzen, who gave himself to the performance of all Christian offices to his living mother. God hath so blessed the former part of your life above the lot of most women, with two such able guides, as have so stored you with spiritual and temporal furniture, that you need not the aid of any your children. Nevertheless, grace and nature will be ascending and expressing themselves, though in weak services. Reuben, when he found but a few flowers, must bring them to his mother Leah. Esau, when he takes venison, gratifies his aged father withal. Samson finds honey by the way, and presents of it to his parents. Here is a posy gathered out of old and new gardens; this savoury meat hath God brought to hand, here is sweet out of the strong. Let your soul eat and bless. The use and fruit of them I wish to every believer, especially in age and sickness, but the handsel and honour of them (if any be) to yourself, whom the law of God and nature binds me to honour above others. Long may you live to bless your children with your daily prayers, especially your sons in that work which needs much watering. Yet every good Christian in years cannot but desire to be forewarned against death approaching; and that is the aim of these endeavours. God prosper and bless them, as the former; and send me my part in the benefit of these (as he hath done of them) in the time of use.

> Your Son in all duty, desirous of the
> birthright of your love and blessing,
> SAMUEL WARD.

THE LIFE OF FAITH IN DEATH.

MOTHER.

THE LIFE OF FAITH IN DEATH.

THAT which hath been already spoken of the life of faith, is to the natural man above all faith. And yet, if that be all it can do, then is all little better than nothing. Say it could fill the mind of man with all content, satiate his life with all delight, and sweeten the bitterness of all afflictions; yet if, for all this, there lurk in his breast a secret and slavish fear of death, the least piece of this leaven, but in a corner of the peck, is enough to sour the whole lump of his joys; the least dram of this coloquintida will mar the relish of all his sweets, and make him cry out, ' There is death in the pot.' And, O death! how bitter is thy mention and memory?

Ask nature, and call to philosophy, and see if they can afford any aid? Must they not confess themselves here quite posed and plunged? Hath not death set and toiled their whole army? For poverty, shame, and sickness, and other such petty crosses, some poor cures and lame shifts have they found out; but, when death comes, all their courage hath failed, and all their rules have left them in dark and desperate uncertainties. It is possible for Pharaoh, with much ado, to stand out the storms of hail, the swarm of flies and lice; but, when once the cry of death is in the houses, then is there no way but yielding; his enchanters and mountebanks could abide the cry of frogs and other such vermin, but this basilisk affrights them. Only faith takes it by the tail, handles it, and turns it into a harmless wand; yea, into a rod budding with glory and immortality.

Quartan agues are not so much the shame of physic, as death is of all natural skill and valour. Death is faith's evil.* Faith only professeth this cure, undertaketh and performeth it with the least touch of Christ's hand; and that as familiarly as the richest balm doth the least cut of the finger. Faith turneth fears into hopes, sighings and groanings into wishings and longings, shaking and trembling into leaping and clapping of hands.

Alas! all troubles are but as pigmies to this giant, who defies all the host of infidels, holds them in bondage all the days of their lives, and makes their whole life no better than a living death and dying life. Only faith encounters this giant, singles him out for her chief prize, and grapples with him not as a match, but as with a vanquished underling; insulting over him as much as he doth over the sons of unbelief; sets her foot upon the

* After the analogy of scrofula being called the king's evil, because the king was supposed to be able to cure it by a touch.—ED.

neck of this king of fears, and so easily becomes conqueror and emperor of all petty fears, which are therefore only fearful, because they tend to death; the last, the worst, the end, and sum of all feared evils. Here, and here only, is the incomparable crown of faith; here only doth she evidently and eminently honour her followers, and difference them from all others with a noble livery of true magnanimity and alacrity. It is true, if we had windows into the breasts of men, a difference one might see in the inward bearing of adversity; but, for the face and outside, both may seem alike hardy, both may seem alike resolute. But, when it comes to the point of death, then the speech, the behaviour, the countenance, palpably distinguish the dull patience perforce of the worldling, from the cheerful welcome of the Christian. Let death put on her mildest vizards, come in the habit of the greatest* sickness to the stoutest champion on his own down-bed; yet shall his heart tremble and his countenance wax pale. Let her dress herself like the cruelest fury, come with all her racks, fires, strappadoes, wild beasts, all her exquisite tortures. Faith will set a woman or a child to make sport with her, to dare and to tire her, and her tormentors.

Alas! what do they tell us of their Socrates, their Cato, their Seneca, and a few such thin examples which a breath will rehearse, and a few lines contain their poor ragged handful, to our legions, whose names or number one may as soon reckon as the sand of the sea-shore: theirs a few choice men of heroical spirits trained up either in arts or arms; ours of the weakest sexes and sorts, only strong in the faith; theirs, either out of windy vain-glory, childishly reckoning of a short death and a long fame, or out of a blockish ignorance venturing upon death, as children and madmen upon dangers without fear or wit; ours out of mature deliberation and firm belief in Christ, who hath drunk out of death's bitter cup an eternal health to all mankind, taken the gall and poison out of it, and made it a wholesome potion of immortality. Faith here proclaims her challenge, and bids nature or art out of all their soldiers and scholars produce any one who, having option to live or die, and that upon equal terms, have embraced death. Whereas infinite of hers have been offered life with promotions, and yet would not be delivered, expecting a better resurrection.

If any shall challenge these for thrasonical flourishes, or carpet vaunts, I appeal and call to witness not the cloud now, but the whole sky of witnesses, such I mean as have died either in the Lord, or for the Lord, who in the very point and article of death have lived, and expressed lively testimonies of this their life, partly in their incredible sufferings, partly in their admirable sayings. For their ' acts and monuments,' if they had all been penned, all the world would not have contained their histories, the sums would swell to large volumes. The valour of the patients, the savageness of the persecutors, striving together, till both exceeding nature and belief, bred wonder and astonishment to beholders and readers. Christians have shewed as glorious power in the faith of martyrdom, as in the faith of miracles. As for their last speeches and apophthegms, pity it is no better mark hath been taken, and memory preserved of them. The choice and the prime I have culled out of ancient stories, and latter martyrologies, English, Dutch, and French. The profit and pleasure hath paid me for the labour of collecting, and the like gain, I hope, shall quit the cost of thy reading. Sweetly and briefly they comprise and couch in them the foundation, the marrow of large and manifold precepts, prescribed by the learned divines for preparation against death.† The art of dying well is easier

---

* Qu. 'Gentlest?'—Ed.   † Beza, Perkins, Hall, Byfield.

learned by examples than by directions. These chalk the way more plainly, these encourage more heartily, these persuade more powerfully, these chide unbelief with more authority : if some work not, others may, some will affect some, some another. Read them over to a sick or to a dying Christian ; if they quicken not, if they comfort not, it is because there is no life of faith in them ; if there be the least spark, these will kindle it, cherish and maintain it in the door, in the valley, in the thought, in the act of death.

THE LIVING SPEECHES OF DYING CHRISTIANS.

PART I.

OLD Simeon's swan-song : ' Lord, let thy servant depart in peace,' &c.

The good thief, the first confessor : ' Lord, remember me when thou comest into thy kindom.'

Stephen, the first martyr : ' Lord Jesus, receive my spirit ; forgive them,' &c.

Peter, the apostle : ' None but Christ, nothing but Christ.'

Andrew the apostle : ' Welcome, O Christ! longed and looked for. I am the scholar of him that did hang on thee, long have coveted to embrace thee, in whom I am that I am.'

Polycarpus to the pro-consul, urging him to deny Christ : ' I have served him eighty-six years, and he hath not once hurt me ; and shall I now deny him ? '

When he should have been tied to the stake, he required to stand untied, saying : ' Let me alone, I pray you ; for he that gave me strength to come to this fire, will also give me patience to abide in the same without your tying.'

Ignatius : ' I am the wheat or grain to be ground with the teeth of beasts, that I may be pure bread for my Master's tooth. Let fire, racks, pulleys, yea, and all the torments of hell come on me, so I may win Christ.'

Lucius to Urbicius, a corrupt judge threatening death : ' I thank you with all my heart, that free me and release me from wicked governors, and send me to my good God and loving Father,' &c.

Pothnius, bishop of Lyons, to the president, asking him in the midst of torments, what that Christ was, answered : ' If thou wert worthy, thou shouldst know.'

Cyprian : ' God Almighty be blessed for this gaol delivery.'

Ambrose to his friends about him : ' I have not so lived, that I am ashamed to live any longer ; nor yet fear I death, because I have a good Lord.'

And the same to Calligon, Valentinian's eunuch, threatening death : ' Well, do you that which becomes an eunuch, I will suffer that which becomes a bishop.'

Augustine : ' Boughs fall off trees, and stones out of buildings, and why should it seem strange that mortal men die ? '

Theodosius : ' I thank God more for that I have been a member of Christ, than an emperor of the world.'

Hilarion : ' Soul, get thee out ; thou hast seventy years served Christ, and art thou now loath to die, or afraid of death ? '

Vincentius : ' Rage, and do the worst that the spirit of malignity can set thee on work to do. Thou shalt see God's Spirit strengthen the tormented more than the devil can do the tormentor.'

Jubentius and Maximinus : ' We are ready to lay off the last garment, the flesh.'

Attalus answered to every question, ' I am a Christian :' being fired in an iron chain. ' Behold, O you Romans ! this is to eat man's flesh; which you falsely object to us Christians.'

Basil to Valens's viceroy, offering him respite : ' No ; I shall be the same to-morrow. I have nothing to lose but a few books ; and my body is now so crazy, that one blow will end my torment.'

Gorgius, to the tyrant offering him promotion : ' Have you anything equal, or more worthy than the kingdom of heaven ? '

Babilas, dying in prison, willed his chains should be buried with him. ' Now,' saith he, ' will God wipe away all tears, and now I shall walk with God in the land of the living.'

Barlaam, holding his hand in the flame over the altar, sung that of the psalmist : ' Thou teachest my hands to war, and my fingers to fight.'

Julitta : ' We women received not only flesh from men, but are bone of their bone, and therefore ought to be as strong and constant as men in Christ's cause.'

Amachus : ' Turn the other side also, lest raw flesh offend.' The like Lawrence.

Symeones : ' Thus to die a Christian is to live, yea, the chief good, and best end of a man.'

Marcus of Arethuse, hung up in a basket, anointed with honey, and so exposed to the stinging of wasps and bees, to his persecutors that stood and beheld him : ' How am I advanced, despising you that are below on earth ! '

Pusices to Ananias, an old man trembling at martyrdom : ' Shut thine eyes but a while, and thou shalt see God's light.'

Bernard : ' Fence the heel void of merit with prayer, that the serpent may not find where to fasten his teeth.'

The Second Part.

Edward VI., king of England : ' Bring me into thy kingdom ; free this kingdom from Antichrist, and keep thine elect in it.'

Cranmer, Archbishop, thrusting his hand into the fire : ' Thou unworthy hand,' saith he, ' shalt first burn ; I will be revenged of thee for subscribing for fear of death to that damned scroll.'

Latimer, Bishop, to one that tempted him to recant, and would not tell him his name : ' Well,' saith he, ' Christ hath named thee in that saying, ' Get thee behind me, Satan.' And being urged to abjure, ' I will,' saith he, ' good people : I once said in a sermon, in King Edward's time, confidently, that Antichrist was for ever expelled England, but God hath shewed me it was but carnal confidence.'

To Bishop Ridley, going before him to the stake : ' Have after as fast as I can follow. We shall light such a candle by God's grace in England this day, as I trust shall never be put out again.

To whom Bishop Ridley : ' Be of good heart, brother, for God will either assuage the fury of the flame, or else strengthen us to abide it.'

Bishop Hooper, to one that tendered a pardon upon recantation : ' If you love my soul, away with it; if you love my soul, away with it.' One of the commissioners prayed him to consider that life is sweet and death is bitter: ' True,' saith he, ' but the death to come is more bitter, and the life to come is more sweet. O Lord Christ, I am hell, thou art heaven, draw me to thee of thy mercy.'

John Rogers, to one that told him he would change his note at the fire: ' If I should trust in myself, I should so do, but I have determined to die, and God is able to enable me.'

Being awakened and bidden to make haste to execution: ' Then (saith he) shall I not need to tie my points.'

John Philpot: ' I will pay my vows in thee, O Smithfield.'

Thomas Bilney: ' I know by sense and philosophy that fire is hot and burning painful, but by faith I know it shall only waste the stubble of my body, and purge my spirit of its corruption.'

Glover to Augustine Brenner: ' He is come, he is come,' meaning the Comforter, God's Spirit.

John Bradford, embracing the reeds and faggots, said: ' Strait is the way, and narrow is the gate, and few that find it.' And speaking to his fellow-martyr: ' Be of good comfort, brother, for we shall have a merry supper with the Lord this night; if there be any way to heaven on horse-back or in fiery chariots, this is it.'

Lawrence Sanders: ' I was in prison till I got into prison, and now (says he, kissing the stake), welcome the cross of Christ, welcome everlasting life. My Saviour began to me in a bitter cup, and shall I not pledge him?'

John Lambert: ' None but Christ, none but Christ.'

Baynam: ' Behold, you papists that look for miracles, I feel no more pain in the fire than if I were in a bed of down; it is as sweet to me as a bed of roses.'

Hugh Laverocke, comforting John-a-Price, his fellow-martyr, said unto him: ' Be of good comfort, my brother, for my Lord of London is our good physician, he will cure thee of all thy blindness, and me of my lameness this day.'

William Hunter to his mother: ' For a momentary pain I shall have a crown of life, and may not you be glad of that?' To whom she answered: ' I count myself happy that bare such a champion for Christ, and thee as well bestowed as any child that ever I bare.'

Adam Damlip, to his fellow-prisoners wondering at his cheerful supping and behaviour after the message of his execution: ' Why (quoth he) think you I have been so long in the Marshalsea, and have not learned to die?' And when they told him his quarters should be hanged up: ' Then (said he) shall I need take no thought for my burial.'

Priest's wife, to one offering her money: ' I am going to a country where money bears no mastery.' When sentence was read: ' Now have I gotten that which many a day I have sought for.'

Kirby, to Master Wingfield pitying him: ' Be at my burning and you shall see and say, There is a soldier of Christ. I know fire, water, and sword are in his hands, that will not suffer them to separate me from him.'

Doctor Taylor: ' I shall this day deceive the worms in Hadley church-yard;' and fetching a leap or two when he came within two miles of Hadley, ' Now (saith he) lack I but two stiles, and I am even at my Father's house.'

Walter Mill, urged to recant at the stake: ' I am no chaff, but corn; I will abide wind and flail by God's grace.'

Bishop Farrar, to a knight's son bemoaning his death: ' If you see me stir in the fire, trust not my doctrine.' And so he stood holding up his stumps till one Garvell struck him down with a staff.

Rawlings to the bishops : ' Rawlings you left me, Rawlings you find me, and so by God's grace I will die.'

John Ardeley : ' If every hair of my head were a man, it should suffer death in the faith I now stand in.' The like Agnes Stanley and William Sparrow.

Thomas Hawkes, being desired to give a sign whether the fire was tolerable to be borne, promised it to his friends ; and, after all expectation was past, he lift up his hands half burned, and being on a light fire, with great rejoicing striketh them three times together.

Lawrence Guest, to his wife meeting him with seven children on her hand : ' Be not a block to me in the way, now I am in a good course and near the mark.'

The Lady Jane Grey, requested by the lieutenant of the Tower to write her symbol in his book before her beheading, wrote this : ' Let the glassy condition of this life never deceive thee. There is a time to be born, a time to die; but the day of death is better than the day of birth.'

Alice Driver, when the chain was about her neck : ' Here is a goodly neckerchief, God be blessed for it.'

John Noyes, kissing the stake : ' Blessed be the time that ever I was born for this day.' To his fellow-martyrs : ' We shall not lose our lives in this fire, but change them for a better, and for coals have pearls,' &c.

Julius Pelmer : ' To them that have the mind linked to the body, as a thief's foot to a pair of stocks, it is hard to die indeed ; but if one be able to separate soul and body, then by the help of God's Spirit it is no more mastery for such a one than for me to drink this cup.'

Elizabeth Folkes, embracing the stake : ' Farewell all the world, farewell faith, farewell hope, and welcome love.'

Roger Bernard, being threatened whipping, stocking, burning, answered : ' I am no better than my Master Christ, and the Prophets which your fathers served after such sort, and I for his name's sake am content to suffer the like at your hands.' So immediately he was condemned, and carried to the fire.

Thomas Sampal, offered a pardon in the midst of the fire : ' Oh ! now I am thus far on my journey, hinder me not to finish my race.'

Latimer, Bishop, when they were about to set fire to him and Bishop Ridley, with an amiable countenance, said these words : ' God is faithful, which doth not suffer us to be tempted above our strength.'

Bishop Ridley, to Mrs Irish, the keeper's wife, and other friends at supper : ' I pray you be at my wedding to-morrow ;' at which words they weeping, ' I perceive you are not so much my friends as I took you to be.'

Tankerfield, when he had put one leg into the fire : ' The flesh shrinks and says, Thou fool, wilt thou burn and needest not ? The spirit says, Hell fire is sharper, and wilt thou adventure that ? The flesh says, Wilt thou leave thy friends ? The spirit answers, Christ and his saints' society is better. The flesh says, Wilt thou shorten thy life ? The spirit says, It is nothing to an eternal life.'

Joyce Lewis : ' When I behold the uglesome* face of death, I am afraid ; but when I consider Christ's amiable countenance, I take heart again.'

---

* That is, " ugly."—ED.

THE THIRD PART.

John Huss, to a countryman who threw a faggot at his head: ' O holy simplicity, God send thee better light! You roast the goose now, but a swan shall come after me, and he shall escape your fire.' Huss, a goose in the Bohemian language, and Luther a swan.

Jerome of Prague: ' Make the fire in my sight; for if I had feared it, I had never come hither.' While it was making, he sung two psalms.

Anonimus, on his deathbed: ' Now, phlegm, do thy duty, and stop thou my vital artery. Now, death, do me that friendly office to rid me of pain, and hasten me to happiness.' To a friend of his that willed him to have his thoughts on heaven: 'I am there already.'

Claudius Monerius being cavilled at by the friars for eating a breakfast before his execution: ' This I do that the flesh may answer the readiness of the spirit.'

Michaela Caignoela, a noble matron, seeing her judges look out of the windows, said to her fellow-martyrs: ' These stay to suffer the torment of their consciences, and are reserved to judgment; but we are going to glory and happiness.' And to certain poor women weeping and crying, ' O madam! we shall never now have more alms:' ' Yes; hold you,' saith she, ' yet once more;' and plucked off her slippers, and such other of her apparel as she could with modesty spare from the fire.

James Delos, to monks that called him proud heretic: ' Alas! here I get nothing but shame; I expect indeed preferment hereafter.'

Madam la Glee, to one Chavique, that upbraided her for denying the faith: ' Your cursed faith is not worthy the name of faith.' She put on her bracelets: ' For I go (said she) to my Spouse.'

Marlorat, to friends that called him deceiver: ' If I have seduced any, God hath seduced me, who cannot lie.'

Castilia Rupea: ' Though you throw my body down off this steep hill, yet will my soul mount upwards again. Your blasphemies more offend my mind, than your torments do my body.'

Christopher Marshall of Antwerp: ' I was from eternal a sheep destined to the slaughter, and now I go to the shambles: gold must be tried in the fire.'

Vidus Bressius: ' If God's Spirit saith true, I shall straight rest from my labours: my soul is even taking her wings to fly to her resting-place.'

The Duke of Wittemberg and Luneburg: ' Many have been mine errors and defects in government; Lord, pardon and cover all in Christ!'

Picus Merandula: ' If Christ's death and our own were ever in eye, how could we sin? Death is welcome, not as an end of trouble, but of sin.'

Martin Luther: ' Thee, O Christ, have I taught, thee have I trusted, thee have I loved; into thy hands I commend my spirit.'

Œcolampadius, to one asking if the light offended him not: ' I have light enough here,' laying his hand on his breast. And to the ministers about him: ' Let the light of your lives shine as well as your doctrine.'

Francisco Varlute: ' Paul and Peter were more honourable members of Christ than I, but I am a member; they had more store of grace than I, but I have my measure, and therefore sure of my glory.'

Peter Berger: ' I see the heavens open to receive my spirit.' And beholding the multitude at the stake: ' Great is the harvest; Lord, send labourers!'

John Mallot, a soldier : ' Often have we hazarded our lives for the emperor Charles the Fifth, and shall we now shrink to die for the King of kings ? Let us follow our Captain.'

John Fillula, to his fellows : ' By these ladders we ascend the heavens. Now begin we to trample under feet sin, the world, the flesh, and the devil.'

Thomas Calberg, to the friars, willing him to repent at the last hour : ' I believe that I am one of those workmen in Christ's vineyard, and shall presently receive my penny.'

Robert Ogner's son, to his father and mother at the stake with him : ' Behold millions of angels about us, and the heavens open to receive us.' To a friar that railed : ' Thy cursings are blessings.' And to a nobleman, that offered him life and promotion : ' Do you think me such a fool, that I would change eternal things for temporary ? ' To the people : ' We suffer as Christians, not as thieves or murderers.'

Constantine, being carried with other martyrs in a dungcart to the place of execution : ' Well (saith he), yet are we a precious odour, and sweet savour to God in Christ.'

Fran. Sanromanus, a Spaniard : ' Work your pleasures on my body, which you have in chains, your captive ; but my soul is even already in heaven, through faith and hope ; and upon that Cæsar himself hath no power.'

Joan, the marshal's wife of France, to her husband at the stake with her : ' Be of good cheer, our wedding was but a shadow, an earnest and contract, of that solemn and blessed marriage which the Lamb will now consummate.'

Anne Audebert of Orleans : ' Blessed be God for this wedding girdle (meaning the chain). My first marriage was on the Lord's day ; and now my second, to my Spouse and Lord Christ, shall be on the same.'

John Bruger, to a friar offering him a wooden cross at the stake : ' No (saith he) ; I have another true cross, imposed by Christ on me, which now I will take up. I worship not the work of man's hands, but the Son of God. I am content with him for my only advocate.'

Martin Hyperius : ' Oh! what a difference there is betwixt this and eternal fire ! who would shun this to leap into that ? '

Augustine of Hannovia, to a nobleman persuading him to have a care of his soul : ' So I will (saith he), for I presently will lay down my body to save my conscience whole.'

Faninus, an Italian, kissed the apparitor that brought him word of his execution. To one reminding him of his children : ' I have left them to an able and faithful Guardian.' To his friends weeping : ' That is well done, that you weep for joy with me.' And to one objecting Christ's agony and sadness to his cheerfulness : ' Yea (saith he), Christ was sad that I might be merry. He had my sins, and I have his merit and righteousness.' And to the friars offering him a wooden crucifix : ' Christ needs not the help of this piece to imprint him in my mind and heart, where he hath his habitation.'

George Carpenter : ' All Bavaria is not so dear to me as my wife and children, yet for Christ's sake I will forsake them cheerfully.'

Adam Wallace, a Scot, to a tempting friar : ' If an angel should say that which thou doest, I would not listen to him. Is the fire ready ? I am ready. Let no man be offended, no disciple is greater than his master.'

John Burgon, to his judges asking him if he would appeal to the high court : 'Is it not enough that your hands are polluted with our blood, but you will make more guilty of it ?'

Frederick Anvill of Berne, to the friars that willed him to call on the virgin Mary, three times repeated : 'Thine, O Lord, is the kingdom, thine is the power and glory, for ever and ever. Let's fight, let's fight! Avaunt, Satan, avaunt !'

Godfrey Varall of Piedmont : ' Hangman, do thine office ; my death will be fruitful to myself and others.'

Hallewine of Antwerp, and Harman of Amsterdam, to the margrave of Antwerp, offering mitigation of torments upon abjuration : ' We are resolved these momentary afflictions are not worthy that exceeding weight of glory that shall be revealed.' Peter and Nicholas Thiesseu, brethren, used the like speech.

Annas Burgius, in the midst of his torments : Lord, forsake me not, lest I forsake thee !'

Peter Clarke, with the root of his tongue plucked out, pronounced audibly (to shew that none ever wanted a tongue to praise God) : ' Blessed be the name of God ;' as of old Romanus the martyr, mentioned in Prudentius.

Godfrey de Hammele, to one that called him heretic : ' No heretic, but an unprofitable servant, yet willing to die for his Lord, and reckoning this death no death, but a life.'

Bucer : 'No man by talk shall withdraw my mind from Christ crucified, from heaven, and my speedy departure, upon which my soul is fixed.' When one advised him to arm himself against Satan's temptation : ' He hath nothing to do with me. God forbid, but now my soul should be sure of sweet consolation.'

Tremelius, a Christian Jew : ' Let Christ live, and Barabbas perish.'

Ferdinand, emperor : ' If mine ancestors and predecessors had not died, how should I have been emperor ? I must, that other may succeed me.'

Frederick the Third, Elector Palatine, to his friends about him, wishing him recovery : ' I have lived enough to you, let me now live to myself, and with my Lord Christ.'

Leonard Cæsar : ' Oh Lord, do thou suffer with me ; Lord, support me and save me.'

Windelmuta, to one that told her she had not yet tasted how bitter death was : ' No (said she), neither ever shall I, for so much hath Christ promised to all that keep his word ; neither will I forsake him for sweet life, or bitter death.'

Henry Voes : ' If I had ten heads, they should all off for Christ. God forbid I should rejoice in anything save in his cross.'

The minister of Brisgo : 'This skin, which scarce cleaves to my bones, I must shortly have laid off by necessity ; how much more willingly now, for my Saviour Christ.'

Adolphus Clarebachius : ' I believe there is not a merrier heart in the world at this instant, than mine is. Behold, you shall see me die by that faith I have lived in.'

Alexander Cane, when a fool's cap was put on his head : ' Can I have a greater honour done me, than to be served as my Lord Christ before Herod ? Lord, seeing my persecutors have no mercy, have thou mercy on me, and receive my soul.'

Almondus a Via: ' My body dies, my spirit lives. God's kingdom abides ever. God hath now given me the accomplishment of all my desires.'

Giles Tilman, urged to know what he believed of purgatory : 'Purgatory and hell I leave to you, but my hope is directly to go into paradise. Neither fear I this great pile of wood, whereof some might have been spared to warm the poor; but will pass through it purged for my Saviour.'

Peter Bruce : 'I thank God my broken leg suffered me not to fly this martyrdom.'

Marion, the wife of Adrian, seeing the coffin hooped with iron, wherein she was to be buried alive : 'Have you provided this pasty-crust to bake my flesh in ?'

Lewis Paschalis : 'It's a small matter to die once for Christ; if it might be, I could wish I might die a thousand deaths for him.'

John Buisson : 'I shall now have a double gaol-delivery ; one out of my sinful flesh, another from the loathsome dungeon I have long lain in.'

Hugh Stallour to John Pike, his fellow-martyr : 'Yet a little while, and we shall see one another before the throne and face of God.'

Levine de Blehere, to his friends that offered to rescue him by tumult : 'Hinder not the magistrates' work, nor my happiness. Father, thou foresawest this sacrifice from eternal : now accept of it, I pray thee.'

Christopher Fabrianus : 'First bitter, then sweet; first battle, the victory when I am dead ; every drop of my blood shall preach Christ, and set forth his praise.'

Francis Soet : 'You deprive me of this life, and promote me to a better, which is, as if you should rob me of counters, and furnish me with gold.'

Guy de Bres : 'The ringing of my chain hath been sweet music in mine ears, my prison an excellent school, wherein God's Spirit hath been my teacher. All my former discourses were as a blind man's of colours in comparison of my present feeling. Oh, what a precious comforter is a good conscience.'

Dionysius Peloquine, to the inquisitor telling him his life was now in his own hands : 'Then (said he) it were in an ill keeping. Christ's school hath taught me to save it by losing it, and not, by the gain of a few days or years, to lose eternity.'

Lewis Marsake, knight, seeing his other brethren go with halters about their necks, which they offered not him because of his dignity : 'Why, I pray you (quoth he), deny me not the badge and ornament of so excellent an order. Is not my cause the same with theirs ?' Which obtaining, he marched valiantly to the stake with them.

Simon Lalœus, to one Silvester, his executioner : 'Never saw I a man in all my life whose coming was more welcome to me than thine.' So cheerful was his death, that Silvester, amazed at it, left his office, became a convert and a Christian himself, went to Geneva for further instruction in the gospel.

Kilian, a Dutch schoolmaster, to such as asked him if he loved not his wife and children: 'Yes (said he); if all the world were gold, and were mine to dispose of, I would give it to live with them, though it were but in prison. Yet my soul and Christ are dearer to me than all.'

Giles Verdict: 'Out of my ashes shall rise innumerable Christians.' Which prophecy God so verified by the effect, that it grew a byword after his death that his ashes flew abroad all the country.

Antony Verdict, brother to the former, condemned to be eaten with beasts, to prevent the like proverb, said to his father: 'O father, how hath God enabled you to have two sons honoured with martyrdom !'

John Barbevill, to friars that called him ignorant ass: 'Well, admit I were so, yet shall my blood witness against such Balaams as you be.'

Francisce Colver, to his two sons, massacred together with himself: ' Sheep we are for the slaughter. This is no new thing. Let us follow millions of martyrs through temporal death to eternal life.'

By all these, which are but a handful of Christ's camp royal, it sufficiently appears they had their faith fresh and lively in the face of this grand enemy, and, by virtue of their faith, their spirits, wits, and tongues untroubled, undismayed, insomuch that an ancient witnesses of the Christian bishops, that they did more ambitiously desire the glory of martyrdom than others did prelacies and preferments; and a late mortal enemy of theirs bade a vengeance on them, for he thought they took delight in burning. What, then, shall we gain by them? I remember Mr Rough, a minister, coming from the burning of one Austo in Smithfield, being asked by Mr Farrar of Halifax where he had been, made answer, There where I would not but have been for one of my eyes, and would you know where? Forsooth, I have been to learn the way; which soon after he made good, by following hîm in the same place, in the same kind of death. Now, if one president made him so good a scholar, what dullards and non-proficients are we if such a cloud of examples work not in us a cheerful ability to expect and encounter the same adversary, so often foiled before our eyes? Yet, lest any should complain that examples without rules are but a dumb and lame help, I will annex unto them a pair of funeral sermons, opening a couple of seals revealed to John in his second vision; the first affording us sundry meditations of death and hell, the second of heaven, and the happiness of such as die in the Lord and rest under the altar.

The use of them I chiefly dedicate and commend to old sick persons, such, especially, as die of lingering diseases, affording them leisure to peruse such themes, though I forbid none; but to all I say, ' Come and see.'

Ἔρχου καὶ ἴδου. *Come and see.*
And behold a pale horse: and his name that sat on him was Death, and hell followed after him: and power was given unto them.'—REV. VI. 7, 8.

' Come and see.' Were it some stately, some pleasing, yea, or but some vain sight, such as Mordecai riding on the king's horse in pomp with the royal furniture, or but a company of players riding through a market, a drum, a trumpet, or the least call would serve the turn, to draw us out to the sight ; but these being serious, yea, to nature somewhat hideous and odious, voices like unto thunders are given to the beasts to call beholders. The crier in the wilderness is willed to cry this theme aloud in the deaf ears of men. A Boanerges, with all the vehemency and contention of his voice and affections, will be too little, unless God bore the ears, open the eyes, and persuade the hearts of men to come and see. Yet it is but our folly to be so shy of this sight, for though it be sad, yet is it of all the sights under the sun the most necessary, the most profitable. Though we turn away our faces and close our eyes, yet see it we must, and see it we shall, nevertheless, never the sooner, never the later. Nay, the truth is, see it we never shall, but with closed eyes. Thou tender, faint-hearted man or woman, thou art so loath to meet with a corpse or bier, to see a skull or anything that minds thee of death, shalt thou by this means protract or escape thy death? No; let me tell thee, prevision is the best prevention, and premonition the best premunition. That which is commonly received of the basilisk, is here no conceited story, but a serious truth. He that sees it before he be seen of it, may avoid the deadly poison of it ; he that sees it before it comes, shall not see it when it comes. He that manageth a horse at an armed stake, fits him to rush into the main battle without fear. And wouldst thou, with Joseph of Arimathea, walk every day a turn or two with death in thy garden, and well fore-acquaint thyself therewithal, thou shoulst have, if not Enoch's, yet every true believer's privilege, not to see death, not to taste of death, viz., in that ugly form, distasteful manner, which other the sons of Adam do, who, because they will not see the face of it, must see the sting of it. To die well and cheerfully, is too busy a work to be well done *ex tempore.* The foundation of death must be laid in life. He that means and desires to die well, must die daily; he that would end his days well, must spend them well, the one will help the other. The thoughts of thy end, as the train of the fowl, and rudder of a ship, will guide thy life, and a good life will lead thee to a peaceable end, that thou shalt neither shame nor fear to die. In a word, Plato's philosophy in this, is true divinity, that the best mean and whole sum of a wise man's life, is the commentation of death, not every fleet and flitting flash, but frequent and fixed contemplations. Death is the knownest and unknownest thing in the world ; that of which men have the most thoughts and fewest meditations. Be therefore persuaded to come and see ; that is, come that thou mayest see. Come from other objects, infinite and vain spectacles, with which the eye is never glutted. Draw near and close to this, that thou mayest see it throughly. Wipe off the clay, spittle, and scales off thine eyes, that thou mayest clearly behold the nature, quality, and consequents of death. No mortal wight but hath some blushes of mortality, such as go and come ; but if they would suffer them to lodge in their minds, they must needs stir some affection, and leave some impression to the memory, and produce some effects in their lives. Socrates had a gift that he could fasten his eyes many hours on one object without change or weariness. Half so staid a thought of one's mortality, might bring a man to immortality. It is not beauty seen, but looked on, that wounds. I met with a story of one that gave a young prodigal a ring with a death's head, with this condition, that he should one hour daily, for seven days together, look and think upon it ; which bred a strange alteration in his life, like that of Thesposius in Plutarch, or that, more remarkable, of Waldus, the rich merchant in Lyons, who seeing one drop down dead in the streets before him, went home, repented, changed his life, studied the Scriptures, and became a worthy preacher, father, and founder of the Christians called Waldenses, or poor men of Lyons. In conference and confessions many one hath acknowledged to myself the like ; some that by dangerous sickness of their own, others that by fear of infection in times of the plague, and general visitation, others by the death of friends, as by shafts that have fallen near them, have been awakened, affrighted, and occasioned to think deeply on their ends, to provide against their ends, to attend the word, which hath proved the mean of their conversion and salvation. And this I think should be enough to persuade young and old, one and another, to come and see.

But what now are we come out to see ?

Behold, First, the seal opened.

Secondly, the horse issuing out.

Thirdly, the colour of the horse.

Fourthly, the rider and his followers, death and hell.

This horse is under seal. Seals we use commonly to confirm and conceal, to make things sure, and to keep things secret. And thus death, as all God's judgments, are said to be sealed, Job. iii. 3, and that with a firmer seal than of the Medes and Persians ; in which sense, this horse, Zech. iv., issueth from between two brazen mountains ; that is, God's inevitable, unalterable decree. He rusheth not out, rangeth not abroad at the will of man or Satan, at hap or by blind destiny, but at the pleasure and by the appointment of the great Master of these God's horses, Jesus Christ (one of whose chief royalties is to keep the lock and key of death and hell, Rev. i.), else would he be ever trampling under feet the sons of men. Look how naturally and continually the sea would overwhelm the whole earth, if the waves were not bounded by providence ; so would this horse overcome the inhabitants of it, were he not tied short, and restrained by his and our Lord. You see him here limited to the fourth part of the earth, else had not one been left alive ; for all are sentenced, and have deserved to die, and it is favour that all die not. In a word, men die not by chance, course of nature, influence of stars, but then and therefore, because it is appointed. A million of Ethiopians perish in one day, in one battle, 2 Chron. xiv., not because all were born under one aspect of planets, but because such a slaughter was sealed of God. And though there be one way in, and twenty out of the world, yet all falls out as God determines and disposeth. That Christian which believes this, though he may desire David's arithmetic to number his days aright, that is, to know the brevity of them, yet will he never study the black and senseless art of calculating his birth and death. None but fools are curious and inquisitive to know that, which is under God's privy signet. We are all as soldiers sent to sea with commission under seal, not to be opened till we come to such and such a point. To guess and conclude we shall die at such an age, in such a climacterical year, what is it but to make a league with death ? not unlike to that frenzic merchant that would make and strike up matches of hundreds and thousands with parties absent, as if they were present. A fond, itching humour, and such as would, for the most part (whatever we think), do us hurt rather than good ; if the day and hour were far off, it would breed security ; if near hand, horror. Sicknesses are sufficient summonses and warnings. Mark such as, sentenced by judges and physicians, foreknow their death, yet without special grace fore-fit themselves never the more carefully. Some deaths, indeed (as some clocks), give warning before they strike, with symptoms and signs infallible ; and so extraordinarily God gives to some Moseses and Hezekiahs a presage, and hearts to prepare ; but generally God hath seen this the best for us, that it should be for the general most certain, for the particular most uncertain, to him sealed, to us concealed ; of which he would have us make these uses.

First, for our bodily health, not to be too careful, nor too careless. With all our physical diet and miserable anxiety, we cannot add one cubit to the length of our days, or measure of our health. We are all sealed up no otherwise than the measure of our wealth, or our crosses and blessings, for the having or avoiding of which, the means we must use without carking care, or cowardly fear, cheerfully relying on Christ, the Lord-keeper of the seal, not wittingly and desperately preventing that sealed date by surfeits, of toil or pleasure, by wilful neglect of diet, contempt of physic, by grief or by melancholy ; nay, not by haste to glory, with Cleombrotus the heathen, or with hasty, self-murdering Christians, such as Augustine's times were full off; but with Job, patiently abide all the days of our life, during the term of our sealed lease, till the very day and date expire, and appointed time of dismission and dissolution come. And,

Secondly, for our soul's provision, not to do as most that have set days of truce and peace, and in which they hang up their armour a-rusting, and their beacons unwatched; but as people that live in perpetual hazard of war, have all things in a daily readiness for service at half an hour's warning, upon the least alarm; who would not live one hour in infidelity or irrepentance, lest in that he be taken napping, as the foolish virgins, and that rich fool that reckoned of many years, and had not one night to continue. Grant it were enough to repent and believe the last day of life, yet how can a man be sure to do that, unless he do it every day; considering that every day may, for aught he knows, be the last. The seal may be opened in a day and hour one least thinks of it, as it is to most that die.

Lastly; Whenever this horse comes to fetch away us, or any of ours, children, or friends, a believer stamps not, and rages not, as mad Marshal Biron; murmurs not, repines not, as the wild Irishmen without hope; expostulates not with destiny, as Alexander for his Hephæstion; but with Aaron, lays his hand on his heart and mouth for his sons' sudden death, knowing what God hath sealed shall be and must be. If the dreams of a blind fatal necessity could quiet heathens, how much more should a Christian be cheerful at the disposal of a wise and loving keeper of the seal? A minute sooner or later it shall not be than he hath foreseen and foresealed for thy especial good, who hath times, and seasons, and seals, in his ordination. Worthy was the speech and resolution of an understanding divine. If Christ hath the key and seal of death, then a fig for death. This, though it be an ordinary notion, yet well digested, it is a singular stay to a believer.

The seal being thus opened, 'come and see' the creature that issues forth. Behold an horse, a fierce, a strong, a warlike, a speedy creature, so described by God himself, Job xxxix.

Look, therefore, how easily Jehu stamped Jezebel into pieces, and Tamerlane's troops of horse the Turkish footmen, or as the sturdy steed dashes out the little whappet's brains, so easily doth death with the least kick and spurn of his heel the halest complexion, the stoutest constitution, triumphing like an emperor over all sorts of people, treading on the necks of kings and princes, as Joshua over them in the cave, insulting in the terms of Rabshakeh, 'Where is Hamath? the kings of Arphad, Ivah, and Sepharvaim?' Elam, Meshech, and Tubal, whose fear was upon the living, are they not descended into the grave? made their beds in the slimy valley, and laid their swords under their heads. Where is Goliah with his brazen boots? Hath wisdom delivered, strength rescued, or wealth ransomed any out of my fingers? For all their confidence, have they not gone to the king of fear? How can it be otherwise, seeing death comes as an armed horseman upon naked footmen? No encountering, no resistance, no running away, no evasion by flight. This winged Pegasus posts and speeds after men, easily gives them law, fetches them up again, gallops and swallows the ground he goes, sets out after every man as soon as he comes into the world, and plays with him, as the cat with the mouse, as the greyhound with the badger; sometimes he follows fair and afar off, lingers aloof and out of sight; anon he spurs after, and by and by is at the heels in some sickness, and then, it may be, gives us some breath again, but in the end overtakes us, and is upon us with a jerk, as the snare over the fish or the fowl. Absalom could not outride him; Pharaoh's chariot wheels fell off in this chase. Jonathan and Saul, swift as the eagles, strong as the lion, yet how were they slain with the mighty? What, then, is the course the Christian takes? He neither foolishly thinks to resist or escape, nor yet cowardly swoons, or cravenly yields; but as a valiant footman that espies an horseman pursue him in a champaign, stays not till he come upon him, but addresseth himself for the encounter. So does a Christian, in his best health and prosperity, put on his armour, get him the helmet of salvation, the shield of faith, and learneth the use of them betimes, before he be unapt to it in sickness or age. As the Parthians teach their very children to handle the bow, the Scythians the dart, the Germans the spear; and so it comes to pass, that believers are not surprised, as worldlings often are, with milk but in their breasts, without oil in their lamps, and all in vain then fondly cry out to this horseman to stay his stroke. As the rich fool Gregory relates of, who entreated death to stay till the next morning, Truce but till to-morrow, and I will be ready for thee. A Christian wisely considereth that he hath no morrow, and therefore, while it is called to-day, is ready for this horse, who never sets any certain day of his coming.

Behold also the colour of this horse, χλωρος, the colour of the withering leaf, pale and wan, symbolizing and noting the effect he hath first upon the living, whom he appals, as he did Belshazzar, whom all his concubines and courtiers could not cheer, nor all his wine in the bowls of the temple fetch colour into his countenance. See we not often prisoners at the bar wane away, and dye as white as a cloth at the sentence of death pronounced on them. Many gulls and gallants we may hear sometimes slight off death with a jest, when they think it out of hearing, and some wish it, and call for it, as Gaal for Abimelech; but when it comes in good earnest, they are not able to look it in the face with the blood in their cheeks. Some foolishly set a face on the matter on their deathbeds, lest neighbours should censure when they are gone for cowards, hypocritically painting their faces, as Jezebel did, affronting Jehu out of the window, God knows with a cold heart, and if her paint had been off, a pale face should one have seen underneath it. Whereas Christians, having a good measure of faith to warm them at the heart, change not their countenance, nor have their colour any whit abated, but as is recorded of Mrs Joyce Lewis at the stake, and sundry other Christians, even of the fearfulest by nature and sex, looked as fresh and cheerfully at the hour of death as at their marriage.

A second effect of this pale horse is after death, bereaving the bodies of all blood and colour, making them lifeless and wan carcases, and so lays them a rotting and mouldering among the worms their sisters, till the fashion of them be utterly altered, the beauty consumed, and shape turned into rottenness. Oh, how grievous is this to such Absaloms, Jezebels, and Rosamonds, who have set much by their painted sheaths and pampered carcases, whose belly is their God, and yet their end must be corruption. Dust they were, and to dust they must return. Favour is deceitful, and beauty is vanity. When the pale horse comes there is no remedy. Here only faith hath an antidote, comforting herself with these sayings: This base and vile body of mine must be thus served, that it may be transfigured and made conformable to the glorious standard, Christ's body, more glorious than the sun in his brightest hue. It must thus be sown in pale ignominy, that it may rise in glorious beauty. What if I lose a little vermilion red, mixture of phlegm and sanguine, shall I not recover a radiant, resplendent lustre? Can the alchemist, with his art, cause a dry, withered flower to shew itself again for a space in its natural verdant shape and colour?

And cannot God, that made me first of clay, and that clay of nothing, reduce and refine the same after it hath been in the earth ? As the Chinese do the materials of their curious dishes for many scores of years, that when it is thoroughly defecate, their posterity may temper and frame some vessel of excellent service withal. Certainly my Redeemer liveth, and with these eyes I shall see him, as he is most admirable to behold, and myself like unto him in my degree, ten thousand times more comely than is here possible to imagine, the most personable creature that ever the sun saw ; when the body shall be enriched with those excellent dowries of impassibility, clarity, subtilty, agility.

Oh, but here is yet a more fearful spectacle behind than all that hath yet come in sight. Hell, even hell itself, in the worst sense, not the grave of the body, but of the soul. For John sees here principally the judgment of the wicked that were slain for the contempt of the gospel by the pale horse, for not yielding to the white and his crowned rider. And their woful state is here opposed to the happy condition of the martyrs under the altar.

Well, then, behold also, even hell, the page and follower of death, attending him wherever he goes among the wicked sort. Whence it is that they are so often coupled in this book, death and hell. Look as the foxes wait upon lions, carrion crows upon armies, gaolers upon sergeants for a prey, so diligently does the devil on death for a booty. No fowler does more cunningly stalk behind the horse, or creep behind brakes or hedges, to get his aim at the shy fowls. No sergeant hides his mace, no angler his hook more warily, knowing that else hell should never swallow so many.

Alack, alack ! we silly fish see one another caught and jerked out of the pond, but see not the fire and frying-pan into which they come. In this consists the devil's chiefest policy and our grossest simplicity, and even this is the cause of our sottish and foolish living and dying.

O that my head were a fountain of tears, to weep for and bewail the stupidity, yea, the desperate madness of infinite sorts of people that rush upon death, and chop into hell blindling. How brutish and beastly are the premises and conclusion of the epicure and his brood, 'Let us eat and drink, for to-morrow we shall die.' Who knows whether the soul of the beast descend, and man's ascend ? Who ever saw the one go downward and the other upward, and then what matter if the life of the one differ not from the other ? What need a man care whether he be a sadducee's swine, an epicure's horse, or himself ? The one many times hath less care and more pleasure than the other, if death be the last line, the full point, and final cessation of the creature. These brutes thank philosophy that hath taught them not to fear any such hobgoblin spirits or old wives' tales as hell. But such philosophy Socrates, Plato, and the wiser sort even of the heathen have hissed out of schools as belluine. Yea, the most savage and unlettered people, the less soiled with art, the more confidently do they, out of nature's instinct and divine impression, conclude of an eternal place of well and ill being after death for the souls of men. But these monsters wilfully shut their eyes, deface and obliterate these stamps and principles of nature, and so dance hoodwinked into perdition. Miserable it is to see how boldly and blindly they think and venture on death. Theramenes, he writes books in praise of death, as the end of all calamities. Augustus, he dies in a jest, calling for a *plaudite*. Tiberius in dissimulation. Diogenes, hearing Antisthenes cry out in his pains, Who shall ease me ? offers him a knife to dispatch himself withal. Caninus, called to execution, bids his fellow remember he had the best of the game. The Earl of Kildare, seeing his writ of death brought in, when he was at shuffle-board, throws his cast, with this in his mouth, ' Whatsoever that is, this is for a huddle.' Little list would these blind bayards have for such idle mirth, if their eyes were opened to see this follower of death. How piti-ful is the frenzy of those brave spirits, as they deem and term themselves (as much as they scorn pity), our duelists I mean, who, as if they never had heard of hell, are as prodigal of their lives as cocks or dogs are of theirs, pouring them out upon every drunken quarrel. I pity not the loss or miss of such, good for little but to set in the front of a battle, or to stop breaches and cannons withal; but I pity the loss of their souls, who serve themselves, as the Jesuit in Lancashire, followed by one that found his glove, with a desire to restore it to him, but pursued inwardly with a guilty conscience, leaps over a hedge, plunges into a marlpit behind it, unseen and unthought of, wherein he was drowned. I marvel not that they fear not a rapier or pistol. Who would not choose it before a lingering and painful sickness, were it not for the after-claps of death? No coward need fear the encounter of it alone in a single combat. But death hath a second, a page ten times more dreadful than himself, with whom we have to begin, when we have done with death, which is but the begin-ning of sorrows. Death is pale, but his follower is a black fellow, a terrible monster, never enough feared. In which respect how lamentable also is the blindness of all self-murderers, who make death the remedy of every grief, and cure of every violent passion. If they find themselves inwardly vexed, or perplexed in conscience, they seek death as a present ease, not considering how they leap out of the smoke into the flame, out of the flame into the fire, out of a curable momentary disturbance into an endless irrecoverable woe (without the extraordinary mercy of God), to which usually the devil speeds them, that he might get them into his clutches, and so pass out of doubt all means of prevention and evasion by faith and repentance.

Oh, senseless Ahithophel! how did thy wisdom fail and befool thee, when thou settest thine house in order, and disposest of thy goods, forgettest thy soul, hangest thyself; which durst thou, or wouldst thou have done, had but one believing thought of an eternal fire come into thy head? How blockish is the manner of dying of many a Nabal, who, strucken with the fear of death and hell, become as insensate as stocks and stones, have no mind nor power to think of one thing or other, cannot abide to hear any mention of the danger of that which they fear, whose senses the devil bewitches and benumbs, lest they should see and avoid? Such was Louis XI., who straitly charged his servants, that, when they saw him sick, they should never once dare to name that bitter word death in his ears. So do cowards and cravens shut their eyes, and choose rather to feel blows than to see and shun them.

Little better is the common course that most people take. Scared some are with a confused and preposterous fear of death, and flashes of hell in their consciences, and yet take no course to get pardon and faith in Christ; but, either taking it to be some melancholy humour, send for merry com-panions to drive it away; or being given up to hardness of heart and im-penitency, wilfully shake off all thoughts of repentance, shut their eyes and ears against all good advice, and desperately put all at adventures, and chop into the jaws of that roaring lion. Some of them ridiculously fearing death, they know not why, more for the pangs of it (which often are less than the toothache) than for the hell following; like fools that fear the thunder crack, and not the bolt; the report of the piece, and not the bullet; the sergeant's arrest, and not the gaoler's imprisonment; labour to escape death which they cannot, and hell which they might. Others of them, scared with some terrible apparitions, affrighted (as Cardinal Crescentius, a little before his death, with a black dog in his chamber), a presage and preludium of hell approaching, they cry out they are damned, the devil, the devil, do they not see him? &c. And so Spira-like, desperately and disconsolately depart in hellish horror. Other of them, a little wiser, and yet little the better for it, admit a cold thought or two, and it may be a little parley about the matter; but, when they have fetched a sigh or two, put all upon a ' Lord, have mercy on them,' trust it shall go as well with them as with others, even as God will have it, and think they do much if they send to a minister to pray with them or for them; never giving all diligence to make their salvation sure, and to escape so great a condemnation.

Oh! if we could consider how fearfully such find themselves deluded, when their souls awake worse than Jonas in the tempest, even in a gulf of fire and brimstone; how would it awaken and arouse us to foresee death and hell in their shapes, and to fore-appoint ourselves thoroughly, not against the first death, which we cannot, but against the second we may, if we get our part in the first resurrection.

This text, methinks, speaks to every sick man bound on his bed with the cords of death, as Delilah to Samson. Up and arise, for the Philistines are at hand. Death is at the door and behind the door; the fiends wait to fetch away thy soul. Bellarmine is of opinion that one glimpse of hell were enough to make a man not only turn Christian and sober, but anchorite and monk, to live after the strictest rule that can be. I am of belief that God's Spirit co-operating a thorough meditation of it, might be a mean to keep one from it. For a man to wish to have a sight of it, or that one might come thence and make report of the intolerable and unutterable pains of it, is superfluous, superstitious; and if it should be granted, yet being not God's ordinance and allowance, it might go without his blessing and do one no good. Thy best course is well to ponder what we that are God's ministers report of it, out of Moses', the prophets', Christ's, and the apostles' descriptions. And if God mean thee any good, our warning may do thee some good. Popish writers are too bold in making maps of heaven and hell, as if they had surveyed them and their regions and inhabitants; but most, I think, are on the other hand too brief and summary in their meditations and writings. To paint it in its own native colours is impossible, or by any contemplation to comprehend the horror of it. Shadows and parables the Scripture useth, by which thou mayest and oughtest to help thy conjectures, and to work on thy affections withal, after this or the like manner.

Here God hath allowed thee on his earth a pleasant habitation, commodiously situate in a good air, richly decked with furniture, compassed with delightful gardens, orchards, and fields, where thou hast liberty to walk and ride at thy pleasure; how would it trouble thee to think of being laid up all thy life in some strait and loathsome prison? By this consideration how ill thou wilt brook to be cast into a doleful, disconsolate dungeon, to lie in utter darkness, blackness of darkness, in eternal chains, in little ease for ever.

Here a great part of thy contentment is to live among good neighbours, with a loving wife, with cheerful companions; and loath thou art at any time to be long in the house of mourning, to be among melancholy, mal-contented, complaining, feeble, or brawling people, in hospitals, or bridewells, or bedlams. How will then thine ears endure to be tired with continual howling, screeching, and gnashing of teeth, to live among dogs, enchanters, unclean birds, reprobate spirits, worse than so many toads, tigers, or serpents?

Here, if thy Father should, in displeasure, bid get thee out of sight, or thy prince banish thee his court and presence, as David did Absalom, for some offence, thou wouldst take it heavily; how shall thine ears tingle to hear God say, ' Depart out of my presence; go, thou cursed, into the lake prepared for the devil and his angels?'

Here thou shrinkest to think of the gout, colic, stone, or strangurian, shiverest to hear of the strappado, the rack, or the lawn; how then wilt thou bear universal tortures in all the parts of thy body, exquisite anguish and pains, such as of which the pangs of childbirth, burnings of material fire and brimstone, gnawings of chest-worms, drinks of gall and wormwood, are but shadows; and to which they are all but sports and flea-bitings, even to the torments thy body shall suffer for its sins against the Creator.

But hast thou ever, here in this world, tasted of a troubled spirit, of the grief and fears of a wounded conscience, possessed with bitter things; strucken and pierced with the venom of God's arrows, fears of the Almighty? By these thou mayest make the best guess how it will fare with thy soul when God shall pour all the vials of his wrath into a vessel of his fury, and vex thy soul in his sore displeasure, scourge thee with the rods of scorpions, make thee drunk with the gall of asps and cockatrices, make thy mind heavy unto the death, holding it ever in those agonies which made his own Son sweat clots of water and blood. Oh, how fearful a thing it is to fall into the hands of God, who is a consuming fire! Think of it whiles there is hope, you that forget God, heaven, and hell, lest you come there where there is no redemption, no hope of ease or end, which is that that makes hell, hell indeed. For if these pains might have an end, were it after million and millions of years, as many as there be sands in the sea-shore, yet mightst thou nourish some miserable comfort of a release in the long run; but this night hath no day, this ague no intermission, this death no death to end it withal.

Here thou wouldst be loath to lie on the rack from morning to night, to be wrung with the colic for a few days or hours, to be haunted with a quartan from Michael to Easter. Oh! then, add eternity to insupportable torments, and let thine ears tingle, and thine heart melt, to think of it, Were it not for hope in small pressures, we say heart would burst. Oh! then, this word *ever and ever*, if thou couldst duly believe and consider it, how would it break that hard heart of thine, which knows not how to repent, nor cares to prevent, the wrath to come.

What thinkest thou? Are these things tales and fables? Is hell but a name and word, a scarebug for to keep fools in awe? Hath not God, thinkest thou, a day of reckoning, a prison and power to punish rebels and traitors? or are not his punishments like to his justice, infinite and eternal? Know these things to be as true as God is truth, save that they are short of the truth itself. Why dost thou not, then, take thy soul apart, and ruminate of these things by thyself, judging thyself here, that thou mayest not be condemned in the world to come? Art thou afraid of a melancholy fit? and fearest thou not this gulf, and whirlpool, and sorrow? Art thou loath to be tormented before thy time, and fearest not to be tormented time without end? I wonder how the souls of wicked men and unbelievers go not out of their bodies, as the devils out of demoniacs, rending, raging, tearing, and foaming. I wonder how any can die in their wits, that die not in the faith of our Lord Christ. Verily, if these things move thee not, thou art in a worse plight than Felix and Belshazzar; yea, the very devils themselves, who believe them, yea, quake and tremble to think of them. How fain would I snatch thy soul out of this fire! Undoubtedly know, that if this warning do thee no good, it is because thou art of old justly ordained to perish in thy impenitency, and to be a fire-brand in these everlasting flames. Now, on the contrary, if thou beest a vessel of mercy and honour, it will do thee no hurt, but drive thee to Christ, in whom there is no condemnation, who only is perfectly able to save and deliver thee out of this lake. If thou beest already in him, it will cause thee to rejoice in thy Lord and Saviour, who hath delivered thee from the fear of two such enemies, that now thou mayest, with the ostrich in Job, despise the horse and his rider, and triumph by faith over hell and death: ' O death, where is thy sting? O hell, where is thy victory?' Death is to men as he that comes attended: to Dives he comes followed with devils, to carry his soul to hell; to Lazarus with troops of angels, to convey him to Abraham's bosom: so that we may in earnest say, that death is the atheist's fear, and the Christian's desire. Diogenes could jestingly call it, the rich man's enemy, and the poor man's friend. This, this is that which makes death so easy, so familiar and dreadless to a believer. He sees death indeed, but death is not death without hell follow him; and hell he sees not, but only as escaped and vanquished, and therefore is said not to see death. Now (says the believer) comes death, and the prince of this world with him; but he hath no part in me; all the bitterness and tears of death lie in the fear of hell, which, thanks be to Christ, hath nothing to do with me, nor I with it, therefore I taste not of death. Now comes God's sergeant, pale death, whom I know I cannot avoid; but this I know, he comes not to arrest me, to carry me to prison, but only to invite me to a feast, attend, and convey me thither. Let such fear him as are in debt and danger, mine are all discharged and cancelled. He comes with his horse to take me up behind him, and to fetch me to my Father's joys, to a paradise as full of pleasures, as he carries the wicked to a prison full of pains. Pharaoh's baker and butler were sent for out of prison, the one to promotion, the other to execution; he that had the ill dream expected the messenger with horror, the other longed for him with comfort. The latter is my case; therefore, though I be reasonably well in this world, as a child at board, yet home is home, therefore will I wait till this pale horse comes, and bid him heartily welcome; and with him the angels of my father, who have a charge to lay my body in a bed of rest, and to bestow my soul under the altar, as it follows in the next seal, which is so pleasing a vision, that we need no voice or preface, such as we had in the former, inviting us to ' Come and see.' The very excellency of the object itself, is of force enough to draw and hold the eyes of our minds unto it.

THE SECOND SERMON.

And when he had opened the first seal, I saw under the altar the souls, &c.—
VERSE 9.

WHEN death hath been viewed in the palest, and hell in the blackest colours that may be, yet, if we have faith enough to see souls in their white robes under the altar, there is comfort enough against the horror of both, enough to enable the believer to despise and trample over them both. In the opening of this fifth seal, I hope to find more solid antidotes, more lively cordials, against the fear of death, than in all the dead and dry precepts of Bellarmine's doting ' Art of Dying.' For this part of the vision was shewed John of purpose to sweeten the harshness of the former, that his spirit, grieved and amazed with the sight of the calamities and mortality under the persecuting butchers, rather than emperors, might yet be relieved and refreshed with a sight of the blessed estate of such as died either in or for the Lord.

Wherein was proposed to his sight, and to our consideration, these severals. *First*, the immortal subsistence of souls, after their separation from the body. *Secondly*, their sure and secure condition under the altar. *Thirdly*, their dignity and felicity, clothed with white robes. *Fourthly*, their complete happiness at the last day, when the number of their brethren shall be accomplished.

Of all these Christ meant John should take notice, and all believers by his testimony, to their full consolation.

First, John, being in the spirit, could see spirits. Men, indeed, clad in flesh, can hardly imagine how a soul can have existence out of the flesh. Eagles can see that which owls cannot ; so is that visible and credible to a spiritual man, which to a natural is invisible, incredible. And yet even nature's dim eyes have been clear enough to see this truth. Nature, I say, pure and mere nature, not only the Platonists, and other learned ones, who resolutely concluded it, and aptly resembled it to the distinct being of the waggoner after the breaking of the coach, the swimming out of the mariner in the wreck of the ship, the creeping of the snail out of the shell, the worm out of the case. Not unto the learned Grecians and civilized Romans, but even the rudest Scythians and unlettered savages ; yea, though there be many languages, and sundry dialects in the world, yet is, and hath this ever been the common voice of them all, that souls die not with the body. And however the body's resurrection hath to them been a problem and paradox, yet is the soul's eternity an inbred instinct sucked from nature's breast, or rather an indelible principle stamped in the souls of men by the finger of God. And indeed, to right reason, what difficulty or absurdity is there in it ? What lets me to conceive a being of it in the air, in the heaven, or in any other place, as well as in the compass of my body? Is not one substance as capable of it as another ? Can it live in the one, and not in the other ?

Hath it not, even whiles it is in the body, thoughts, motives, passions by itself, of its own, different from the body, many cross and contrary to the disposition of the body ; cheerful ones when that is in pain or melancholy, choleric ones when that is phlegmatic ? Doth it wait upon the body for joy, sorrow, anger, and the like ? doth it not more often begin unto it ? Not to speak of martyrs innumerable, who have been exceedingly pleasant in the midst of torments, as if they had been spirits without flesh ; how many ancient stories and daily examples have we of cheerful minds, in distempered, pained, languishing, dying bodies ? Reason will then conclude, that the soul may well be, and be sensible after death without the body, which even in the body can be well when that is ill, cheerily when that is hurt or sick, grieved or troubled when that is in perfect temper and health. And, on the contrary, small reason have we to think it sleeps out of the body, or that it is seized by death out of the body, which never was overcome by sleep, which is but death's image and younger brother, in the body, but ever was working and discoursing in the deepest and deadest sleeps of the body.

Besides, is it likely God would enrich it with such noble and divine dowries, to be salt only to the body, to exhale with it as brutes do ? The admirable invention of arts, letters, engines, the strange forecasts, prospects and presages of the understanding part, the infinite lodgings, the firm retainings of the memory, do they not argue an immortality ? Do men engrave curiously in snow, ice, or transient stuff ?

What means the greatest anxiety of men about their surviving name, if the mind perished with the body, if death were the cessation of the man, and destruction of the whole substance ? What should nature care for an airy accident without a subject, whereof no part of him should be sensible ?

What means the very fear of death, if that were the end of all fears, and cares, and sorrows, if nothing remained sensible, and capable of any thing to be feared ?

Lastly, the fresh vigour, the unimpaired ability, that nimble agility of the mind in sickness, yea, many times the freer use of the faculties of it in the confines, yea, in the act and article of death, than in former health ; do they not tell the body, the soul means not to fall with the carcase (which hath the name* of falling), lies not a dying with it, but erects itself, means only to leave it as an inhabitant doth a ruinous house, or as a musician lays down a lute whose strings are broken, a carpenter a worn instrument unfit any longer for service and employment, and as a guest makes haste out of his inn, to his long home and place of abode.

Loath I am to mingle philosophical cordials with divine, as water with wine, lest my consolations should be flash and dilute ; yet, even these and such like arguments have taught all philosophy (the brutish school of the Epicure excepted) to see and acknowledge that the soul is not a vapour but a spirit, not an accident but a substance, and elder and more excellent sister to the body, immixt and separable ; a guest that dies not with it, but diverts out of it, intending to revisit and reunite it again unto itself. But divinity certainly knows all this to be most certain, that it is a particle of divine breath, imbreathed into the red loam at the first, not arising out of it, but infused from heaven into it, and therefore may as well exist without the clay after it, as it did before it ; and when the dust returns to the dust, heaven goes to heaven, both to their originals, the soul first, because first and principal in every action, the body after, as an accessory and second : and so the day of death to the body, is the birth of eternity to the soul.

This undying and ever-living condition of the soul, throughly rolled in the mind, firmly embraced, and undoubtedly apprehended by faith, works admirable effects, as in life, so in the approach of death. Seneca, that saw it but through clouds, crannies, and crevices, with *ifs* and *ands*, yet professeth that when he thought but a little of it, and had some pleasant dreams of it, he loathed himself and all his trifling greatness. But most divinely and resolutely, Julius Palmer : ' He that hath his soul linked and tied to the body, as a thief's feet to a clog with gyves and fetters, no marvel he knows not how to die, is loath to endure a division ; but he that useth, and can by faith separate the spirit from the body, to him it is as to drink this :' and with that drinks off a cup of wine in his hand, and within a while after, as cheerfully drinks of death's cup in the sight of the same witnesses. Even

* I suppose ' *Cadaver*,' from ' *Cadare*,' to fall.—ED.

Socrates himself sweetened his cup of poison, with his discourse of the soul's immortality, to the amazement of the beholders. Such souls indeed as place all their felicity to be in a full-fed and well-complexioned body, and to partake of the senses' corporeal delights, hath not accustomed itself to its own retired delights of abstracted meditations, knows not how to be merry without a playfellow, no marvel though it be as loath to part with the body, as a crooked, deformed body to part with rich robes, gorgeous apparel, which were its only ornaments.

But such noble and regenerate spirits as know their own dowries, have inured themselves to sublimate contemplations, and to have their conversation in heaven, whiles they were in the body ; such, I say, though they do not cynically revile the body as a clog, a prison, a lump of mire, &c., but know it to be the temple of the Holy Ghost, yet are they willing, yea, and sigh to be unclothed, to sow it awhile in the earth, being a dark and thick lantern, hindering the clear sight of it, till they may reassume it clarified, a spiritual, an angelified body made apt and obsequious to all divine services, to celestial offices without weariness, intermission, and such like vanity, which here it is subject unto : as willing as David to lay aside Saul's cumbersome armour, and to betake him to such as he could better wield and command at pleasure.

This is the first and lowest help faith hath to comfort the soul withal in the approach of death. When the strong men buckle, the keepers of the house fail ; they wax dim that look out at the windows, when the whole outward man decays. That the inner man ages not, faints not, languisheth not, but rather lifts up the head, is more fresh than formerly, and expects to be unburdened, and to be at liberty, freed from corporeal, tedious, unpleasing works of sleeping, eating, drinking, and other meaner drudgery, that it may once come to higher and more spiritual employments better suiting with its native condition ; even as the lion longeth to be out of the grate, and the eagle out of the cage, that they may have their free scope and fuller liberty.

Under the Altar.

Now if this much revived John (as no doubt it did) to see the soul's continuance after death, how much more to see their safety and rest under the altar ; that is, under Christ's protection and custody, under the shadow of his wings ; who makes them grateful to his Father, covers them from his wrath, safeguards them from all molestation, procures them absolute quiet and security. The phrase alluding to the altar in the tabernacle, which gave the offerings grace and acceptation ; and partly to the safety of such as fled from the avenger to the altar. Christ is our altar, and all the souls of such as die in his faith, are as Stephen bequeathed to him ; he presents them to his Father, shelters them from accusation and condemnation, gathers them, as the hen her chickens, under his wings, being fully able to keep what is committed to him from all disquiet. He that could keep the three young men in the furnace, with whom he walked, yea, their very garments from the violence of fire ; the Israelites and their apparel in the wilderness ; Jonah in the whale's belly ; how much more easily, now he sits at the right hand of his Father in majesty and glory, can he defend saved and glorified souls from external and internal annoyance, and settle them in absolute peace with him in his paradise, according to his frequent promise to such as overcome, ' They shall sit with me upon thrones.'

And long white Robes were given unto every one.

If John had seen souls at rest, though in poor and mean condition, yet were a corner of an house with peace to be preferred to a wide palace with disquiet; a poor diet with green herbs, with quiet, to a feast with stalled oxen, and crammed fowls, sauced with bitter contention. But behold, he sees not naked, beggarly, ragged souls, but adorned with white robes ; that is, endowed now, and glorified with perfect righteousness, purity, clarity, dignity, and festivity, of all which white apparel hath ever been an emblem and symbol in divine and human heraldry, a clothing of princes in their great solemnities of coronation, triumphs and ovations, says Eusebius ; so was Herod arrayed in cloth of silver, with which the sunbeams meeting, made such a glister, as amazed the people, that styled him a God ; so says Tertullian, were they wont to dignify servants at their manumissions with white apparel, in token of their new liberty and preferment. At feasts great persons were wont to change their guests' ordinary clothes with a white synthesis, a colour fit to express alacrity. Christians the whole Easter week wore white apparel. All the graces the souls had here in this their infancy of regeneration, were but stained and polluted clouts ; their knowledge dark and obscured with ignorance, their memories clouded with oblivion, their wills and affections tempested with mutinies and perturbations, their habits of holiness and charity sullied with defects and infirmities, their delights dusk and parti-coloured and spotted with mixture of sorrow ; all their apparel black and sad russet at the best ; but they are purer than the crystal, whiter than the snow, or than fullers' earth is able to make them. The lilies, and Solomon, in all their royalties, not like unto the meanest of them. Call us no more *Marah*, may they say, but *Naomi*. For fulness of beauty is conferred upon them, God becoming fulness of clarity and light unto the understanding, without error or darkness, continuation of eternity to the memory without forgetfulness, multitude of peace to the will and affections without disturbance or disorder ; the superior part of the soul pleasing itself in the blessed vision of God, and the inferior satiate with the fruition of rivers of pleasures, and variety of monthly fruits. All this joy increased by the amity and magnificence of the place, being God's palace, built and prepared for eternity, for the honour of his majesty, and habitation of his saints, all shining like precious jasper ; enchanted by the full choir of angels, and communion of holy men, excellent when they were on earth, now perfected in their virtues, and freed from frailties, never mourning, but ever singing and lauding their Creator with hallelujahs, without defatigation or satiety ; all this made up and consummate by the addition, not of a number of years, but of eternity uncountable, unalterable, incomprehensible. What are the chief miseries of this life, but the sordid apparel of the soul, the black thoughts, the speckled phantasies, dark oblivion, roiled, soiled affections, all the habit of it squalid, jagged and tattered ? Now then was Joseph loath to change his prison rags, or Esther her old and mean clothes, with stately and royal array ? Promise a child a new satin suit, and see whether he will not long for it, and call for it ; see whether he will cry when you bid him lay off his russets. Whence is it then that men die so dully, so unwillingly, so heavily ? Or whence can it be, but because they do not live and certainly believe, and expect these white robes for their souls ? When the beauty of a man's mind is here obfuscate and defaced with melancholy tentations, opaque imaginations, with yellow choler, with pallid fear, with ruddy shame, with sable despair ; O what would he give for a

candid, calm, and serene state of his mind! And when again it pleaseth God
to afford him sunshine holidays of joy and tranquillity, wherein his mind is
clad, and decked with golden, silver, and precious ornaments of peace,
meekness, temperance, patience, O what an heaven would he think he had
here on earth, if all his days were but such days! Whereas this a Christian
may well assure himself of, that whatever grace doth here prepare and begin,
there glory will absolve and perpetuate, for matter of sanctity, purity, and
alacrity of the mind, typified in these white robes; yea, further for matter of
dignity and triumph, which then shall be most complete, where they shall
see Christ at that day come in the glory of the Father with millions of his
angels, descending and bringing down his heavenly Jerusalem, meeting
them half way in the clouds, and there avenging them on their enemies,
sitting with them as assessors upon thrones, to judge the angels, and the
world of wicked ones, and such as have insulted over them on the earth, in
which they shall then without any malignity of envy, anger, or appetite of
revenge, take admirable and unspeakable content and comfort, yea, reckon
it as the accomplishment of their inchoate glory, for which they are here
said to long for and groan under the altar, till the number of all their
brethren being consummate, God shall openly acquit and applaud them,
condemn and confound their opposites. These, these are the only, stately,
and kingly dignities ; the meditations whereof are only able to beget and
foster true heroical and Christian resolutions against the fear of death and
hell, otherwise unvanquished. To conclude, then: to the man that would
both in health and sickness nourish ever in his breast undaunted and more
conquering thoughts of these two enemies, instead of Bellarmine's many
frivolous and tedious rules, I prescribe but these two practices of faith.
The first is to work in his mind a settled and undoubted certainty; and the
second, a lively and frequent representation of them.

Were heaven nothing else but an haven of rest, we know how welcome
the one is to a sea-sick weather-beaten traveller, and may by that guess
how desirable the other should be to a soul that long hath been tossed in
the waves of this world, sick of its own sinful imaginations, and tired with
external tentations. The happiest soul that ever hath sailed over this
Euripus, in the best ship, in the healthfulest body that ever was, never had so
calm a passage but that it hath had cause enough often to wish itself on shore.
What with self-groaning phantasies, and injected tentations, how little respite or rest is here to be found! Is there any palace or tower here so
high or strong that can keep diseases from the body? how much less cares,
sorrows, fears, and Satan's assaults from the soul! Were there but such
an island as some have dreamed of here on earth, that might free our
bodies or minds from disquiet, but for the space of the moment of this life,
how would people covet to dwell in it! In the times of the late wars in
the Netherlands, how did the boors forsake their farms and fly into walled
cities for security from dangers! What violence then should our heavenly
Jerusalem suffer of our wishes and desires! were it but for the sweet and
amiable name of peace whereof it is denominated, having indeed the God
of peace for the king and keeper of it; walls many cubits high, into which
no Sennacherib can shoot an arrow, nor the dragon-beast, nor the false prophet to seduce or to accuse; strong gates and bars excluding all enemies
and annoyances, and so affording perfect tranquillity to all the inhabitants,
out of which they insult ten times more safely than the Jebusites did over
the blind and lame, over the pale horse and his riders, death and hell.
Consider and compare a little the simplicity of the worldling with the wis-

dom of the Christian, the happy stability of the one with the woful uncertainty of the other, at the time of their departure. Even foxes and hares and other such vermin, fore-acquaint themselves with muses, thickets, and burrows, into which, when they are chased and hunted, they may repair for safety; but these fools, while they live in health and prosperity, never think of the evil day: and when away they see they must go, how unshiftable are they ! Some of the meaner sort, they take care for their winding-sheet; or if richer, for a marble or painted sepulchre, which yet cannot preserve their bodies or names from putrefaction ; the supersitious sort, to be buried in a friar's cowl or under an altar of stone; the desperater sort, wishing the mountains might cover them from the wrath of the Lamb. An harbour or receptacle for their souls they never think of; whence it is that they are as loath to have them turned out of their bodies as Hagar and Ishmael to be out of doors, and exposed to misery and dangers ; or rather as Cain, to be cast as a vagabond out of God's presence, fearing lest every one that met him next should cut his throat for a cursed caitiff. And indeed what else can they look for, but instantly to be devoured of the roaring lion that waits at the door of death, to fetch away their souls into the place where there is no night nor day. Only the wise believer, he hath provided a sanctuary, or city of refuge, against time of danger, hath learned wisdom of the conies, who, though a little nation, yet wise and forecasting, have their refuge in the rocks. Christ is the believer's rock and his strong tower, his altar, and therefore he fears not what death can do unto him. Christ hath assured him on his word, that he shall have all tears wiped away, and the Spirit secured him that he shall rest from his labours. In which regard he is so far from lingering and hankering after a continuance in this *Baca* of tears, this wilderness of fears, that he studies rather to enter into this rest, cries out with David, 'Woe is me, that I dwell in Meshek and Kedar ! when I think of peace, there is war at hand.' With Jeremiah, ' Woe is me, that I dwell with a contentious people.' With Elias, ' I am weary of my life; an end, good Lord.' Or with blessed Simeon, ' Now, Lord, let thy servant depart in peace, into that land of peace. Here I have seen that there is no peace to be had ; all here is vanity and vexation of spirit.' For a minute of peace, months of vanity ; for a dram of honey, pounds of aloes and gall. Souls here find no resting-place for the soles of their feet, till they come to the Mount Ararat, whither their works follow them, where their sorrows leave them. And so conclude with Vidus Bressius: ' O that my soul had the wings of the dove, to fly and make haste to that mountain of God, and hill of tranquillity and eternity.' Thus the one dies howling, the other singing; because the one knows he changeth for the better, the other for the worse. The one takes death for a gulf of sorrow, the other for a port of liberty and ease ; the one because he is stripped for a scourging, the other because he lays off his clothes to go to bed after his toil.

If Queen Elizabeth, whiles she was a prisoner in her sister's days, could have been fully assured, and had clearly foreseen her own long, glorious, and prosperous reign ensuing, would she have wished herself a milkmaid for the present? No ; it had been impossible. All our fears and doubts arise from infidelity, and the uncertainty, or else from the deadness and dulness, of our hopes; to put life into which there can be no better, no other help than first to ground and root our faith in Christ through the word and Spirit, and then often to be setting before our eyes a state and condition happy above all that cities, kingdoms, crowns, pearls and jewels, marriages, feasts, and all other metaphors and parables of Scripture, do but shadow out unto us: which supereminent and superabundant felicity Paul, that had been an eye-witness, not able to describe, much less to amplify, sums it up, ' An exceeding-exceeding, eternal weight of glory.'

A superlative, transcendent phrase, such as is not to be found in all the rhetoric of the heathens, because they never wrote of such a theme, nor with such a spirit. If any of us had but half the strength of Paul's faith, or life of his hope, or cheerful fore-imaginations, which he had of this felicity, we could not but have the same desires and longings for our dissolution and fruition of them. If we thoroughly believed and remembered this to be the state of ourselves and dead friends, would we or could we so fear for ourselves or mourn for them in blacks whiles they are in whites, as Jacob for Joseph, thinking him devoured by some evil beast, when he was lording it in Egypt? No, verily; but think of it and look for it we would with the same affections that children do for their plays, apprentices their freedom, spouses their marriage, labourers their wages, husbandmen their harvest, heirs their inheritance, princes their kingdoms. Amongst many thousands, I choose to instance and end with Monica and Augustine's examples, the mother using this speech to her son: ' All that I have desired to live to see is that which I now see—thee, my son, a Christian. And now, what do I any longer in this base and impure world?' And he of his mother: ' What cause have I to mourn for a mother of whose happiness I may be so well assured?'

When I Awake I shall be Satisfied.

Write, O Christ, these meditations in our hearts, imprint these patterns so fast in our memories, that we may all the days of our lives have frequent forethoughts of our appointed change, chiefly in that last and solemn day of our death, when the prince of this world will be busy and we shall be weak. Let thy Comforter then bring them to mind, that by faith we may overcome, and, having the ark of thy covenant in eye, cheerfully pass through the waters of Jordan, and so take possession of that land which flows with all variety of delights, without either end or satiety. ' Even so, come, Lord Jesus, come quickly.'

A COAL FROM THE ALTAR TO KINDLE THE HOLY FIRE OF ZEAL.

IN A SERMON PREACHED AT A GENERAL VISITATION AT IPSWICH.

TO MY REVEREND FRIEND

MR SAMUEL WARD

SIR—Your sermon, which I copied partly from your mouth, and partly from your notes, I have adventured into the light; encouraged by the approbation and earnest entreaty of such whose judgments you reverence and whose love you embrace; who also have made bold here and there to vary some things, not of any great consequence, if I can judge. I was loath to smother such fire in my breast, but to vent it, to inflame others. If you shall blame me, I know others will thank me. What I have done is out of zeal to God and his church.

Your affectionate Friend,

AMBROSE WOOD.

Be zealous.—REV. III. 19.

THIS watch-word of Christ, if it be not now a word in season, I know not when ever it was, or will be.   Would he now vouchsafe to bestow a letter upon his church here on earth, should he need to alter the tenor of this ? Which being the last to the last of the seven churches, why may it not (saith an ancient, upon this text) typify the estate of the last age of his churches ? the coldness whereof himself hath expressly foretold.   And if God should now send through the earth such surveying angels as Zachariah mentions, chap. i., could they return any other observation of their travels than theirs, ' The whole world lies in lukewarmness ' ? which makes me often, in my thoughts, proportion these ends of time to the like period of David's age, when no clothes were enough to keep heat in him, 1 Kings i. 1. Faith, I grant, is a more radical, vital, and necessary grace ; but yet not so wholly out of grace with the times as poor zeal, which yet, if by any means it might once again be reduced into favour and practice, before time sets, and be no more, I doubt not but Christ would also yet once again, in this evening of the world, come and sup with us, a favour including all other in it.

My desire especially is, that this our island might take it to itself, as well as if it had by name been directed to it ; what would it hurt us to make an especial benefit and use of it ?   Some of our own have so applied it (either out of their judgments or affections, I say not). Learned Fulke marvels if it were not by a prophetical spirit penned for us ; others more resolutely have made it a singular type of purpose for us.   Their warrant I know not, especially if it be true, which all travellers tell you, that they find more zeal at home than abroad.   We are, I grant, in sundry respects equal to Laodicea.   Even the very names thereof, as well the first and oldest in regard of the blessings of God,   Διοσπολις, God's darling, as the latter in regard of good laws and civility, *Laodicea*, how well do they become us ?   As rich as they, and that in the very same commodity of wools, abounding as they with many learned Zenos, and bountiful Hieros, parallel in all regards, I would I could say lukewarmness excepted.   But I must be a faithful and true witness, and yet this is all I have to say ; it was, as I conceive, Laodicea's complexion, and not her constitution ; her practice, not her orders ; personal lukewarmness, not legal, which Christ strikes at.   That fault I find in my text, the same I find in our common Christians, whose spiritual condition and state is too like the external situation of our country, between the torrid and the frigid zones, neither hot nor cold ; and so like Laodicea, that if we take not warning, or warming, we may, I fear, in time to come be spued out of God's mouth.

For this present assembly of ministers, could all the choice and time in the world have better fitted me than mine ordinary lot ?   If fire be set upon the beacons, will not the whole country soon be warned and enlightened ?

For myself also, methinks it will better beseem my years to heat, than to teach, my ancients ; to enkindle their affections, then to inform their judgments.   And whereas Paul bids Titus preach zeal with all authority, though in mine own name I crave your patience and audience, yet in his name that is the first of the creatures, and *Amen*, I counsel him that hath an ear, to hear what the Spirit saith to the churches.

Ζηλωσον, ' *Be zealous.*'

A COAL FROM THE ALTAR.

Ζηλῶσον, ' *Be zealous.*'—Rev. III. 19.

Zeal hath been little practised, less studied. This heavenly fire hath ever been a stranger upon earth; few in all ages that have felt the heat of it, few that have known the nature of it. A description will rake it out of the embers of obscurity; and it may be that many, when they shall know it better, will better affect it.

2. Zeal hath many counterfeits and allies.* There are many strange fires, which, having sought to carry away the credit of it, have brought in an ill name upon it. From these it would be distinguished.

3. Zeal is everywhere spoken against; it hath many enemies and few friends. The world can no more abide it, than beasts can the elementary fire; the rebukes of many have fallen upon it, the devil weaves cunning lies to bring down the honour of it. Oh, that we could raise and maintain it, by setting forth the deserved praise of it, and challenge it from the false imputations of such as hate it without a cause.

4. Zeal hath in this our earthly mould little fuel, much quench-coal; is hardly fired, soon cooled. A good Christian, therefore, would be glad to know the incentives and preservatives of it, which might enkindle it, inflame it, feed it, and revive it when it is going out.

5. Zeal, in the world's opinion, is as common as fire on every man's hearth; no man's heart without zeal, if every man might be his own judge. If most might be heard, there is too much of it. But the contrary will appear if the right marks be taken, and the true rules of trial and conviction be observed, and the heart thereby examined.

6. Zeal generally handled will break as lightning in the air, and seize upon no subject. Application must set it on men's hearts, and exhortation warm this old and cold age of the world, chiefly this temperate climate of our nation.

THE FIRST PART.

It was said of old, that zeal was an intention of love; of late, that it is a compound of love and anger, or indignation.

The ancients aimed right and shot near, if not somewhat with the shortest. The modern well discovered the use and exercise of more affec-

* Qu. ' Alloys?'—Ed.

tions than love within the fathom and compass of zeal; but in helping that default went themselves somewhat wide, and came not close to the mark; which I ascribe not to any defect of eyesight in those sharp-sighted eagles, but only to the want of fixed contemplation. And, to speak truth, I have oft wondered why poor zeal, a virtue so high in God's books, could never be so much beholden to men's writings as to obtain a just treatise, which hath been the lot of many particular virtues of inferior worth, a plain sign of too much undervalue and neglect.

He that shall stedfastly view it shall find it not to be a degree or intention of love, or any single affection (as the schools rather confined than defined zeal), neither yet any mixed affection (as the latter rather compounded than comprehended the nature of it), but a hot temper, higher degree or intention of them all. As varnish is no one colour, but that which gives gloss and lustre to all, so the opposites of zeal, key-coldness and lukewarmness, which by the law of contraries must be of the same nature, are no affections, but several tempers of them all.

Paul warrants this description where he speaks of the twelve tribes. They served God with intention or vehemency, Acts xxvi. 7.

The root shews the nature of the branch. Zeal comes of a word framed of the very sound and hissing noise which hot coals or burning iron make when they meet with their contrary. In plain English, zeal is nothing but heat; from whence it is that zealous men are oft in Scripture said to burn in the Spirit.

He that doth moderately or remissly affect anything may be styled *Philemon*, a lover; he that earnestly or extremely, *Zelotes*, a zealot; who to all the objects of his affections is excessively and passionately disposed; his love is ever fervent, his desires eager, his delights ravishing, his hopes longing, his hatred deadly, his anger fierce, his grief deep, his fear terrible. The Hebrews express these intentions by doubling the word.

This being the nature of zeal in general, Christian zeal, of which we desire only to speak, differs from carnal and worldly chiefly in the causes and objects.

It is a spiritual heat wrought in the heart of man by the holy Ghost, improving the good affections of love, joy, hope, &c., for the best service and furtherance of God's glory, with all the appurtenances thereof, his word, his house, his saints, and salvation of souls; using the contrary of hatred, anger, grief, &c., as so many mastiffs to fly upon the throat of God's enemies, the devil, his angels, sin, the world, with the lusts thereof. By the virtue whereof a zealot may run all through all his affections, and with David breathe zeal out of every pipe, after this manner for a taste.

Love.—' How do I love thy law, O Lord, more than the honey or the honeycomb, more than the thousands of silver and gold?'

Hatred.—' Thine enemies I hate with a perfect hatred.'

Joy.—' Thy testimonies are my delight. I rejoice more in them than they that find great spoils, more than in my appointed food.'

Grief.—' Mine eyes gush out rivers of tears. O that my head were a fountain of tears, because they destroy thy law!'

Hope.—' Mine eyes are dim with waiting: how do I long for thy salvation!'

Fear.—Thy judgments are terrible, I tremble and quake,' &c.

Look what pitch of affection the natural man bestows upon his dearest darling, what insatiable thirst the covetous worldling upon his Mammon, the ambitious upon his honour, the voluptuous upon his pleasure, the same the Christian striveth in equal, yea (if possible), far exceeding terms to convert and confer upon God and his worship.

In brief, to open a little crevice of further light, and to give a little glimpse of heat; zeal is to the soul, that which the spirits are to the body, wine to the spirits, putting vigour and agility into them. Whence comes that elegant antithesis in the Scripture, ' Be not drunk with wine, wherein is excess, but be filled with the Spirit.'

Christ is said to lead his spouse into the wine-cellar ; which simile Bernard * delighting oft to repeat, in two or three sermons interprets of a special measure of zeal inspired into his church. Thus (saith he) Christ led his disciples into the wine-cellar on the day of Pentecost, Acts ii., and filled them and the house with such zeal, as they came forth like giants refreshed with wine, and seemed to the people as men drunk with new wine.

It is to the soul as wings to the fowl. This also is a Scripture emblem to picture the angels with wings, as in the hangings of the temple, and in the visions of the Revelation, in token of their ardent and zealous execution of God's will, whence also they have their name *seraphim;* ' he maketh his ministers a flame of fire,' Heb. i. 7.

To this fire and these wings, which we in the Lord's prayer desire to imitate, there is nothing in us answerable but our zeal ; as wheels to the chariot, which makes us not go, but run the ways of God's commandments, and so run that we may obtain. As sails to the wind, and wind to the sails, to which alludes the phrase so frequent in Scripture, *Plerophory.*

As courage to the soldier, mettle to the horse, lust † to the ground, which makes it bring forth much fruit, yea, a hundredfold, vivacity to all creatures. To conclude this, this is that celestial fire which was shadowed out unto us by that poor element in comparison and beggarly rudiment, the fire (I mean) of such necessary use in the law, which rather than it should be wanting, the Lord caused it to descend from heaven, that it might cause the sacrifices to ascend thither again, as a sweet incense unto the Lord, without which no burnt-offering was acceptable.

The Second Part.

But now, as then, there are certain false fires, abominable to God, odious to men, dangerous to the Nadabs and Abihues that meddle with them, bringing thereby coals upon their own heads, and ill favour upon all their services ; and not only so, but that which is worse, an ill report and surmise even on those that offer the right fire, and serve the Lord in spirit and truth ; yet for their sakes is the name of zeal blasphemed all the day long.

Against these, as then, so now, severe caveats and clear distinctions must be laid, lest such as have not their senses exercised to put a difference, mistake poisonful weeds for wholesome herbs, to their own destruction, and for the sake of one revile the other, to the wrong of God and his saints.

It fares not otherwise with the soul than with the body ; besides the native and radical heat, the principal instrument of life, there are aguish and distempered heats, the causes of sickness and death.

To discern of those requires some skill and judgment; yet a good empiric, a Christian of experience, will give a shrewd guess at them, the easier and the better if he mark these following signs and symptoms common to all the kinds of zeal, here also following.

First,. They are deeply sick of the -pharisaical humour, they love to be

* Serm. xli. in Can. iv. 9.   † That is, ' fatness or fertility.'—ED.

seen of men, and say with Jehu, ' Come and see how zealous I am for the Lord of Hosts.' They proclaim their alms with a trumpet, paint their good deeds upon church windows, engrave their legacies upon tombs, have their acts upon record. Thus, comets blaze more than fixed stars; aguish heats breed flushings, and are more seen in the face than natural warmth at the heart. Scholars count hiding of art the best art; the godly man studies by all means how to conceal the one hand from the other in doing well. Hiding of zeal is the best zeal.

Secondly, Of Ahab's disease; exceeding in external humiliation, affected gestures, passionate sighs, loudness of voice, odd attires, and such like. These know how to rend the garment, hang the head with the bulrush, to whip and lance their skins with Baal's priests, and yet strangers to a wounded spirit; not but that true and hearty zeal doth lift up the eyes, knock the breast, dance before the ark. Therefore, this character may deceive the unwary. Let Eli take heed of judging Hannah's spirit rashly by the moving of her lips; yet hypocrites so usually strain nature, and without a cause exceed, and that in public, and upon the stage, that for the most part their actions and affections are palpable; as Jesuits, Capuchins, &c., yea, in many histrionical protestants. Horse-coursers' jades will bound, curvet, and shew more tricks, than a horse well mettled for the road or cart.

Thirdly, You may know them by their diligence and curiosity in lighter matters, joined with omission and neglect of greater, wise in circumstance and careless in substance, tithing mint, straining at gnats, &c. In all cheap and easy duties, prodigal; niggardly and slothful in the weighty things of the law. These have at command good words, countenance, yet tears from their eyes sooner than a farthing from their purse, having this world's goods, and see their brother want; these stick up feathers for the carcase, beguiling the simple, cozening the world, but chiefly themselves.

Fourthly, These fires cannot keep themselves within their own hearths, these spirits cannot keep themselves within their own circles. True zeal loves to keep home, studieth to be quiet in other men's dioceses; false zeal loves to be gadding, is eagle-eyed abroad, and mole-eyed at home. Instead of burning bright and shining clear, like brinish lights, they sparkle and spit at others, or, like ill-couched fireworks, let fly on all sides; only out of their wisdom they know how to spare Agag and the great ones, and be sure they anger not their great masters, and meddle with their matches; whereas it is the property of fire that comes from above, to spare the yielding sheath, and melt the resisting metal, to pass by the lower roofs, and strike the towered pinnacle, as Nathan, David; Elias, Ahab; John, Herod; Jonas, Nineveh, &c.

Fifthly, Note, also, in all their proceedings with others, instead of wholesome severity (which rightly zealous men never come unto but by compulsion, and not without compassion of the offender, weeping with Moses and Samuel over the people, being sorry with the emperor, that they know how to write sentences of condemnation), these delight in cruelty, the brand of the malignant church; feed their eyes with massacres, as the queen-mother.* No diet so pleasing to these ravening wolves as the warm blood of the sheep. These are they that cry fire and faggot, away with them, not worthy to live; their very mercies are cruelty; especially in their own cause, they heat the furnace seven times hotter than in God's.

Lastly, These meteors and vapours have no constant light, or continued heat (as the fixed stars, ever like themselves), but have only their aguish

* I presume the reference is to the massacre of St Bartholomew.—ED.

fits and lunatic moods; sometimes, in adversity, they are good under the rod, as Pharaoh; again, in prosperity, like the fat kine of Bashan, ungrateful and forgetful. Sometimes in prosperity, when the sun of peace shineth on them, and the favourable influence of great ones, they shoot forth their blade with the corn on the housetop, running with the stream, and sailing with the wind; sometimes their zeal depends upon the life òf Jehoiada; sometimes on the company of the prophets. Commonly in the beginning they blaze like straw-fire, but in the end go out in smoke, and smother; whereas in their entrance into profession, they galloped into shows, and made some girds at hand, they tire, give in, and end in the flesh, whereas all natural motions are swiftest toward their end.

The vestal fires were perpetual, and the fire of the altar never went out. Spices and wefts of these evils may be found in the sincerest Christians; but they suffer not the dead flies to lie and putrefy in the precious boxes of true zeal. Of all these the preacher's caveat may be construed, ' be not over just,'* though it may also admit other interpretations, as after shall appear.

These are the special notes and symptoms of strange fires. The kinds, also, are many, and might be distributed into many heads; but I will reduce them into three, which are known by their names :—

1. Counterfeit zeal, false fire.
2. Blind zeal, smoky fire, or fool's fire, *ignis fatuus*.
3. Turbulent zeal, wild fire.

The first, wanting truth and sincerity, propounds sinister ends.
The second, knowledge and discretion, takes wrong ways.
The third, love and humility, exceeds measure.
The first abounds amongst subtle and crafty professors, and is to be abhorred and detected.†
The second, among simple and devout, is to be pitied and directed.
The third, amongst passionate and affectionate, and is to be moderated and corrected.

The first is the mere vizor of zeal, looking asquint one way, and tending another; pretending God and his glory, intending some private and sinister end; first either of honour and promotion, as Jehu, who marched furiously, and his word was the Lord of hosts, but his project was the kingdom.

Secondly, at filthy lucre; as Demetrius and his fellows, who cried, Great is Diana of Ephesus, but meant her little silver shrines. It cannot be denied, but many such there were who helped to pull down the abbeys, not out of any hatred to those unclean cages, but to rear their own houses out of the ruins, and spoiled copies to make cushions.‡ Judas complained of superfluity, but grieved it fell besides his bag. Many hold temporalities, tithes, and glebes unlawful, because they are loath to forego them. If Jezebel proclaimed a fast, let Naboth look to his vineyard. If the usurer and tradesman frequent sermons, let the buyer and borrower look to themselves. It is too common a thing to make zeal a lure and stale to draw customers, a bait of fraud, a net to entrap; with malicious Doegs, to make it a stalking horse for revenge against the priest, thereby to discharge their gall at ministers and other Christians, for the omission and commission of such things as themselves care not for. With the strumpet in the Proverbs, to wipe their mouths, and frequent the sacrifices, that they may be free from suspicion.

* ' Be not over just ' hath seven expositions here, two or three more hereafter.
† Qu. ' detested ?'—ED.
That is, ' tore up manuscripts, and stuffed cushions with the fragments.'—ED.

All these evils have I seen under the sunshine of the gospel ; but by how much zeal is more glorious than common profession, by so much is dissembled fervency more detestable than usual hypocrisy ; yea, no better than devilish villainy and double iniquity. Such painted walls and whited sepulchres the Lord will break down. Let all Timothies and Nathanaels learn to descry them, and discard them. The cure of this was deeply forelaid by Christ, 'I counsel thee to buy gold tried in the fire.' All is not gold that glistereth ; an image of faith breeds but a show of zeal. Many seemed to trust in Christ, but Christ would not trust them ; but such faith as will abide the fire brings forth zeal that will abide the touchstone.

The second is erroneous or blind zeal, not according to knowledge, Rom. x. I bear many devout papists witness (though I fear the learnedst of them be self-condemned) that they have this zeal, persuading themselves they do God best service when they please the devil most in their will-worship. The same witness I bear many separatists, though I fear most of them be sick of self-conceitedness, new-fangleness, and desire of mastership. For who would not suspect such zeal, which condemns all reformed churches, and refuseth communion with such as they themselves confess to be Christians, and consequently such as have communion with Christ ? It would grieve a man, indeed, to see zeal misplaced, like mettle in a blind horse ; to see men take such pains, and yet fall into the pit. This made Paul to wish himself Anathema for the sake of such ; and yet the multitude and common people reason thus : Is it possible but these men have the right ? But, alas ! how should it be otherwise, when a blind company will follow a blind sect-master ? This being one property of blind zeal (κακοζηλία), a fond admiration and apish imitation of some person, for some excellence they see in him, which so dazzles their eyes, that they cannot discern their errors and infirmities, which they oftener inherit than their virtues ; as appears in the Lutherans, and the Jews, that would sacrifice their children to Moloch, in imitation of Abraham. In these the devil becomes an angel of light, and playeth that dragon, Rev. xii., pouring out floods of persecution against the church, causing devout men and women to raise tragedies, breathe out threatenings, and persecute without measure. Than these the devil hath no better soldiers ; but when their scales fall from their eyes, and they come into God's tents, God hath none like unto them. The cure of this divinely is forelaid by Christ also, to buy eye-salve of him. Angels have eyes as well as wings to guide their flight ; when the ship is under sail, and hath the freshest way, it hath most need to look to the steerage, keep the watch, have an eye to the compass and landmarks.

The third kind is turbulent zeal, called by James bitter zeal, a kind of wild fire transporting men beyond all bounds and compass of moderation ; proceeding sometime of a weakness of nature in men, that have no stay of their passion, like to clocks whose springs are broken, and cities whose walls are down. Zeal is a good servant, but an ill master ; mettle is dangerous in a head-strong horse. And so the poets (which were the heathen's prophets) shadowed out the cure of this in Minerva's golden bridle, wherewith she managed her winged Pegasus. There is too much of this bitter zeal, of this Hierapicra, in all our books of controversies ; but, especially, there hath been too much in our domestical wars ; some sons of Bichri have blown the trumpet of contention, trumpets of anger. The churches of God should have no such custom ; Oh, that our churches understood that saying !

In quarrels of this nature Paul spends his zeal, not in partaking, but in parting the fray, beating down the weapons on both sides. Who art thou that judgest? who art thou that condemnest thy brother? Rom. xiv. 10; as if he should say, 'the matters are not *tanti*, we have made the devil too much sport already; who threw in these bones to set us together by the ears, whilst he lets in the common enemy upon us. Charity, charity is the builder of churches; strife about trifles hath wasted many famous ones, and placed the temples of Mahomet where the golden candlestick was wont to stand. We pity the former ages contending about leavened and unleavened bread, keeping of Easter, fasting on Sundays, &c. The future ages will do the like for us. Oh! that the Lord would put into the hearts both of the governors and parties to these quarrels, once to make an end of these Midianitish wars, that we might jointly pour out the vials of our zeal upon the throne of the beast.

Thus have you heard the errors and counterfeits of zeal, through whose sides, and upon the back of which, divers of the malicious world use to beat those whom it hates, because their works are better than their own; injuriously concluding that all zealots are alike. Thus I have heard our merchants complain that the set up blues have made strangers loathe the rich woaded blues, only in request; this is an old sophism. True judgment would teach us to conclude that the best drugs have their adulterates; the most current coins their slips; and that virtue which so many hypocrites put on, to grace themselves withal, is surely some rare and excellent jewel.

The Third Part.

The true zealot, whose fervency is in the spirit, not in show; in substance, not in circumstance; for God, not himself; guided by the word, not with humours; tempered with charity, not with bitterness: such a man's praise is of God though not of men; such a man's worth cannot be set forth with the tongues of men and of angels.

Oh! that I had so much zeal as to steep it in its own liquor; to set it forth in its own colours, that the Lord would touch my tongue with a coal from his altar, that I might regain the decayed credit of it with the sons of men.

It is good to be zealous in good things, and is it not best in the best? Or is there any better than God, or the kingdom of heaven? Is it comely whatever we do, to do it with all our might? Only uncomely when we serve God? Is mean and mediocrity in all excellent arts excluded, and only to be admitted in religion? Were it not better to forbear poetry or painting, than to rhyme and daub? And were it not better to be of no religion, than to be cold or lukewarm in any? Is it good to be earnest for a friend, and cold for the Lord of hosts? For whom dost thou reserve the top of thy affections? for thy gold? for thy Herodias? &c. O ye adulterers and adulteresses, can ye offer God a baser indignity? What aileth the world? Is it afraid, think we, that God can have too much love; who, in regard of his own infinite beauty, and the beams he vouchsafeth to cast upon us, deserves the best, yea all, and a thousand times more than all? Ought not all the springs and brooks of our affection to run into this main? May not he justly disdain that the least riveret should be drained another way? That anything in the world should be respected before him, equalled with him, or loved out of him, of whom, for whom, and through whom are all things? Who, or what can be sufficient for him, our Maker and Saviour? In other objects fear excess; here no ecstasy is high enough.

Consider and reason thus with thyself (O man), canst thou brook a sluggard in thy work, if thou be of any spirit thyself? Is not a slothful messenger as vinegar to thy teeth, and as smoke to thine eyes? Hast thou
any sharpness of wit? is not dulness tedious unto thee? And shall he that
is all spirit (for whom the angels are slow and cold enough) take pleasure
in thy drowsy and heavy service? Do men choose the forwardest deer in
the herd, the liveliest colt in the drove? and is the backwardest man fittest
for God? Is not all his delight in the quickest and cheerfulest givers and
servitors? Even to Judas he saith, That thou doest, do quickly; so odious
is dulness unto him. What else moved him to ordain that the neck of the
consecrated ass should be broken rather than offered up in sacrifice? Doth
God hate the ass? Or is it not for the sake of the quality of the creature;
which hath ever among the heathens been an hieroglyphic of heaviness and
tardity.

Thirdly, This zeal is so gracious a favourite with God, that it graces with
him all the rest of his graces. Prayer, if it be frequent,* prevaileth much;
the zealous witnesses had power to shut and open heaven, Rev. xii. By this
Israel wrestled with God, overcame, and was called a prince with God; this
strengthened the heart of Moses (as Aaron and Hur supported his hands)
till the Lord said, Let me alone; this made Cornelius's prayer to come into
heaven, whither our cold suits can no more ascend than vapours from the
still, unless there be fire under it. Repentance, a needful and primary
grace, which the Baptist so urged; but then we must be zealous and repent
(as my text joins them), or else no repentance pleaseth God; nor are there
fruits worthy repentance. Alms and good deeds are sacrifices pleasing to
God; but, without zeal, the widow's mites are no better than the rest; it
is the cheerful lose† that doubleth the gift. Generally, as some man's mark
and name furthereth the sale of his commodity, so zeal enhanceth all the
graces of God. It pitieth me for Laodicea that lost so much cost, had as
many virtues, did as many duties as other churches; but, for want of this,
Christ could not sup with them. Furnish a table with the principallest
fare and daintiest dishes that may be had; let them be roasted and boiled
to the halves, or stand on the table till they be lukewarm! what will the
guests say? All that we can do, is but the deed done, *opus operatum*, unless zeal confer grace.

Fourthly, Zeal is the richest evidence of faith, and the clearest demonstration of the Spirit. The baptism of water is but a cold proof of man's
Christendom, being common to all comers; but if any be baptized with fire,
the same is sealed up till the day of redemption. If any shall say, Friend,
what doest thou profess a religion without it? how can he choose but be
struck dumb? Can we suppose wormwood without bitterness, a man without reason? then may we imagine a religion, and a Christian, without spirit
and zeal.

The Jesuit saith, I am zealous; the Separatist, I am zealous; their plea
is more probable than the lukewarm worldlings', that serve God without
life. If the colour be pale and wan, and the motion insensible, the party
is dead or in a swoon; if good and swift, we make no question. The
zealous Christian is never to seek for a proof of his salvation; what makes
one Christian differ from another in grace, as stars do in glory, but zeal?
All believers have a like precious faith; all true Christians have all graces
in their seeds; but the degrees of them are no way better discerned than by
zeal. Men of place distinguish themselves by glistering pearls. A Christian

* Qu. 'fervent?'—ED.   † That is, 'eagerness.'—ED.

of degrees shines above others in zeal. Comparisons I know are odious to the world, that fain would have all alike ; but the righteous is better than his neighbour. All Christians are the excellent of the earth ; the zealot surmounteth them all, as Saul the people by the head and shoulders ; he is ever striving to excel and exceed others and himself.

One of these is worth a thousand others, one doth the work of many, which made him speak of Elisha* in the plural number, 'The horsemen and chariots of Israel;' besides his own work, he wins and procures others, makes proselytes. It is the nature of fire to multiply, one coal kindles another ; his work so shines, that others come in and glorify God, marvelling and inquiring what such forwardness should mean, concluding with Nebuchadnezzar, 'Surely the servants of the most high God.'

These are good factors and agents, doing God as good service, as Boutefews† do the devil, and Jesuits the pope, sparing no cost nor labour, and what they cannot do themselves, they do by their friends ; 'Who is on my side, who ?' &c.

As for lets and impediments, they overlook and overleap them, as fire passeth from one house to another; neither is there any standing for any of God's enemies before them ; they make havoc of their own and others' corruptions. If you will rightly conceive of Peter's zeal in converting and confounding, you must imagine (saith Chrysostom) a man made all of fire walking in stubble. All difficulties are but whetstones of their fortitude. The sluggard saith, 'There is a lion in the way.' Tell Samson and David so ; they will the rather go out to meet them. Tell Nehemiah of Sanballat ; he answereth, 'Shall such a man as I fear ?' Tell Caleb there are Anakims, and he will say, 'Let us go up at once,' &c. Let Agabus put off his girdle and bind Paul, let him be told in every city that bonds await him ; he is not only ready for bonds, but for death. Tell Jubentius he must lay down his life ; he is as willing as to lay off his clothes. Tell Luther of enemies in Worms ; he will go, if all the tiles of the houses were devils. The horse neighs at the trumpet, the leviathan laughs at the spear. They that mean to take the kingdom of God by violence, provide themselves to go through fire and water, carry their lives in their hands, embrace fagots ; they say to father and mother, 'I know you not,' to carnal counsellors and friendly enemies, 'Get you behind me, Satan.' Zeal is as strong as death, hot as the coals of juniper, floods of many waters cannot quench it. Agar, Prov. xxx., speaks of four things, stately in their kind ; I will make bold to add a fifth, comprehending and excelling them all, namely, the zealous Christian, strong and bold as the lion, not turning his head for any ; as swift as the greyhound in the ways of God's commandments, in the race to heaven ; as nimble as the goat, climbing the steep and craggy mountains of piety and virtue ; a victorious king, overcoming the world and his lusts ; Solomon in all his royalty is not clothed like one of these in his fiery chariot.

To cut off the infinite praises of zeal, let us hear what honourable testimonies and glorious rewards it pleaseth God to confer upon it. David's ruddy complexion, and his skill in music, made him amiable in the eyes of men ; but the zeal of his heart styled him a man after God's own heart, and the sweet singer of Israel. Abraham, that could find in his heart to sacrifice his Isaac, was called the friend of God. The same virtue denominated Jacob a prince with God. Elisha,* the chariots and horsemen ; Paul, a chosen vessel, &c.

* 'Elijah.'—ED.   † This is the French *Boute-feu*, an incendiary.—ED.

Neither doth God put them off with names and empty favours, but upon these he bestows his grace. David dedicateth his Psalms to him that excelled ; God, in dispensing of favours, observeth the same rule, : '. To him that overcometh will I give,' &c. To him that hath shall be given. Husbandmen cast their seed upon the fertilest ground, which returns it with the greatest interest ; God gives most talents to those that improve them in the best bank. Joseph shall have a parti-coloured coat, of all kinds of graces and blessings ; and because he knows this will purchase them hatred and envy, he takes them in special tuition ; if any will hurt his zealous witnesses, there goeth out a fire out of their mouths to devour their enemies, Rev. xii. A man were better anger all the witches in the world than one of these. If God bring any common judgments, he sets his seal, Rev. vii. 3, and *thau*, Ezek. ix., on their foreheads, and sprinkles their posts, Exod. xii. ; snatcheth Lot out of the fire (who burneth in zeal, as Sodom in lust) as men do their plate whiles they let the baser stuff burn. In fine, he taketh Enoch and Elijah in triumphant chariots up to heaven, and after their labours and toils, setteth them in special thrones, to rest in glory ; the apostles in their twelve, the rest in their orders, according to their zeal. And though he may well reckon the best of these unprofitable servants, yet such congruity (not of merits, but of favour) it pleaseth him to observe in crowning his graces, that the most zealous here are the most glorious there.

Who would not now wonder, how ever this royal virtue should have lost its grace with the world ? how ever any should admit a low thought of it ? But what ? shall all the indignity which hell can cast upon it, make it vile in our eyes ? Or rather, shall we not reason from the opposition, as Tertullian did of Nero ? That religion which Nero so persecutes, must needs be excellent.

If zeal were not some admirable good, the devil and world would not so hate it ; yet lest silence should be thought to baulk some unanswerable reasons, let us see how they labour to be mad with reason. Let Festus be the speaker for the rest, for he speaks what all the rest think ; you know his mad objection, and Paul's sober answer in that place, Acts xxvi. 24, and the like, 2 Cor. v. 13 ; whether he be mad or sober, it is for God and you.

This text bids us be zealous and repent ; the word signifies, be wise again, or return to your wits. The prodigal is said to come to himself, when he was first heated with this fire. We may well answer the world as old men do young ; you think us Christians to be mad that follow heaven so eagerly, but we know you to be mad, that run a madding so after vanity.

A Christian indeed is never right, till he seems to the world to be beside himself ; Christ's own kindred were afraid of him. The apostles are said to be full of new wine, Acts ii. ; besides, with these the world is mad, they run with Stephen like mad men, Acts vii. ; Nicodemus, and such as he, never offends them.

You know also what Ahab laid to the charge of Elijah, with the apology he made for himself. This is a stale imputation in ages. Haman accused Mordecai and the Jews of it. The apostles are said to be troublers of the whole earth. In the primitive church all mutinies and contentions were laid to the martyrs. True it is, where zeal is there is opposition, and so consequently troubles. Christ sets this fire on earth, not as an author, but by accident. The thief is the author of the fray, though the true man strike never so many blows ; but the Ahabs of the world trouble Israel, then complain of Elijah. The papists will blow up the state, then father it upon the puritans. It is not for any wise man to believe the tithe of the tales and slanders which fly abroad of the zealous. Lewd men would fain strike at all goodness through their sides.

You may remember also Eliab's uncharitable censure of David, I know the pride of thine heart. So do all worldlings measure others by their own length. If they see any forwardness in the peaceablest spirit, they ascribe it either to vainglory or covetousness, the only springs that set their wheels on going; but of this the knower of the heart must judge between us.

When slandering will not serve, then they fall to glavering, cunningly glancing at zeal, whiles they commend the golden mean wherein virtue consists. But Christians, take heed none spoil you through such philosophy, or rather sophistry; for true philosophy will tell you that the mean wherein virtue is placed is the middle betwixt two kinds, and not degrees. And it is but mean virtue that loves the mean in their sense.

Oh, say they, but some discretion would do well. It is true, but take withal Calvin's caveat to Melancthon, that he affect not so the name of a moderate man, and listen to such syrens' songs till he lose his zeal.

I have observed that which the world miscalls discretion to eat up zeal, as that which they call policy doth wisdom. As Joab stabbed Abner under a colour of friendship, antichrist undermineth Christ by pretending to be his vicar. The fear of overdoing makes most come too short. Of the two extremities we should most fear lukewarmness. Rather let your milk boil over than be raw.

From glavering they fall to scoffing. Young saints will prove but old devils. These hot-spurs will soon run themselves out of breath. But we say such were never right bred. Such as prove falling stars never were aught but meteors; the other never lose light or motion. Spiritual motions may be violent and perpetual.

When none of these will take, they fall to right down railing. These puritans, these singular fellows, &c., unfit for all honest company. I hope the state's puritan* and the common puritan be two creatures. For with that staff the multitude beats all that are better than themselves, and lets fly at all that have any show of goodness. But with that which most call puritanism I desire to worship God. For singularity, Christ calls for it, and presseth and urgeth it. What singular thing do you? or what odd thing do you? Shall God's peculiar people do nothing peculiar? The world thinks it strange we run not with them into excesses, and do as most do, that we might escape derision. Judge you which of these men shall please. I believe none shall ever please Christ till they appear odd, strange, and precise men to the common sort, and yet need not be over just neither. Let them that have tender ears stop them against the charms of the world and scorns of Michal, unless they were wiser. Let him that hath a right ear hear what Christ saith to the churches; Be zealous.

THE FOURTH PART.

Yea, but by what means shall a Christian attain this fire, and maintain it when he hath gotten it?

Say not in thine heart, What Prometheus shall ascend into heaven and fetch it thence? Thou mayest fetch it thence by thine own prayer, as did

* That is, the political puritan.—ED.

Elias and the apostles, men of infirmities as well as thyself. Pray continually and instantly. The Lord that breathed first thy soul into thee, will also breathe on thy soul. I speak not of miraculous (which was but a type), but of ordinary inspiration. Prayer and zeal are as water and ice, mutually producing each other. When it is once come down upon thine altar, though no water can quench it, yet must it be preserved fresh by ordinary fuel, especially the priest's lips must keep it alive.

Sermons are bellows ordained for this purpose. The word read is of divine use, but doth not with that motion stir these coals.

Experience sheweth the best oration will not so much move as the meanest orator.

After the sparkles once by these means kindled, cherish and feed them by reading the word. Let it dwell richly in thine heart. Excite thy dulness by spiritual hymns. Love songs inflame not lust more than the Song of songs doth zeal. Read or sing the 116th psalm; and if thou be not zealous, every verse will check thee in thy throat. Meditation is another help, approved by Isaac's and David's practice; an art lately so taught, as I shall need only to point at the choice themes suiting and furthering this argument. I need not go far to fetch this fire. I may strike it out of every word of this epistle to Laodicea. Behold the Lord God, especially thy Lord Christ, in his glorious titles and majesty; for so he begins his visions to John, and his epistles to the churches, exciting their dull hearts. By such apparitions did he set on fire the heart of Moses in the burning bush, and inflamed Stephen, his first martyr. Answerable and proportionable to which are our serious contemplations. Behold him as one that seeth thee, and knoweth thy works, the rousing preface of all these letters. Cæsar's eye made his soldiers prodigal of their blood. The atheist thinks God takes as much notice of him and his prayers as he doth of the humming of flies and bees; and therefore no marvel if his service be formal and fashionable. The faithful Christian, by faith's prospective, sees him at home, and hears him saying, Well done, thou good servant, which maketh him to work out his heart. Behold him as the beginning of creatures, especially of the new creature. Oh, what love hath he shewed thee in thy redemption! Out of what misery into what happiness, by what a price, to what end, but that thou shouldest be zealous of good works. Behold him as the faithful witness, that witnessed himself for thee a good witness, and here faithfully counsels thee to follow his pattern. Behold him as a speedy and royal rewarder of his followers. Take thyself into paradise, represent to thyself thy crown, thy throne, thy white robes. Look not on the things that are seen, but on the far most excellent weight of glory. Look upon these, and faint if thou canst.

Behold, also, he is a consuming fire, a jealous God, hating lukewarmness, not only destroying Sodom with fire and brimstone, and providing Tophet for his enemies, but awaking also his drowsy servants by judgments (as Absalom Joab, by firing his corn), his Israelites by fiery serpents. Whom he loveth he chasteneth, and keepeth them in the furnace of fiery trials, till they come to their right temper. He standeth and knocketh. If nothing will arouse us, a time will come when heaven and earth shall burn with fire, and Christ shall come in flaming fire, to render vengeance with fire unquenchable, We, therefore, that know the terror of that day, what manner of persons ought we to be?

From God turn thine eyes unto man; set before thee the pillar and cloud of fiery examples, that have led us the way into Canaan. He is but a dull jade that will not follow. The stories of the Scriptures, the lives of the fathers, the acts and monuments of the church, have a special virtue for this effect. The very pictures of the fires and martyrs cannot but warm thee. If thou canst meet with any living examples, follow them, as they follow Christ, frequent their company ; even Saul amongst the prophets will prophesy. No bangling hawk, but with a high flier will mend her pitch ; the poorest good companion will do thee some good. When Silas came Paul burnt in the spirit. A lesser stick may fire a billet. If thou findest none, let the coldness of the times heat thee, as frosts do fire. Let every indignation make thee zealous, as the dunstery of the monks made Erasmus studious. One way to be rich in times of dearth, is to engross a rare commodity, such as zeal is. Now, if ever ' they have destroyed thy law,' it is now high time to be zealous.

Consider and emulate the children of this generation, to see how eager every Demas is for worldly promotion. How did that worthy bishop disdain to see an harlot more curiously to adorn her body unto sin and death, than he could his soul unto life everlasting. It angered Demosthenes to see a smith earlier at his anvil than he was at his desk.

When thou hast thus heat thyself, take heed of catching of cold again, as many have done, and brought their zeal to death's door.

The fire may go out divers ways : first by subtraction of fuel ; if a man forbear his accustomed meals, will not his natural heat decay ? The Levites that kept God's watch in the temple, were charged expressly, morning and evening, if not oftener, to look to the lights and the fire. He that shall forget (at the least) with the curfew-bell in the evening to rake up his zeal by prayer, and with the day-bell in the morning to stir up and kindle the same, if not oftener, with Daniel; I cannot conceive how he can possibly keep fire in his heart. Will God bless such as bid him not so much as good-morrow and good-even ?

He that shall despise or neglect prophecy, must he not needs quench the Spirit ? Have I not marked glorious professors, who for some farm's sake, or other commodities, have flitted from Jerusalem to Jericho, where the situation was good, but the waters naught! and their zeal hath perished, because vision hath failed !

Such as read the Bible by fits upon rainy days, not eating the book with John, but tasting only with the tip of the tongue ; such as meditate by snatches, never chewing the cud and digesting their meat, they may happily get a smackering, for discourse and table-talk, but not enough to keep soul and life together, much less for strength and vigour. Such as forsake the best fellowship, and wax strange to holy assemblies (as now the manner of many is) ; how can they but take cold ? Can one coal alone keep itself glowing ?

Though it go not out for want of matter, yet may it be put out by sundry accidents ; when it is newly kindled, it may be put out with scoffs and reproaches, if Peter take not heed, and fence himself well against them; but if once thoroughly grown, such breath will but spread and increase it.

It is possible fire may be oppressed with too much wood, and heat suffocated with too much nourishment ; over-much prayer, reading, and study, may be a weariness both to flesh and spirit ; but it so rarely happeneth, that I need not mention it ; and yet the soul hath its satiety. There be some such perchance over-nice men in this sense also, who have not learned that God will have them merciful to themselves. It is often smothered for want of vent and exercise. Let such as use not, and express not their zeal, brag of their good hearts ; surely they have none such, or not like to have them such. If Nicodemus had not buried Christ by day, we might have feared his zeal had gone out, for all his coming by night.

Yet this is not so ordinary as to extinguish it by the quench-coal of sin. Gross sin every man knows will waste the conscience, and make shipwreck of zeal. But I say, the least known evil unrepented of, is as a thief in the candle, or an obstruction in the liver. I fear David served God but reasonably, till he published his repentance ; he that steals his meat, though poverty tempt him, yet giveth thanks but coldly ; zeal and sin will soon expel the one or the other out of their subject. Can you imagine in the same roof God and Belial, the ark and Dagon ? Lastly, and most commonly, foreign heat will extract the inward, and adventitious heat consume the natural.

The sun will put out the fire ; and so will the love of the world, the love of the Father ; they cannot stand together in intense degrees, one cannot serve both these masters with such affection as both would have. Seldom seest thou a man make haste to be rich, and thrive in religion. Christ's message to John holds true. The poor are most forward in receiving and following the gospel; as thou lovest thy zeal, beware of resolving to be rich, lest gain prove thy godliness ; take heed of ambitious aspiring, lest courts and great places prove ill airs for zeal, whither it is as easy to go zealous as to return wise. Peter, whiles he warmed his hands, cooled his heart. Not that greatness and zeal cannot agree, but for that our weakness many times severs them. If thou beest willing to die poor in estate, thou mayest the more easily live in grace. Smyrna, the poorest of the seven candlesticks, hath the richest price upon it.

The diligent practice of these courses will make easy the practice of this counsel, Be zealous, &c.

THE FIFTH PART.

But here methinks I hear the lukewarm worldling of our times fume and chafe, and ask what needs all this ado for zeal, as if all God's people were not zealous enough.

Such as think they are, or can be zealous enough, need no other conviction to be poor, blind, naked, wretched, and pitiful Laodiceans. Fire is ever climbing and aspiring higher ; zeal is ever aiming at that which is before ; carried toward perfection ; thinking meanly of that which is past, and already attained, condemning his unprofitable service, as Calvin in his last will; this rule tries full conceited Christians.

What would you have us to do ? We profess, keep our church, hear sermons, as Christians ought to do.

Affectionate friendship and service is not only for public show and pomp upon festival days in chambers of presence, but for domestical, ordinary, and private use ; to such holiday and church retainers, God may well say, Let us have some of this zeal at home and apart.

All affections are most passionate, without a witness. Such as whose families, closets, fields, beds, walks do testify of their worship, as well as temples and synagogues, are right servitors. God much respects their devotions ; and they have strong proof of the power of godliness.

We would you should know, that we are such as have prayers said or read in our families and household ; or else we say some to ourselves at our lying down and uprising; and more than that, say you what you will, we hold more than needs.

First, know that zeal knows no such unmannerly courses as to slubber over a few prayers, whiles you are dressing and undressing yourselves; as most do, half asleep half awake. Know further, that such as hold only a certain stint of daily duties, as malt-horses their pace or mill-horses their round, out of custom or form, are far from that mettle which is ever putting forward, growing from strength to strength, and instant in duties, in season, out of season; and this says hard to lazy Christians.

May not we go too far on the right hand?

It is true; but liberality baulks and fears covetousness and niggardness more a great deal than prodigality; so does zeal, lukewarmness, and coldness more than too much heat and forwardness; the defect is more opposite and dangerous to some virtues than the excess.

Why, are not some, think you, too strait-laced; that dare not use their Christian liberty in some recreations; swear by small oaths, or lend money for reasonable use? Hath not God left many things indifferent, wherein some shew themselves more nice than wise?

Zeal will cut off the right hand if it cause to offend, much more to pare nails and superfluities; it consumes the strongest, dearest corruptions, much more will it singe off such hair and dross as these. If aught be praiseworthy, it embraceth such things; if any be doubtful, carrying show of evil, of ill report, it dares not meddle with them; it fears that some of these are as indifferent, as fornication was among the heathen.

There are but few such, no, not of the better sort you speak of.

Grant there be any, and zealous emulation culleth the highest examples. Such as mean to excel in any art, travel to find out the rarest workmen, purchase the choicest copies. He that hath true zeal, will strive to purge himself, as Christ is pure.

Will you have us run before our neighbours, or live without example, or company?

Cowards and cravens stand and look who goes first; soldiers of courage will cast lots for the onset and fore-rank, for desperate services and single combats. Jades will not go without the way be led.

So we may soon come to trouble and danger enough.

What danger can there be for an honest, peaceable, religious forwardness?

The slug or snail puts out its tender horns to feel for lets in the way, and pulls them in where there is no cause; so do the fearful that shall be without; but zeal either finds no dangers or makes them none: it neither fears to do well, or to reprove ill-doers, let whoso will be displeased.

Some indeed care not whom they offend, they are so harsh and fiery; they can bear with nothing.

Will true Christianity allow us to bear with any sin?

Can tin or hot iron choose but to hiss again, if cold water be cast on it? Can a righteous soul choose but vex itself at open evil? Such ostriches as can digest oaths, profane and filthy speeches, shew what mettle they have for the Lord of hosts; who will yet be ready enough to offer the challenge, or stab, for the least disgrace to themselves or their mistress. Phinehas had rather, if it were lawful, fight in God's quarrels than in his own.

All are not by nature of so hot dispositions, or so fiery-spirited, as others.

If there be such a dull, phlegmatic creature as hath no life or spirit in anything he goes about, or whom nothing will move; he may plead complexion; and yet grace is above nature. But the best way is, see every man compare his devotion in matters of God with his spirits and mettle in other affairs, wherein his element or delight lies. If the one equal not the other, the fault is not in nature : the oldest man hath memory enough for his gold, and the coldest constitution heat enough where it likes.

Well, our hearts may be as good as the best, though we cannot shew it.

Fire cannot be long smothered, it will either find a vent or go out; zeal will either find word or deed to express itself withal.

All have not the gift of utterance.

Violent affections have made the dumb to find a tongue. If it be low water, the mill may stand; but abundance of heart will set the wheels on going. What earnest discourses will unlearned mariners make of their voyages, huntsmen of their game, &c.

All have not ability and means : many have great charges.

Love and zeal are munificent, make money their servant, not their master; wheresoever the heart is enlarged, the hand cannot be strained; where the bowels are open, the purse is not shut. Herod, for his pleasure, cares not for half his kingdom : what will not some gentlemen give for hawks and hounds ? Not only the poor woman that spent the rich ointment on Christ, the widow that gave all her substance, the converts that sold all and threw all at the feet of the apostles; but even the bounty of the superstitious papists shall rise in judgment against such as profess a religion, will give it good words and countenance, but be at no cost with it, and know a cheaper way to save charge withal.

All have not so much leisure to spend so much time and study about matters of religion; they have somewhat else to do.

There are indeed many vanities which distract and divide the mind of worldlings; but zeal counts one thing needful, to which it makes all other vail and stand by. Is there any so good a husband of his time, that will not steal some hour for his pleasure; that cannot spare his God and his soul half an hour, morning and evening; that bestows not idly as much time as a sermon or two would take up in the week ? The soul, I confess, hath his satiety as well as the body; but why should we sit on thorns more at a sermon than at a play, think the Sabbaths longer than holidays, but for want of zeal ? If thou beest not a vain and willing deceiver of thyself and others, deal honestly and plainly with thy soul, try thyself by these few rules; and if thou judgest thyself to come short of them, amend and ' be zealous.'

THE SIXTH PART.

Which little round fire-ball coming to hand, as David's small stone, by ordinary lot, knowing the insufficiency of mine own, I pray that God with his arm would scatter it far and wide into those wild parts of the world, without the pale of Christendom, which lie so frozen and benumbed in their paganism, that they feel not the coldness of their religions; as also in those regions, that being within the tropics of the church, have just so much and so little heat, as to think they have enough, and need no more. Chiefly mine affections burn within me for the good of mine own nation, for which I would I had but so much zeal as truly to wish myself *anathema*, upon condition it had heat suitable to its light. For I must bear it record, it hath knowledge, I would I could say according to zeal. But the Spirit, knowing that which is spoken to all to be in effect as spoken to none, directs me what I should speak to churches, to speak to particular angels. Now the principal in our church, under that Archangel of the covenant, I most willingly acknowledge to be my lord the king, as an angel of light. And why not that very angel, who by his writing hath begun to pour out the fifth vial upon the throne of the beast, darkened his kingdom, caused them to gnaw their tongues for grief, and blaspheme for the smart of their wounds ; though as yet they will not repent of their errors ? The Lord anoint him more and more with this oil above all the princes of the earth, that from his head it may run down upon our skirts ; make him shine in zeal above all other stars, to the warming and enlightening of this whole horizon ; set him up as a standard for his people ; clothe him with zeal as with a cloak, to recompense the fury of the adversaries, that he may strike the Aramites, not three but five times, till they be consumed ; that he may put the Ammonites under the iron saws, harrows, axes, which have provoked him as much as ever they did David, 2 Sam. xii. But yet, as in the time of the Old Testament, the custody of the fire and light was the charge of the priest, so here I observe Christ to lay it upon his ministers, interpreting his rule by his practice : ' Tell the church, tell the angel of the church ;' honouring that despised office with that stately style ; intimating the union between people and minister, that they should be as one. What is spoken to the one, is spoken to the other ; not as some, that ever make clergy and laity two members, in division and opposition ; neither yet as some spirits, that lay all level, but implying a property, especially in grace and zeal in the ministers, whom the preacher calls the master of the assemblies ; that they should exceed as far the people as angels do men, and that he will reckon with them for the religion of the people, because cold priests make bold sinners. Zealous Jehoiada may make Jehoash the king zealous, so long as he lives with him. We therefore, men and brethren, or rather, men and angels, upon whom it lies to keep life and heat in the devotion of the world, to consume the dross of vices and heresies, that have fallen into the sink of our times ; we that are to make ready our people for the second coming of Christ, is the spirit of Eli, think we, sufficient for us ? What manner of persons ought we to be, burning in spirit, fervent in prayer, thundering in preaching, shining in life and conversation ? Why is it then, my brethren (Oh, let my plainest rebukes be the fruits and signs of my best love to mine own tribe ; let them not be as breakings of the head, but as precious balm to those whose honour with the people I prefer to my life), why is it that some of us pray so rarely and so coldly in private (the evils of our times will not out but by frequent fasting and fervent prayer), in public so briefly, so perfunctorily, and feebly, that we scarce have any witnesses of what we say ? Why are there yet remaining any mutes amongst us ? Why are there any tongues that dare speak against often or zealous preaching ? Doth not Paul adjure us before Him that shall judge the elect angels, that we preach instantly, in season and out of season ? Read we the commentaries of that text, or let the practice of ancients expound it ; and tell me if ever old or new interpreted that charge, of bare reading, of quarterly, or monthly, yea, or of once on the Sabbath, preaching only, as if that were fully sufficient, without endeavouring or desiring any more. If always often preaching be prating, what meant the practice, I say, not only of Calvin and Beza, but of Chrysostom, Basil, Ambrose, with other of the fathers, preaching every day in the week, some of them twice in the week, none of them so seldom, as such would bear the world in hand ? What

meant sundry ancient councils, the eleventh of Tolet in Spain, yea, even of
Trent itself, to excite the torpor of the bishops of their times, as their
canons speak, enjoining frequent preaching, calling for more than almost any
man is able to perform?

But here I may turn reproving into rejoicing, that preaching is grown in
any better fashion and grace with our times, by royal and reverend, both
examples and countenance: only I wish that every Archippus may fulfil
his ministry, be instant and constant in preaching.   Solomon, the older and
wiser he grew, the more he taught the people, sharpened his goads, and
fastened his nails; whereas many amongst us are so wise in their youth,
as to affect the foolishness of preaching, but in their dotage ease slays the
fool; when the door is oiled, it leaves creaking.   They must then fall to
make much of themselves, till, contrary with the prophet, they cry out,
' My fatness, my fatness, my belly, my belly!' so favouring their lungs that
they will be sure never to die of David's consumption of zeal.   Let such
preach, say they, that want livings; and if for shame they preach at all, it
must be rarely and easily for breaking of their wind (my meaning is not to
tax such whom God disenables by weakness of body, or such as recompense
their rarity with industry, as Perkins, &c.); and yet, forsooth, these think
they may justly challenge, and wear the double honour of countenance and
maintenance, I marvel with what right or with what face, so long as there
remains express canon of Scripture bequeathing it to those that toil in word
and doctrine.   Neither will zeal set us on work only to preach, or to preach
often, to avoid the infamy of bare readers; but it will teach us to preach
painfully, and that in the evidence and demonstration, not so much of art
or nature, as of the Spirit and grace, regarding only that the people know
Christ and him crucified, not caring whether they know what we have read,
how many quotations our memory will carry level, how roundly we can
utter our mind in new-minted words, in like sounding, idle, vain, and
offensive paranomasies.   I blush to fall into the least touch of that kind;
yet, at once to shew and reprove that childish folly, ' It is a vein of vain
preaching, turning sound preaching into a sound of preaching, tickling
men's ears like a tinkling cymbal, feeding them ἡδύσμασι κὶ ἐκ ἐδεσμασι,
spoiling the plain song with descant and division.'   What is this but to
shew our own levity and want of true art; indeed, affecting such a dancing,
piperly, and effeminate eloquence (as Tully, Demosthenes, or any masculine
orator would scorn), instead of that divine, powerful delivery which be-
cometh him that speaks the oracles of God?   If ever we mean to do any
good, we must exhort and reprove with all vehemency and authority, lifting
up our voice as a trumpet, as the sons of thunder, piercing their ears, witnessing, striving, and contending, according to our gift, whatsoever it be,
to manifest our affections, that we may work upon the people, which all the
art in the world will not teach us to do; only zeal at the heart will naturally produce it, without straining or affecting.   If God require the heart
as well as the head, why should we not labour to move the affections as well
as inform the judgment?   There is a doctrinal, and, as some term it, a
doctorly kind of preaching, which is admired of some that understand it
not; of others, that could be content with the mass again, because it was
gentle and had no teeth in it.   And such sermons I have sometimes heard
for matter void of exception, but so delivered, as if one were acting a part,
or saying a lesson by heart.   It hath called to mind a song which sometimes I have met, withal excellently composed, full of sweet air, surely and
truly sung, but with flat and dead voices without spirit, which hath marred

the music. Of such a sermon and preacher the countryman's verdict did well that said, This man may be a great scholar, but he wants beetle and wedges to hew our knotted timber withal; our green wood will not burn unless it be better blown. You shall sometimes see an excellent horse of shape and colour, having many of those marks Du Bartas describes in Cain's supposed horse, which yet, wanting mettle, hath been of little worth and less use. If there were no other preachers than these, which hold themselves the only profound and learned preachers, I muse what should become of conversion of souls, which they that covet must come with the spirit of Elias, to turn the hearts of the fathers to their children. I may in truth, and I hope with modesty, speak with the preacher, that in observing I have observed and have found that divers great clerks have had but little fruit of their ministry; but hardly any truly zealous man of God (though of lesser gifts) but have had much comfort of labours in their own and bordering parishes, being in this likened by Gregory to the iron on the smith's anvil, sparkling round about. And if for this any bordering neighbours, whose cold labours work not the like success, shall accuse them of some kind (I know not what) of policy in bewitching the people, they may well reply, Behold our zealous affections are our charms, and zeal all our witchcraft; as Latimer well answered one that accused the people of partiality for not affecting him that preached one of his printed sermons, that he had indeed his stick, but wanted his rosin, meaning his zealous manner of preaching and living, without which last all the former will do but little good, if a good ensample of life accompany not their doctrine, as lightning doth thunder. For there are some (I speak it with sorrow of heart) that seem to have fire in their preaching, but carry water in their life ; being notoriously proud, covetous, or debauched, stained with odious vices. Let us hear the sum of all. Do we love Christ more than ordinary? Would we give proof of our treble love to him? Let us, then, feed his flock with a treble zeal, expressed in our prayer, preaching, and living. Let us make it appear to the consciences of all, that the top of our ambition is God's glory ; and that we prefer the winning of souls to the winning of the world.

This title of angels, why may it not also be extended to magistrates, as well as that higher style of gods? Sure I am that the scarlet robe of zeal would exceeding well become them. Jethro maketh it their prime and essential character ; God and Moses their only and sole, in the charge and commission to Joshua so oft repeated, 'Only be of good courage.' And if David were now to re-pen his psalm, I think he might alter the form of his counsel and say, 'Be zealous, ye rulers and judges of the world,' and not wise and politic ; or rather, under the terms of wisdom, he comprehends indeed the zeal we call for, the most now-a-days being Gallios, wise only for the matters of the commonwealth : not having a spark of that spirit which was in Phinehas, Daniel, and Nehemiah, &c., for the Lord of hosts, or to his laws and commandments ; as if God had made magistrates keepers only of the second table, governors of men, and not of Christians ; guardians only of civil societies, and not of his church, and shepherds also of his flock. Are idolatries, blasphemies, profaning of Sabbaths, no sins? Why then either have not the laws force and strength enough in them, as sometime we are answered when we complain? or why are they not executed for the suppressing of these raging sins? Are not all they punished with death in the Scriptures, as well as breaches of the second table? Blood I leave to the malignant church, and admire clemency in rulers as much as any ; but yet I know the profane dissoluteness of the times requires a three-stringed whip of severity to purge our Augean stable of the foul abuses, whipped often with pens and tongues, but spared by them that bear the sword (a man may say, of many governors), altogether in vain for matters of religion. Are not kings of the earth charged to render double to the bloody strumpet of Rome? Why, then, doth the hurtful pity of our times embolden and increase their numbers? Laodicea itself, I doubt not, for matters of mine and thine, had, as their name reports, good civil justice and justicers; but was God the nearer for it? Doth he not threaten, for all that, to spew them out of his mouth? Shall he not curse those that do his work negligently, fearfully, and partially? Our times complain of two special cankerworms of justice, which eat up zeal in magistrates. The first is covetousness, which makes men of place transgress for a morsel of bread: the zeal of their own houses consumes the zeal of God's house. The building of great houses, keeping of great houses, and matching with great houses, raising and leaving of great houses behind them, makes them so ravenous, that they devour so much as chokes all their zeal; which would teach them to shake their laps of bribes, and scorn to accept gifts, though men would augment them for the perverting of judgment. The other, cowardice and fearfulness, which how unfit and base a quality did Nehemiah think it for a man of his place! No better than shyness in a fore-horse, whose eyes men fence on both sides, that they may lead the way, and go without starting; unto which zeal is answerable to magistrates, causing them only to see him that is invisible, without casting a squint eye at men; to sing to God only of judgment and mercy, without tuning their songs to man's care; to walk in the perfect way, without turning either to the right or left hand, for fear or favour. O that there were such a heart in our leaders! how easily would our people follow! What a spring-tide of zeal should we have, if the sun and moon would cast out a benign aspect upon them! Doth it not flourish in all those shires and towns, where the word and sword do jointly cherish it? In others, which are the greatest number, how doth it languish and wane away, and hang down the head! Where is it in divers places of the land to be seen? I had almost said, in my haste and heat, there is none that hath zeal, no, not one, there is no courage for the truth; but that I remember that Elijah was checked for overshooting himself in his too short and quick computation. I hope the Lord hath his fifties amongst us, though but thin sown in comparison of the swarms of professed recusants, and church-papists, of profane atheists, key-cold worldlings, and lukewarm professors. The bodies of our many several congregations, yea, even of the better sort, whereunto have they been likened by our separated adversaries, but unto the prophet Hosea's cake, half-baked upon the hearth, having one side, that is, the outside to the world-ward, in public service, scorched a little and browned over; but the inside to God-ward, in private and family duties, no better than dough; many of them making, indeed, some show, as the outlandish fruits that are plashed upon our walls, but, wanting heat, never come to maturity. If we should make good their resemblances, how then should we please the stomach of God? who hath indeed brooked and borne us a long time. I doubt but wamblingly. How near were we going in '88, and in the powder treason? Do we think he will ever digest us, in the temper we are in? which (to confess the truth of the fashionable Christian) what is it but a state of neutrality, indifference, or such a mediocrity as will just serve the time, satisfy law, or stand with reputation of neighbours? Beyond which, if any step a little forward, do not the rest hunt upon the stop? If there hap to break out a sparkle of zeal in any one house in a parish, is not the whole town in an uproar? as when the bells ring awke,* every man brings his bucket to the quenching of this fire. If hell be in an ale-house, who cries out of it? and as for our Sundays, church service, which is all that God gets at our hands, how perfunctorily and fashionably is it slubbered over. How are his Sabbaths made the voider and dunghill for all refuse business, divided between the church and the ale-house, the Maypole commonly beguiling the pulpit! What man would not spew to see God thus worshipped? This want of devotion makes the foul-mouthed papists to spit at us; this want of reformation makes the queasy-stomached Brownists cast themselves out of the church; and shall God always suffer the land to bear us? But behold, he stands at the door and knocks, by treasons, by plagues, by the hammer of dearths, discontents, fires, inundations, especially by the word; his locks are wet with waiting. O, before he shake off the dust of his feet against us, and turn to some other nation more worthy, let us open the door, that he may come in and sup with us. If he loves us, he will purge us and scour us, by one chastisement or other; if he have no pleasure in us, he cannot but unburthen his stomach of us. If all the land besides should turn the deaf ear, yet let me entreat and charge you of my flock to hear his voice, and be zealous. Since my coming amongst you, I have handled some books of the Old Testament, the Epistles to the Romans, to the Hebrews, of Saint James, Peter, and John; out of them taught the doctrine of the law, of faith, love, and good works. Now, in the choice of this epistle of Christ to Laodicea, my desire was to boil up the former to their just temper, in which work I can willingly be content to spend my strength and days, if God see it fit. I cannot be a better sacrifice than to God, and for you. If I waste myself, so you may have light and heat, what else is the end of my life? God hath given you a name, your zeal is gone abroad; and I hope you have many names among you. The Lord increase their number and zeal. If but one of us this day shall open this door of his heart with Joshua, 'Let others choose, I and my house will serve the Lord' more zealously than heretofore, neither I nor he shall have lost our labours. A lively picture casts its eye upon every one that comes near it; such is the word with whom, and with which, we have to do. Let him that is now cold, grow colder and colder; but let him that hath an ear, hear what hath been said to the churches, and be zealous and amend.

The Lord give us not only understanding, but zeal in all things; he baptize us with fire; he breathe on us, and inspire into us the Spirit of life and power, &c. So shall we run the ways of his commandments.

---

* I suppose 'awake,' an alarm.—ED.

BALM FROM GILEAD TO RECOVER CONSCIENCE.

IN A SERMON PREACHED AT PAUL'S CROSS, OCTOBER 20. 1616.

TO THE READER.

VOUCHSAFE, good reader, in a word or two, to understand the occasion of bringing this Meditation to the press, that was purposed only for the pulpit: the rather for that it cometh not from the author's own hand, who would, no doubt, more exactly have polished it, could he have been persuaded to publish it himself; but he, out of his modesty, as he delivered it not like a scholar, his lesson learned without book, nor brought with him any intent to have it further made public, so could not be induced, though instantly laboured both by myself and many others desiring further fruit of so learned a labour, either to publish it himself, or to have any hand at all in the publishing of it.

Howbeit at length, upon extreme importunity (rather to prevent the wrong that, by imperfect copies printed, he might otherwise sustain, than to satisfy such as were earnest suitors to him for the same), he was with much ado drawn, before his departure from the city, to deliver his notes to a friend, with reference of the whole business to the judgment and discretion of others, to deal in, and dispose of, as they should deem fit; who being present at the speaking of it, with the author's notes, and his own helps, hath done his endeavour to pen it as near as he could to that which by the author himself was then delivered; which, though it be not altogether *verbatim* the same, yet it is hoped that there is not anything material wanting that the diligent hearer shall desire; besides, that he shall find some things over and above, that straits of time, and default of memory, were then a means to keep back.

If any ask, what needed such importunity in this business, there being already so many sermons abroad that even printers themselves complain that the press is oppressed with them? I answer: True it is that there are sermons indeed abroad, by some, more than enough, but yet not enough (I dare say it) such as this is, that deal so pithily, so effectually, in points of practice so necessary, so ordinary, as this doth, wherein learning and piety, delightful manner of handling, together with profitable and useful matter, so concur, that if it please not any, they are those alone, whose profane palates can relish nothing that savoureth of grace, though never so delightful otherwise. If it profit not any, it is to be feared they are such whose corrupt consciences are grown well-near irrecoverable, if not wholly incurable. But I am loath to be long where the work itself is not. This little be spoken rather in way of apology for myself and such others as urged the publishing of it, than in commendation of the work, which, in the very reading of it, to any judicious, ingenious, and religious, will sufficiently commend itself. For myself, considering the general approbation given it by all sorts that heard it, together with the earnest suits of many others so instantly desiring it upon their reports, and finding, upon view and survey, the thing itself fully to answer both the reports of the one and the desires of the other, I was right willing and ready (as he speaketh in Plato), though one barren hitherto in this kind myself, to perform some midwife-like office to another, for the further enlargement of so generally blessed and so deservedly desired a birth. Wherein, if thou shalt chance to find any defects, consider but (I pray thee) how hard a thing it is for another (though not unskilful) to perfect a work that some curious artist hath left unfinished.

And so, wishing only that it may, through God's gracious assistance, either work into or increase in thee a good conscience, and the comfort thereof, I leave the work to thy perusal, and it to his blessing whose gift a good conscience is, and with whom, beside the present comfort of it here, is a plentiful reward reserved for it elsewhere.

Thine in Christ,

THOMAS GATACRE.

BALM FROM GILEAD TO RECOVER CONSCIENCE.

For we are assured that we have a good conscience, desiring in all things to walk honestly.—HEB. XIII. 18.

I WILL use no other preface but the short one before my text, and that not as a preface, but in way of earnest suit, 'Pray for me.' For I desire this day, entreating of a good conscience, both so myself to keep and discharge one, and so to speak home to yours, that the dead consciences may hear the voice of God in my text, and be quickened, the secure ones awakened, the troubled ones comforted, the tender confirmed, the good bettered, and all receive some light and life, that we may all depart hence in the peace of a good conscience, 'assured (with our apostle) that we have a good one, desiring in all things to walk honestly.'

This work, God witnessing to my conscience, I much desire to do; and in so doing I know I desire a worthy work, a work so highly and peculiarly needful for these times, that a sharp seer of them was often heard to pray that God would stir up some to write and preach of this argument, and another to Augustine's wish, that he might hear Paul preach, addeth his own, that the text and theme might be conscience. They both saw it gasping, drawing on, and dying, and therefore desired that some life might be put into and kept in it, before it should be utterly overwhelmed in death and darkness.

The time, indeed, was in the beginning of time, when Adam by his first sin brought death upon his soul, and caused it to reign over all the powers of it, that this faculty had most life left in it, like Job's messengers, to tell news of the great loss. This little spark was left fresh, to shew what great light had been extinguished;* but now this also, through affected blindness and wilful malice, is so smothered and suffocated, through a daily custom of sinning, the eyes of it so pecked out, the mouth so stopped, the very heart of it so wounded and quelled, that (as the world justly complains) it is dead long since, yea, long since buried in the grave of habitual sinning, with the stone of hardness rolled upon it, that, as Mary said of Lazarus, the very name of it is grown unsavoury, odious, and, I fear, ridiculous in the ears of many. Is it not, then, high time for the Lord to work? and for us to see it, by crying aloud (as Elias said of the dead idol) we may

* Scintilla reliqua rectæ rationis.—Lips.

fetch life again into it, which is the very life of our spiritual life, and soul of our soul.

The time is now come upon us wherein men affect and desire good names, estates, wives, houses, good clothes, good everything, but content themselves with mean and vile consciences, which ought to be the chief and only good. Wherein men love to exercise and shew, in preaching, in hearing, in trading, and all manner of conversing, their memory, their skill and cunning, and all other their good parts, as they call them, neglecting this, which is the whole of a man, and despising Paul's exercise and Paul's policy, 'to have a good conscience before God and man,' Acts xxiv. 16, 33. Wherein men love preaching, indeed, and knowledge, but not wholesome doctrine, preaching to the conscience and knowledge of themselves, which makes this pulpit and churchyard full of polemical and school divinity, while the plain, practical, and ascetical part lieth untilled and unregarded, which maketh city and country full of craft and cunning, but void and destitute, not only of the power, but show, of conscience. All which maketh me to choose rather, with the apostle, to speak five words to the heart than ten thousand to the ear, 1 Cor. xiv., yea, one to shew you a good conscience, than ten thousand to shew all the science in the world. Sermon you hear upon sermon, till this manna comes out at your nostrils; but, as one said of laws, one is yet wanting for the practising of all the rest. Now conscience is the spring of practice, and the wheel that must set all the rest on going. Is it not high time to speak to conscience, that we be no longer hearers only, but doers also?

The time is now approaching, as we may easily discern, if we have not drunk or slept out our eyes, as in the times of Noah, in which Christ is pouring out his vials upon the earth; and, shortly, wherein the books shall be opened, these clasped and sealed books of our consciences, the contents whereof are now like letters written with the juice of oranges, that cannot be read till it come to that fire which shall make the secrets of all hearts legible; yea every the least fraction, even the least idle thought or speech; all which are faithfully registered in them. Is it not then high time to look into these books, to cast up these books, yea, to be well skilled and versed in them, for the sake and rectifying whereof all other good books are written, that we might be able to prove and examine ourselves, whether upon good ground we can say, with our apostle, 'We are assured we have a good conscience'? &c.

Which text, when I read and pronounce, which I do that you may well understand, methinks I hear Paul's voice, and discern his spirit, as the maid knew Peter's voice. I hear him use the like appeal in the very like case, when the Hebrews accused him, and Ananias had smitten him on the mouth: 'I have, in all good conscience, served God to this day.' In the self-same case, when they hired Tertullus to paint him out with his rhetoric for a pestilent fellow, a troubler and commotioner of the whole world, he used the like provocation: 'I endeavour always to have a good conscience towards God and man.' The very like protestation against the surmises of the same Hebrews, Rom. ix. Yea, so often that, 2 Cor. i. 12, he calls this and claims it as his own glory: 'This is my boasting, a good conscience.' So that, as we discern ships by their flags, so may we Paul by this flag of comfort and defiance, which he hangs out almost in every epistle; and if we may guess at the whole cloth by the list, this epistle, as this triumph, is his. And worthily, indeed, becomes it this chosen vessel, to glory in this choice jewel, with which the whole world, compared and weighed in the balance, will be found as light as dross and vanity; and, without this, loss, dung, and vexation of spirit. For mine own part, when I view this triumph, and the apostle so frequently and so confidently using it, I profess myself deeply affected therewithal. The world hath many stately sights, glorious objects, as, namely, strong towers, tall ships under sail, armies under banners, sumptuous buildings, pleasant orchards and groves; but when I represent to myself, when I seriously conceive and consider Paul, riding in this triumphant chariot, advanced above the reach of men's thoughts and tongues, yea, above all sublunary changes, all the fore-mentioned are in mine eyes but stately Babels, pompous fantasies, painted pageants. Did Paul, in the fruition of this, envy Agrippa's golden chain? No; it was but for manner's sake Paul excepted his chain.* And he that hath this good, needs not envy, I say, not any greatness here present; no, not Nebuchadnezzar's stalking in his magnificent galleries, built for his honour, the great Turk guarded with his Janissaries, the triple-crowned man of pride riding upon men's shoulders, and treading upon emperors' necks; much less the rich fool in the gospel, with his goods increasing and barns enlarged, or the rich glutton, with his delicate fare and purple raiment, or any other glistering appearances of happiness which dazzle the eyes of the doting world. Let become of the rest what will, so that this be my lot and portion (which ever let be my wish above all wishes) that, through God's grace and Christ's blood, I may have a good conscience, and be assured that I have one, desiring, in all things, to walk honestly.

In which text or †woof of Scripture, which I may call Paul's triumph, I find these threads: 1. The excellent matter, a good conscience. 2. The glorious manner, a certain confidence.

The trophies are not mean and base, but the richest gift which Christ ascending on high left us to rejoice in, a good conscience.‡

The boasting is not vain; it is no fantastical opinion, no fanatical revelation, but a true persuasion, 'we are assured.' It is no audacious presumption, but a grounded assertion, built upon these four pillars, as so many characters of a good conscience: (1.) Desiring; (2.) In all things; (3.) To walk or converse; (4.) Honestly.

Now, that we may more distinctly apprehend the contents of the text, and that which is best of all, attain the scope and subject matter thereof, which is the end of all, a good conscience (because many talk of conscience, few know it); I will first discover the nature of it, which hath been darkened by school definitions and rhetorical descriptions.

Secondly, because many slips and bad coins go for current and good ones (most brag of a good one, and fewest have it); I will shew you the goodness thereof, wherein it consists, how it is made good, and how it is distinguished from seeming good ones, and how by four infallible characters it is certainly approved and known to be good.

Because it is a dead commodity, a grape of Canaan, the sweetness whereof few have tasted, and they that have it cannot utter it; I will shadow out the excellency of it, as my poor skill and experience will allow me.

Lastly, when I have taught conscience to know itself and its own worth, I will set it a work to do its office in the application of the points of this and all other sermons.

Briefly collect and remark the heads.

* That is, he wished Agrippa were altogether like himself; only 'for manner's sake,' he added, 'except these bonds.'—ED.

† Σῶμα καί ὑφος τῆς γραφης.   ‡ Seges gloriæ.

What conscience is.

What a good one is ; how it may be discerned from bad ones, and known to be good.

3. How good a thing it is. And

4. What is the use, office, and effect of a good one.

1. For the nature of it. Things that are nearest, and most nearly concern us, are commonly farthest off our knowledge and respect. As God, that is in us and near unto us, our own faces and visages, are hardliest known, hardliest remembered. Some fools doubt whether there be such a thing in them, yea or no. Origen thought it a spirit or *genius*, associated to our souls, to guide and tutor them : but this is like some of his other conceits. The carnal atheist thinks it a melancholy humour of the body, and so thinks all the checks thereof to be effects of humour. The schoolmen, somewhat acuter, thought it, some, an habit ; some, an act of the soul. The latter divines, a faculty of the intellectual part. But the truth is, it is no such inmate, no such guest of the soul, but an inbred faculty of it : ' a noble and divine power, planted of God in the soul, working upon itself by reflection :' or thus, ' the soul of a man recoiling upon itself.'*

A faculty I call it, because it produceth acts, and is not got and lost as habits are, but is inseparable from the soul, immoveable from the subject, as neither acts nor habits are, which is Thomas's chief reason to prove conscience an act, *quia deponi potest ;* the clean contrary whereof is true, though indeed one might think some had laid aside and lost their conscience.

A noble faculty I call it, because so admirably strange in the reciprocal working of it. The eye of man sees not itself but by the help of a lookingglass ; neither hath any creature in this world this privilege and property, besides the soul of man. I give it room, and place it in the whole soul, and thrust it not, as some have done, like a spider, into some corner of it, as if it were a part of a part ; whereas the operation and power of it is circumscribed in no narrower bounds than the soul itself, and therefore the Hebrews more aptly call it לב, heart or soul, and the Grecians καρδία. 'If our heart condemn us,' (1 John iii. 20).

It hath indeed the understanding for the throne and palace thereof, where it is chiefly resident, whereby it exerciseth the principal functions, from whence commonly it hath its name conscience, as the emperor of Russia from Moscow, his chief city ; and look how the soul itself is chiefly seated in the head, and there performeth the chief actions of reason, discourse, and sense, yet is in all and every part of the body, and in them performeth baser and meaner offices of nourishment and motion : right so the conscience keepeth a complete court in the whole soul, commonly called *forum conscientiæ.*

In the understanding part it is a judge, determining and prescribing, absolving and condemning *de jure.* In the memory it is a register, a recorder, and witness, testifying *de facto.* In the will and affections, a jailor and executioner, punishing and rewarding. Say we not in common use of speech, which is the emperor of words, My conscience tells me I did or did not such a thing, which is an action of the memory? My conscience bids me do, or forbids me to do this or this, which is but an action of the will. It smites me, it checks me, it comforts or it torments me; what are these but actions of the affections recoiling upon the soul? But if any list to

* Cum alia scit animus, Scientia dicitur, cum seipsum, Conscientia, &c.—Hugo et Bernardus.

contend about these subtilties, conscience tells them it hath no such custom.
Conscience, falsely so called, delighteth to languish about questions not
tending to edification.   Let us rather turn our eyes to behold and wonder
at the divine royalties and endowments of it, it being in man the principal
part of God's image, and that by which man resembleth most the autarchy
and self-sufficiency of God, which I grant is proper to his infiniteness, to
be content and complete within itself, but under him, and with his leave
and love.   This faculty makes him self-sufficient and independent of other
creatures, like unto those self-moving engines which have their principle of
motion within themselves.   Thus Adam, when he was alone, was not yet
alone and desolate, but might converse with this his conscience, as well as
with a thousand companions and acquaintances.

Secondly, God hath given it more force and power to work upon men
than all other agents whatsoever.   It, being internal and domestical, hath
the advantage of all foreign and outward.   Man in this respect being like
to the earth, immoveable of all the winds, though at once they should blow
from all the points of the compass, yet easily shaken by a vapour from
within; whence it is that the approofs and reproofs of it are so powerful
and terrible, the one cheering more than any cordial, the other gnawing
more than any chestworm, tormenting worse than hot pincers, boiling
caldrons, racks, strappadoes, or what other the cruelty of tyrants hath in-
vented.   If one had angels daily ascending and descending, as Jacob had,
to comfort him, it were not so comfortable; or if langold or coupled to
devils, no more terrible.

Thirdly, It being individual* and inseparable, there is no putting of
it to flight or flying from it.   *Nec fugere, nec fugare poteris.*†   It was
bred and born with us; it will live and die with us.   Agues a man may
shake off, tyrants and ill masters a man may fly from; but this saith
(as Ruth to Naomi), ' I will go with thee whithersoever thou goest.'   It
hath more immediate deputation and authority from God (of whom
all principalities and powers receive theirs) than angels, kings, magistrates, father, mother, or any other superior.   It is only inferior to
God.   It is a certain middle thing between God and man, and hath the
dignity of earls and nobles, that are *comites regum.*   And so Paul is bold,
Romans ix., to call his conscience a co-witness with God, whence it hath
the name conscience, where being no other creature with whom it can bear
witness, none knowing what is in man, save God, and the spirit, or conscience, which is man; which makes Paul join them in one appeal, Romans
xi.   It is his spy and intelligencer in our bosoms and bedchambers; a most
exact notary of whatever we think or do.   It is his lieutenant, and under
him the principal commander, and chief controller of man's life; yea, every
man's God, in that sense that Moses was Aaron's.   It is the surest prog-
nostication and pre-judgment of God's last judgment;‡ and best almanac
within a man's own breast, foretelling him what will become of him at that day.

Wonderful is the greatness and sovereignty of it.   O men therefore, and
O consciences, know yourselves, and in this sense, love, respect, and reverence yourselves more than all other creatures, friends, and acquaintance.
If they could speak, they would say to man's conscience, as the people to
David, A thousand of us are not equal to thee in worth.   It fares with conscience as with simple constables.   Many an officer, if he knew his place,
would stand more upon it, and take more upon him than he doth.   The

* That is, "indivisible."—ED.   † Lyps. Pol.
‡ Præjudicium extremi judicii.—Tertul.

husbandman were happy, if he knew his happiness. The horse were strong, if he knew his strength. Conscience, if it knew its power and authority, would not suffer itself so to be silenced, abused, snibbed, and kept under, being under God, the lord-controller of the soul, and supervisor of our life.

2. Thus have we seen in part the greatness of conscience. Doth it not concern us now to see the goodness of it ? The greatness of it maketh it, if good, nothing better ; if bad, nothing worse ; the surest friend and the severest foe. Whose heart burns not within him, to hear wherein that goodness consists, and how he may come by it ?

The goodness of it is the peace of it ; for stirring, accusing, and galling consciences are consequents of sin, and presuppose some evil.

They, secondly, prove good unto us only by accident, and God's goodness, which maketh them as afflictions, gather grapes of thorns ; yea, all things work to the best of his beloved, as physicians do poisons in their confections.

And thirdly, they do not always produce this effect. Sometimes as sicknesses and purgations, they are in order to health, as in the Jews, Acts ii. Oftentimes as in Cain, Judas, Ahithophel, they destroy their owners.

Good consciences, therefore, properly to speak, are only quiet ones, excusing and comforting ; but here take heed the devil, the great impostor of our souls, put not upon our folly and simplicity, three sorts of quiet ones, as he doth to most : the blind, the secure, and the seared.

Blind and ignorant consciences speak peace, or hold their peace, because they have not skill enough to accuse and find fault ; they swallow many a fly, and digest all well enough. While the scales were upon Paul's eyes, he was alive and quiet ; he thought concupiscence, the sink and breeder of all sin, to be no sin. Such consciences discern sins as we do stars in a dark night ; see only the great ones of the first magnitude, whereas a bright even discovers millions ; or as we see a few motes in dark houses, which sunlight shews to be infinite. Such think good meaning will serve the turn, that all religions will save, or a ' Lord, have mercy on us,' at the last gasp ; and that which is worst of all, they love to live under blind Sir Johns, seek dark corners, say they are not book-learned, nor indeed will suffer their consciences to prove good lawyers in God's book, lest they should prove common barrotters.* The law which nature hath engraven they tread out with sins, as men do the engravings of tombs they walk on with foul shoes ; they dare not look in the glass of God's law, which makes sin abound, lest the foulness of their souls should affright them. A number of such sottish souls there be, whose consciences, if God opens as he did the eyes of the prophet's servant, they shall see armies and legions of sins and devils in them.

In as pitiful a plight as this, are secure, sleepy, and drowsy consciences, who see, but will not see, with whom sin, Satan, and their conscience is not at peace, but at truce for a time. Safe they are not, only secure they be and careless. These sleep and delight in sleeping ; and two ways especially the devil pipes and lulls them asleep : by mirth and by business. Ease and prosperity slay some fools ; wealth and hearts-ease, like Delilah, rock them asleep on her lap ; jesting and merry tales, eating and drinking, cast them into a spirit of slumber, and put their sin and judgment far away, and make them say they shall never be moved. While they prosper and flourish in the world, their consciences deal as creditors with their debtors ; whiles they are in trading and doing, say nothing to them, but if once down the wind, in sickness, crosses, and poverty, then arrest upon arrest, action upon action, then come the fowls of the air and seize upon

* That is, ' blackguards.'—ED.

the sick soul, as the ravens upon sick sheep, write bitter things against
them, and make them possess the sin of their youth. Mark this, you that
dwell at ease, and swim in wealth in London. Your consciences that lie
still like sleepy mastiffs, in plague times and sweating sicknesses, they
fly in the throat; they flatter like parasites in prosperity, and like sycophants
accuse in adversity. Business also and cares of this life choke the conscience, and the voice of manifold employments drown the voice of conscience,
as the drums in the sacrifices to Moloch the cry of the infants. And such
consciences are quiet, not because they are at peace, but because they are
not at leisure. Mark then, you that have mills of business in your heads,
whole *Westminster Halls, Bourses, Exchanges,* and *East Indies* (as I fear many
of you have whilst I am speaking to your conscience), that making haste to be
rich, overlay your brains with affairs, are so busy in your counting-house
and books, and that upon this very day, that you never have once in a
week, or year, an hour's space to confer with your poor consciences ; yea,
when did you ? Let your consciences answer within you. No; but if at a
sermon you appoint them a time, and say you will, you disappoint them
and say, as Agrippa* to Paul, ' We will hear thee another time ;' and for
the most part do as he did, that is, never hear them again.

All these sleepers have but a frenzy man's sleep. This tranquillity will
be sure to end in a tempest.

Yet in a more horrible case, and step nearer hell, are such as sear their
consciences with a hot iron, harden them of purpose, as men do steel, by
quenching the motions of them ; brand them with often sinning against
their checking, fleshing tender novices with this counsel, when their consciences trouble them for anything, then to do it the rather, and so they
shall hear no more of them. And so it proves, through God's just judgment giving them over to a reprobate sense, that their consciences serve
them as Moses did Pharaoh, having received many repulses, and at last
commanded to come no more in sight, forbare to lose any more breath unto
him, but complained to God, who swept him and his host with a final
destruction.

When tutors and pedagogues are weary with pupils, they give them
over to their parents' fury. These are αὐτοχαταχριτοι, and to these villains,
there is no peace, saith my God, and my text. These men's consciences,
if ever they awake (as seldom they do), they awake as Jonah, in fearful
astonishment ; and if they sleep out this life till their long sleep, yet their
condemnation sleepeth not. Think of this, you monsters, scorners, and
mock-gods, that forget your consciences, lest they awake and tear you in
pieces. Be not, my brethren, deceived with any of these deceiving consciences, children of darkness. Though conscience be not usually mocked,
yet many ' deceive their own heart,' James i. 26, for want of examination.
Many say, and think in their consciences, that they have good consciences,
when God saith, O that this people had such a conscience ; and so Paul
speaks in my text, as once to Agrippa, ' O that you were as I am,'
' assured that you have a good conscience, desiring,' &c.

What, then, is a good conscience ? That which speaks peace with God's
allowance, which is a messenger of good things between God and us, that
upon good grounds is in good terms with God. It lies in the lawful peace
of it, and not in integrity and freedom from sin. If my conscience accuse
me not, yet am I not thereby justified ; God is greater than my conscience.
If any conscience say to any man, he hath no sin, it lies in the throat, and

* Qu. 'Felix ?'—ED.

is a liar. Adam only had such a paradise, such a good conscience, walking with God, without sin, without fear, in the state of innocency. There is but one way now to come to it; our peace is now to be had by mediation and reconciliation; being justified by Christ's blood, we have this peace. Instead of many, mark one remarkable place of Scripture for this purpose. If you ask what makes a good conscience, there is but one thing in the world will make it: 'the blood of Christ, once offered by his eternal Spirit, without fault, purgeth our consciences from dead works,' Heb. ix. 14. Yea, so admirable is the force of this blood, that it leaves no more conscience of sin within it. This Lamb takes them away (Heb. x. 2), and carries them out of God's remembrance into the wilderness of oblivion. If any conscience rage as the sea, Christ cast into it, as Jonah, whists all the waves of it. If the law make it as Mount Sinai, covered with dark-ness, the gospel calms and lightens it presently. If tossed as the ship where the disciples sailed in the night, he rebukes the winds, and they are still; if the devils rend and rage in it, he casts them out presently.

The jailor came in trembling, ready to for-do himself; 'Believe on Christ,' sent him out leaping and rejoicing. It is strange how freely, effectually, and speedily he quiets all. O all ill consciences, hear and believe! this is the honour, royalty, and peculiar dignity of Christ's blood, to pacify and make good our consciences. I do not so much admire at all his miraculous healings of diseases, leprosies, blindness, and lameness, demoniacs of all sorts, as I do at his gracious and sudden quieting of the conscience of Mary Magdalene, of Zaccheus, of Paul; and so the like virtue this blood hath still, to-day and yesterday the same. Nothing else in the world hath this virtue save his blood: all other merriments have no more power to quiet conscience than holy-water and charms to conjure the devil.

I find in a French comedy one brought in as troubled in conscience for sin, and he runs up and down like a hart with an arrow in its side: for remedy he buys a pardon, runs to shrift, whips himself, goes on pilgrim-ages, and all this while, like an aguish man that drinks water, or leaps into a pool, his disease increaseth; then falls he to seek merry company, to see if he can play away his trouble; but, like Saul's ill spirit, it re-turns with greater violence, and brings seven worse with it to torment. In the end he finds Christ, or rather is found of Christ, and so finds peace. And this is the good conscience we speak of, to which being in Christ there is no condemnation, no accusation. Wouldst thou purchase a good conscience at an easier rate? wouldst thou have it for sleeping? When thou hast tried all conclusions, come hither and buy salve for thy con-science without money. When thou hast spent all thy time and money about what will not quiet thy mind, as alchemists smoke out all in seeking the philosopher's-stone, here is that which will do it: believe and prove, and thou and thy conscience shall be safe and quiet. This is approved, thus Paul got his. Yea, but is this all? Is it so cheap and easy a thing? May we now sing a *requiem* to our souls, lay the reins on our necks, cast care away, and do what we list? I fear not such an objection from a true believing conscience. They that prattle thus know not *ingenium fidei et bonæ conscientiæ*, the good nature of faith and a good conscience.

Let me not daub your consciences with untempered mortar. Faith, as it pacifieth, so it purifieth, conscience. Christ purgeth our consciences to serve the living God; and, after all his cures, bids the healed go away and walk after the Spirit, and sin no more. There are indeed a generation of libertines and hypocrites, that serve Christ as Louis the XI. is reported to have served his leaden crucifix, which he used to wear in his hat; and when he had blasphemed or done any villany, he would pull it off and kiss it, and so sin over and over again: like our common swearers, that cry God mercy, and ask him leave to abuse his name again, and that wittingly and willingly.

These and such like let their consciences speak peace to them, as the friar in Stephan absolved a gentleman that would needs pay well, yet would not promise to amend his fault, instead of an absolution he pronounced a curse upon him in Latin, which he took for pay: ' Christ absolve thee, which I believe he will not; and bring thee to heaven, which is impossible.'

Many sentences hath the master of sentences * borrowed from Ambrose against such consciences, which I omit to rehearse; lest, as Abner's body, they hinder the passing of the people by. A good conscience stands not with a purpose of sinning; no, not with an irresolution against sin. He is a fool and a vain mocker, no true penitent, that mourns for sin past, and yet means at the same time to sin for the time to come. With which sophism the most perish at this day, with this in their mouths : ' They believe on Christ, and have as good a conscience as the best,' and yet walk in sin. But O thou vain fellow, shew me Paul's good conscience by Paul's proof, by his ' desire in all things,' &c. Is Christ able to save thee, and is he not able to sanctify thee ? Let me with Tertullian tell thee that, the promises standing true, thy faith is false; and, the gospel remaining safe, thou shalt perish.

Titus, a tradesman or lawyer here present, haply is desirous to have peace of conscience, is sorry for his oaths and fraudulent courses this week past, but knows he shall fall to the like the week coming, hates them not, and means not to strive against them, but to return to the mire ; my text saith not to him, ' Go in peace,' to such loose and licentious consciences that make Christ a bawd of sinning, and faith a cloak of liberty. I have heard that the pope hath sold a pardon for a murder past, with a dispensation annexed for the next; but Christ, my Lord and Master (as bountiful and gracious as he is), grants no such. If he forgive that which is past, he gives at least so much grace, as to deny ungodliness for the time to come. To conclude this point. Thou desirest a good conscience, without intending or conditioning : I bid thee believe in Christ, and thou hast one ; yet take this, not into the bargain, but as an after proviso. Art thou willing to have a good conscience ? and to be assured thereof ? here follow four infallible characters and marks of a good one, which I desire you to mark attentively, and by them to try your consciences thoroughly. Hitherto I have shewed how you may get one ; now how you may prove one. Here are four elements or humours ; which, well compounded and mixed, make up a perfect healthful conscience ; if any one be wanting, or fail in a just measure or proportion, conscience is accordingly defective and sick.

The first is, that which must be the first in every good action, that is, the will—(θέλοντες) ; that the bent and inclination of that be set right. I would the word had been plainly translated as it is in other places, *verbatim*, ' willing.' It implies first, that he that hath a good conscience, doth not only do well, but wills to do well, doth it voluntarily, not forcedly, or out of external and sinister motions, but from an internal principle, a sanctified and rectified will, which God accepts for the deed, and above the deed. Secondly, that he doth not only wish and faintly desire, which translation

* Lib. iv. Dist. 14.

may flatter an hypocrite¯that hath some sluggish lusts, and some sudden good pangs and moods, and such as for the time little differ in sickness and starts from a regenerate will; but the word notes a strong and settled resolution, a constant purpose, and such as produceth endeavour. 'He that *will* be rich, pierceth himself through with many sorrows;' where the same word is used. I grant it is *carnificina*, a rack to a good conscience, to say, it must always do well; and contrarily, it is a true ground of comfort to say, that a will and purpose is sufficient testimony and approof of a good one; but then it must be meant, not every languishing and lazy flash of every wisher and woulder, but of a willer; and this word is equal with the other two, which are good synonimas and glosses upon this used by Paul, Acts xxiii. 24, ' I labour,' or ' exercise myself,' and πεπολιτευμαι, ' I lay my policy,' or bend my wit and will to have a good conscience, and to serve God, &c.

It may be said of some, they would be good, but they have no will to it. There is none so prodigal or slothful but would be rich; yet we say not such will be rich, that is, set it down determining it *ultimata voluntate*. There are none so wicked, but at some times would be good and leave sin; but these dispositions breed imperfect essays and proffers, ripen not, hold not, discern not the name of will. Corrupt flesh hath many such propensities and bubbles, and is very prodigal in momentary purposes and promises; but David saith he will keep God's commandments, 'I have vowed, sworn,' &c.; when Michal mocked, ' I will yet be more vile,' as resolute swaggerers, whose will is set and sold to sin. They sin and will sin, say preachers what they can. Ahab will go, cry Micaiah what he please; so Joshua will serve God, let others do what they will. Sanctified will may be crossed, and captivated, and hindered, but yet it holds its own bent, and overcomes the law of rebellion, is predominant, and can never be forced to sin, or to will to sin, without a curb in the mouth; the more stiff and steady this will is, the better symptom of a good conscience.

Secondly, this will must extend itself to all (εν πασι), though in many things our deeds fail: which extent let Paul expound with a distribution, towards God and man. In duties divine, human, of charity and piety, whatsoever is done for God's sake and conscience sake, is done equally. No man makes a conscience of one, but he that doth of all; he that delights in the breach of one commandment, hates all the rest. The rich and precious box of a good conscience, is polluted and made impure, if but one dead fly be suffered, I say not, if one fly of infirmity light in it, against the will forementioned; but if with our will it lie, and die, and putrefy in it. When Christ purgeth Mary's conscience, he casts out, not six, but seven devils, yea, he leaves not one of the legion remaining, not one spot of leprosy in any one member, but saith, ' Faith hath made thee whole.' Here I see many fall short, and I pity to see so many civil men and hypocrites to come so near the kingdom of heaven and a good conscience, and yet one thing is wanting. Foolish Herod, that doest many things and stickest at one; foolish Ananias, that spillest and losest all thy cost with a small reservation: foolish hypocrite, why takest thou pains to climb so high on the hill of piety, and yet for one step of injustice to thy neighbour, ascends not into God's mountain, though thou comest often into God's tabernacle? Thou civil, honest man, why givest thou alms, livest fairly with man, and forgettest the main, art so far short of this ' all things,' that thou forgettest that which should be all in all, that is, piety to God? Universal and catholic obedience, is the best distinguishing touchstone of truth and falsehood, of good and bad consciences. This universality must also extend to great and small duties. I say universality, not equality; a good conscience mainly desires to please God in the great commandments, as Christ calls them, and then in every complement, in every hoof and nail, so near as he can, yet observing a due proportion. It most of all strains at gross sins, yet swallows not gnats. It trembles at wounds and blood, fears faith and truth; it abhors adultery, hates dalliance; it pays tithe-sheaves carefully, it detains not tithe, mint, and aniseed; it says not, an inch breaks no square, and small faults must be winked at, and in this sense may well be said to be scrupulous, because it being tender feels scruples; only here I lay a caveat, that it be not erroneous, or ignorantly dubious and scrupulous, like the wall-eyed or bird-eyed horse, that starts upon every shadow without occasion or cause, makes conscience where God and his word makes none, makes many questions for conscience sake. Light and information is as good as tenderness, both together make an excellent conscience; and *obiter* for the sake of scrupulous consciences, that desire unfeignedly in all things to walk honestly, I give them these solemn charges:

First, That they study the peace of the church.

Secondly, That they study their liberties.

Thirdly, That they be humble towards God and their superiors, and willing to illuminate and regulate their consciences by the word, and be established in what they are to do, not admitting every fear of the contrary without ground, yet remembering Paul's rule, to follow the dictates of conscience, rather than of angel, potentate, or prelate, yea, of apostle. For, after the apostle had determined that, in the 14th to the Romans, he yet requires in the eater a plerophory, and blesseth him that doth it with consent of conscience, and makes all other sin a sin against conscience, being worse than a sin against man, yea, next to the sin aginst the Holy Ghost. An erroneous conscience holds the wolf by the ears, binds to the act, frees not from the fault. Oh! therefore labour to get a salve, and think not your own eyesight to be sharper than the eagles'. Endeavour to inform your consciences aright; and, having so done, be careful in all things to keep a good conscience, and that through the whole tenor and course of your lives, which is required in the next term of conversation.

A word that adds to the former, constancy and equality. There are in the life of man many turnings (ἀναστρεφεσθαι), references, and divers respects, in all these; at every turn to be the same man, requires the strength of a good conscience. To take a step or two well, a child or a drunkard may; but to walk evenly, and to turn hither and thither well, argues strength. A jade, or a broken-paced horse, may rack or strike a stroke or two right; but to maintain the thorough pace at every stop and turn, to be at the command of the rider, argues mettle and goodness. This term is expressed by Paul: 'I have always, or thoroughly, to this day' (ἄχρι τῆς ἡμέρας ταύτης, δια παντος), Acts xxiii. 1; and, xxiv. 16, ἀπροβσκοπον ἔχων συνειδησιν. That is, without tripping or stumbling, or without offence to other, &c. A weak conscience falls at every turn: godly in one company, profane in another; a good one, as a square cube, is the same which way soever you turn him. Turn him to God, to his neighbour, turn him to company, turn him alone, turn him loose to all occurrences, he holds his own, and walks honestly. For example, one day is the brief of a man's whole life, and is a little life, bounded with the night and the morning, as with birth and death: wherein a conscionable man first turns to God in prayer alone, then with his family, then to his calling, then to his recreation, to society, eating and drinking, and at night returns to God and his rest; in all these walking godly, soberly, righteously, and is able to say trulier than the epicure at night, 'I have lived this day:' βεβιώκα, I have walked honestly. He is a good day's-man, or journeyman, or tasker, which is an excellent mystery of well living and redemption of time, a working up our salvation in holiness and righteousness all the days of our life. He that lets slip one day's watch and work may sleep at night in a whole skin, but not in a sound conscience. Such crazy consciences have, as broken brains, their good and evil days, *turbida et lucida intervalla.* Conscience, as a vessel, may easily be kept pure and clean if rinsed every day; but if it go longer, it gathers soil, and asks harder scouring by more than ordinary repentance. Daily washing will keep it pure and fair, which is the last thing which is yet wanting to perfection, such perfection as is to be found in the way; and that being added, will set on the roof and pinnacle upon this building.

Καλως, *honestly;* I could wish the translators had used some other word, because this is so disgraceful and contemptible as the world goes, though the word in its due signification is honourable, *honesty* in truth (as ironically as the world useth it) being only truly honourable, forcing honour from the breasts of men, which is the seat of honour, which bravery doth but beg. The word is comprehensive, and compasseth in the fathom of it as much as any of all the other adverbs in Scripture: worthily, decently, accurately, circumspectly, gravely, after the best fashion or comely, praise-worthy, lively, famously (ἀξίως, εὐπρεπῶς, ἀκριβῶς, σεμνῶς, εὐσχημονῶς). It notes the lustre and grace of an action, which makes our conversation shine before men, and sets out God's glory. Τὸ καλὸν, a thing that citizen and courtier much stand upon in their actions; yea, all men now-a-days build, feast, wear apparel, not for bare necessity, but for their credit, so as they may get honesty by them. Unconscionable men slubber over their work, and think anything good enough for God, as in Malachi; and content themselves with reasonable service, for so they translate that, λογικην λατρείαν, Rom. xii. Whereas Paul often requires Christians should be excellent ringleaders in fair works (καλῶν ἔργων προιςασθε), and provide honest or honourable things before men, and to possess their vessels, much more their consciences, in honour, that they may be fit temples for the Holy Ghost. As Theodoret most divinely upon Exodus, look how the temple was adorned with the finest gold, silver, silk, purple, scarlet, jewels, &c, so must thy conscience, of which temples this was but a type.

There is in every duty, besides the deed done, an honourable decorum annexed, as in hearing, to hear swiftly; in preaching, to labour and to be instant in season, &c.; in giving alms, to do it cheerfully; in trading, to be at a word; in payments and promises, to keep day and touch: and thus it becomes a Christian to exceed the pharisee and the civil man, or else it is not for his and his Master's honour.

David did excellently when he would not offer a sacrifice without cost; the woman that spent her costly spikenard on Christ, the smell whereof perfumed all the house, and holds the scent to this day; the widow that gave all her substance. Our honourable personages, how mean are they in allowances to ministers, in alms to the poor, or any expenses that respect God and their souls! A good conscience, for the sake of this honesty, avoids and flies, not only scandalous blemishes and stains, but all the least blushes and appearances of evil, all brackish-tasted things, his stomach goes against them. If he knew never so well cards, dice, usury, non-residency, plurality to be never so lawful, yet because they stand not with this honour, he will none of them. He asks not what he may do with a safe conscience, but with an excellent one; not what is lawful and expedient, but honourable.

Thus have we seen the apostle riding in this triumphant chariot, drawn, as it were, with these four horses, the four evidences of conscience.

The first proves it good; the second, true; the third, strong; the fourth, excellent.

He that hath ' the will,' hath the seeds of religion, and is a Christian, and no atheist.

He that willeth ' in all things' is a sound Christian, and no hypocrite.

He that ' converseth or walketh,' is a grown Christian, no babe or weakling.

He that walks ' honourably,' is an excellent Christian, no ordinary one.

He that hath ' all these,' may well say and glory with the apostle's confidence, that he is assured.

He that hath them not, as most have them not, may well conclude, We are assured that our consciences are evil and impure, willing to sin, and walk after the flesh.

The word (πέπεισμαι)* is Paul's word, and yet he speaks it in the plural number by way of syllepsis, changing the number, because he would have it the word of every Christian. πέπεισμαι is a word of as good certainty as ὃιδα, it seconds and binds it as the better word, Rom. xiv., ' I know and am assured.' Of it, as of the root, springs πίςις, for all Bellarmine would elevate it. It implies a grounded persuasion, not from inspiration or revelation, but from arguments and experience. Faith is the subsistence and evidence (ὑωόστασις, ἕλεγχος); and the persuasion or assurance of a Christian is as firm as is any wordling's for his estate; yea, a thousand times surer. You rich men think yourselves sure of estates here upon earth, but we Christians know ourselves sure of heaven. Conscience knows itself, as well as science any principle, or sense any object. Without which certainty, Christians were, of all men, most miserable. Popery and nature, and the old leaven of Pelagius, newly worse soured by Arminius, never having had experience of this plerophory, serve Christians, when they boast of this their confidence, as Ananias did Paul, strike them on the face with the term of pride and presumption, yea, stick not to give them the lie; but such betray themselves with their own noise. I would ask them but Paul's question, ' Do not you know?' If they answer, as usually they do, No, nor they think any man living on earth, I would pray them to mark what follows : ' Except you be reprobate,' refuse, or *rejectanii*, as yet in the state of reprobation, for aught they know.

Indeed, it becomes the strumpet and adulteress to doubt of her husband, and not to call him *ishi*, Hosea ii. ; but let him mark (saith Bernard) the spouse's language, ' My beloved is mine, and I am his.' See (saith he) what a good conscience dares do. *Habet ecclesia spirituales suos, qui fiducialiter agunt cum Christo:* ' The church hath her spiritual ones that rely boldly on Christ,' or ' confidently;' the very term that Bellarmine excepts against. And, *id audet unus, quod audet universitas; ego pulvis et cinis*, &c. Yea, every particular person dares do as much as the Catholic Church; I that am dust and ashes, dare apply this to myself. And Thompson upon that text, ' These things (saith he) are not written, for I know not what

* Qu. πέποιμεθα ? πέπεισμαι is not Paul's word, neither is it plural.—ED.

airy notions or ideas, but for me and thee.'* Without which, who would be a Christian? A man's conscience is deep and deceitful; but the spirit of man, especially helped by the Spirit of God, and upon examination and trial, may and doth know as well (saith Augustine), his charity wherewith he loves, as his brother whom he loves; and if his charity, then his faith.

Three *scioes* I find in the end of John's epistle. The major, or proposition, is God's word, 'The believer is saved.' The minor is assumed by God's Spirit and the conscience, two sufficient witnesses, fortified and assisted by many premises, by the compass within, the landmarks without faith, and the fruits of faith. 'Dost thou believe?' saith Christ; 'I believe,' saith the man. And this is the restipulation of a good conscience in baptism, and in every true believer. *Credis?* *Credo* was the ancient form, which answer all waverers must reverse and innovate. Latitudes of assurance I grant in babes and old men. David knew, when he came to Hebron, that God meant to establish the kingdom to him and his, which he knew before, but now with a confirmed knowledge. The balances of the scale shake and tremble at the first; after the weight is in a while, it settles and rests, and so our souls. And even this certainty is of the nature of all precious faith, though experienced faith increaseth it. It is this confidence that makes a good conscience; this valour makes the value of it invaluable and unutterable.

3. Look upon my text, and see how valiantly, by the right and interest of it, Paul first challengeth and commands prayers, even at the hands of the Jews. Who waters a dry stake with any heart? What comfort hath Peter to pray for Simon Magus in the gall of bitterness? But with what hope of audience might he pray for Cornelius, and such as he was? So John for Gaius and the elect lady, walking in the truth; not so for Diotrephes. Secondly, see how he begs, not their good opinion and good words of him, though he knew they had strange surmises and suggestions of him from the false apostles, to be a very *Proteus* and *Polypus*, the grand cheater of the world; but instead of apologies and captation of good will, he relies to this fort, passeth not for man's day; he is happy enough without them; he carries his comforter in his bosom and breast, and hath a self-sufficiency. A dependent and beholden happiness is half a misery, like mills that cannot grind without wind or water. Saul cannot be merry without a fiddler; Ahab without Naboth's vineyard; Haman without Mordecai's courtesy. A good conscience without music, or money, or honour, is happy and merry alone, and is like the late engine of the perpetual motion.

As rich men stand upon terms, I can live by you and without you; so saith a good conscience to the world.

It lays claim not only to the prayers and communion of saints, but to the attendance of angels. As Luther is said to have said, they are cooks and butlers to this continual feast; they ascend and descend to them with messages from heaven. Christ, as Ahasuerus with Esther, delights to sup with such. The Holy Ghost takes up in them his abode and temple. See in the Canticles how Christ is enamoured with the beauty and familiarity of his spouse, and they often mutually invite one another to walks and feasts.

Thirdly, which is more, in the fail of all other comforts; yea, in despite of the greatest discomforts and disgraces that can be, in the greatest storms and stress, in the foulest weather, this ship reigns and rides at anchor, as

* Hæc non sunt scripta pro idæis nescio quibus, sed pro me et te.

in a harbour and lee, hangs out the flag of comfort and defiance. Let the Jews think and speak what they will, it stirs not Paul; he soars like an eagle, not respecting the chitting of sparrows; is above the scourges and razors of tongues.

I am much taken up with admiration, when I read Acts xxvii. How Paul in the angry Adriatical Sea, at midnight, when the tempestuous Euroclydon blew, after fourteen days' want of meat and light, when the mariners despaired, how courageous he was; but I wonder as much and more, to see his conscience pass with topsail and banners displayed, through the sea and waves of good report and bad report, to see him singing and praying at midnight in the dungeon, all manacled and fettered, in a wounded skin, but whole and merry conscience.

Censures and rumours the world is full of; who escapes? Not Paul himself; yet is above them, and gives a secret *item* to all such as censure him, that they wronged him in judging a good conscience. The fashion is, to judge and censure all courses we reach not, or favour not; and so we smite many a good conscience. In this respect what need have we all of good consciences, seeing tongues spare none!

There be three days especially, the day of sickness, of death, of judgment, in which comfort is worth a world, and then all worldly comforts and comforters, like runaway servants and drunken serving-men, are to seek when one hath most use and need of them, as Job complaineth of the brooks of Teman in the drought of summer; which makes the triumph of the wicked (Job xx.) momentary, and as a night vision, whenas the prophet said, ' One dreams of bread, and wakes hungry.' In these times you shall see the merry and jolly worldling hang the head like a bulrush, and the ruffian's brags lag like a starched ruff in a storm. How do such droop, even in old age, and say, The days are come, wherein there is no pleasure! The storm comes after the rain; that which is worst, an ill conscience, like a bloodhound, hunts dry-foot, and brings the scent of sins of his youth; whereas the conscience of a well-passed life is the staff of age, *pabulum senile*, better than all the sack and sugars, and such pitiful comforters. When the stomach fails, and the grinders wax few, and appetite ceaseth, this is a continual feast. In the decay of sleep this is a down pillow. In all our tribulation, this Simon helps us to bear our crosses. In all our evil days it is at hand. It sustains the infirmities of the body. When princes sat in council against David, this was his Jonathan to solace him. When the lion roars, the righteous is bold as the lion, and fears not what man can do unto him.

But if once death begin to look us in the face, how doth Nabal die like a stone! How do Ahithophel and Judas die the death of cowardly harts and hares, pursued with the full cry of their sins, that makes them dead in the nest before they die! Then a kingdom for a good conscience! Then send (as in the sweating sickness and the plague) for Mr Minister, but alas! he is come; he can but speak to the ear, and all in vain, unless God open the conscience to hear and be quiet, to hear and embrace comfort. But when speech fails, and all thy senses shut up their doors and windows, then who or what can avail but a good conscience? When thy wife and thy friends do augment thy grief with parting, and loath to depart, as Paul's friends broke his heart with weeping, then this only and alone dies, or rather lives with thee, and seeing land approaching, bids thee be of good comfort. More cheerfully have I seen it make some die than others wed.

All the martyrs, from Stephen the proto-martyr, down to the last that suffered, are clouds of witnesses; it hath enabled them to embrace their stakes, clap their hands, leap, as Dr Taylor did, within two stiles of the stake, or (as he said) of his home and Father's house.

Lastly, at the last day, and after the last day, when all these shadows shall fly away, this substance shall abide. A good wife is a good thing, but Sarah must part with Abraham; and these relations shall cease in heaven; but a good conscience, attended with good works, shall follow, and the better it hath been here, the better in degree it shall be there, the wider entrance and entertainment it shall find there. When all books shall perish, and heaven melt like a parchment scroll, this book shall be of use; when all devils and damned shall tremble, and wish the hills to cover them, this shall lift up thy head, for thy redemption approacheth; when neither friends nor a full purse shall plead, nor the wicked stand upright in judgment, then, then, well-fare a good conscience; then shall conscience have its mouth opened, tongue untied, and God will bid it speak. Happy he then that hath an excusing one, miserable he that hath it an accusing adversary.

Yet still further: faith and hope are excellent things here in this valley; these shall cease, but conscience abides. A good one was a petty heaven upon earth, a Mount Tabor, a glimpse of glory here; a bad one was a hell, a purgatory, or a limbo at the least, tasting of the flashes and smoke of hell; but hereafter how intolerable shall be the horror of the one, and how inconceivable the joys of the other. Without this worm that dies not, hell should not be hell; without this continual feast, heaven should not be heaven. Next the happy vision of God shall be the company of a good conscience, and next to that the society of saints and angels.

4. But, O Lord, who believes our report, or to whom is the benefit and excellency of this creature of thine revealed? O Lord, to whom shall we speak and apply what hath been said? You, the sons of men, have lost your hearing; charm we never so wisely, thunder we never so earnestly, you despise us ministers. You think we come hither to play our prizes, to speak out of form and not of conscience, or to speak out of choler and passion.

Besides, if you would hear us, we are strangers to your secrets, to your hearts and ways. We are confined to our cells and studies, and are not acquainted with the tithe of the world's villanies; besides, when the hour-glass is out we can say no more to you, and perhaps shall never see you again. But your consciences know you, though happily you be strangers to them; they compass your paths, your lying down, and accustomed ways.

I will therefore turn my speech (as the prophet to the earth and heaven) to your consciences. Hearken, O consciences! hear the word of the Lord. I call you to record this day, that it is your office to preach over our sermons again, or else all our sermons and labours are lost. You are the cuds of the soul, to chew over again. Against your reproofs, and against your secret and faithful admonitions, what exception can any take? Your balm is precious; your smitings break not the head, nor bring any disgrace. God hath given you a faculty to work wonders in private and solitude. Follow them home, therefore, cry aloud in their ears and bosoms, and apply what hath now and at other times been delivered.

Conscience, if the house and owner where thou dwellest be a son of peace, let thy peace and thy Master's peace abide and rest on him; that peace which the world never knows, nor can give, nor take away. Be thou propitious and benign, speak good things, cherish the least sparks and smoke of grace; if thou findest desire in truth, and in all things, bid them not fear and doubt of their election and calling. With those that desire to walk honestly, walk thou comfortably. Handle the tender and fearful gently and sweetly; be not rough and rigorous to them. Bind up the broken-hearted. Say unto them, Why art thou so disquieted and sad? When thou seest them melancholy for losses and crosses, say unto them in cheer, as Elkanah to Hannah, ' What dost thou want? Am not I a thousand friends, wives, and children unto thee ? '

Clap them on the back, hearten them in well-doing, spur them on to walk forward; yea, wind them up to the highest pitch of excellency, and then applaud them. Delight in the excellent of the earth.

Be a light to the blind and scrupulous.

Be a goad in the sides of the dull ones.

Be an alarm and trumpet of judgment to the sleepers and dreamers.

But as for the hypocrite, gall him and prick him at the heart. Let him well know that thou art God's spy in his bosom, a secret intelligencer, and wilt be faithful to God.

Bid the hypocrite walk ' in all things.'

Bid the civil add piety to charity.

Bid the wavering, inconstant, and licentious ' walk constantly.'

Bid the lukewarm and common Protestant for shame amend, be zealous, and ' walk honestly.'

But with the sons of Belial, the profane scorners, walk frowardly with them, haunt and molest them, give them no rest till they repent, be the gall of bitterness unto them. When they are swilling and drinking, serve them as Absalom's servants did Amnon, stab him at the heart. Yet remember, so long as there is any hope, that thine office is to be a pedagogue to Christ, to wound and kill, only to the end they may live in Christ, not so much to gaster and affright as to lead to him; and, to that purpose, to be instant in season and out of season, that they may believe and repent.

But if they refuse to hear, and sin against thee, and the Holy Ghost also, then shake off the dust of thy feet, and either fall to torment them before their time, and drive them to despair; or if thou give them ease here, tell them thou wilt fly in their throat at the day of hearing, when thou shalt and must speak, and they shall and must hear.

Conscience, thou hast commission to go into princes' chambers and council tables; be a faithful man of their counsel. Oh, that they would in all courts of Christendom set policy beneath thee, and make thee president of their councils, and hear thy voice, and not croaking Jesuits, sycophants, and liars. Thou mayest speak to them, subjects must pray for them, and be subject, for thy sake, to honour and obey them in the Lord.

Charge the courtiers not to trust in uncertain favours of princes, but to be trusty and faithful, as Nehemiah, Daniel, Joseph; whose histories pray them to read, imitate, and believe above Machiavelli's oracles.

Tell the foxes and politicians, that make the *main* the *by*, and the *by* the *main*, that an ill conscience hanged Ahithophel, overthrew Haman, Shebna, &c. Tell them it is the best policy, and Solomon's, who knew the best, to get and keep thy favour; to exalt thee, and thou shalt exalt them, be a shield to them, and make them as bold as the lion in the day of trouble, not fearing the envy of all the beasts of the forest, no, nor the roaring of the lion, in righteous causes.

Conscience, thou art the judge of judges, and shalt one day judge them; in the meanwhile, if they fear neither God nor man, be as the importunate widow, and urge them to do justice. Oh! that thou sattest highest in all courts, especially in such courts as are of thy jurisdiction, and receive their denomination from thee, suffer not thyself to be exiled, make Felix tremble, discourse of judgment to them.

To the just judges, bid them please God and thee, and fear no other fear; assure them, for whatever they do of partiality or popularity, thou wilt leave them in the lurch; but what upon thy suit and command, thou wilt bear them out in it, and be their exceeding great reward.

If thou meetest in those courts and findest any such pleaders as are of thine acquaintance and followers, be their fee and their promoter, tell them if they durst trust thee, and leave Sunday works, bribing on both sides, selling of silence, pleading in ill causes, and making the law a nose of wax, if they durst plead all and only rightful causes, thou hast riches in one hand, and honour in the other, to bestow on them.

As for the tribe of Levi, there mayest thou be a little bolder, as being men of God, and men of conscience, by profession. Be earnest with them to add *con* to their *science*, as a number to cyphers, that will make it something worth. Desire them to preach, not for filthy lucre or vainglory, but for thy sake; wish them to keep thee pure, and in thee to keep the mystery of faith; assure them thou art the only ship and cabinet of orthodoxal faith, of which, if they make shipwreck by laziness and covetousness, they shall be given over to popery and Arminianism, and lose the faith, and then write books of the apostasy, and intercision of faith, and a good conscience, which they never were acquainted withal, nor some drunkards of them ever so much as seemed to have.

And whereas thou knowest that many of all sorts are discouraged with the taxation and slanders; some that confer, some that are fearful and doubtful, if they do it to the Lord and thee (as who knows but God?) bid the world as Paul doth here, turn censuring into praying; and, if they will not, let them, as they preach thee, so regard thee in all godly simplicity, ἐξ εἰλικρινέιας κατενώπιον τῦ Θεῦ, and expect their reward at the hand of the great Shepherd.

For the city get thou into the high places, into the pulpits, into the entries and gates of the city; cry aloud and utter thy words in the streets. Oh! that thou wert free of it, and hadst freedom of speech and audience in all their courts and companies; and that, for thy sake, they would make and keep wholesome constitutions for the Sabbath, and orderly keeping of it, and see that well executed and observed, which is the nurse of all piety and conscience.

Charge them that are rich citizens, and in their thousands, that they lay no weak foundation, no three-halfpenny foundation, but be bountiful to pious uses, to the poor, and to the ministry of the city, that they take away the scandal of the times, and upbraiding of the Romish Peninnah against the Hannah of our times. Let the hospital, widows, and orphans, taste of their bounty; with such sacrifices (if they come from faith and a good conscience) God is pleased. Bid them not trust in the shadow of silver and gold, which will wither as Jonah's gourd, but in thy shelter. Go home with them this day, I invite thee to their table. If I had liberty (as they say it is a courtesy for the preacher to invite a guest), Conscience, thou shouldst be my guest. Defer not till to-morrow, lest business hinder thee. This day reckon and walk with them, and talk with them. Bid them lay aside all reckoning books and reckon with thee, and often reckoning will make you friends.

Be at their elbows when they use false weights and balances, and give them privy nips; let the mutual profit of buyer and seller be the rule of buying and selling, and not the gain of the one of them alone. Assure them that are hoarders by fraud, that they hatch as the hen the partridge's egg, that hath wings and will fly away ; and that they heap up wrath against the day of wrath, and are in the mean time self-condemned; whereas thou wouldst make them rich and add no sorrow, nor gravelly grit in their mouth, but such gain as will stand with content and self-sufficiency.

If thou meetest with Simonaical patrons, tell them, they and their money shall perish, for selling thee and the souls of the people.

I have not, as Ezekiel, a map of the city, but thou knowest all the lurking dens, stews, and infinite books.* I send thee to preach and cry unto them.

Roar and thunder in the ears of the roaring boys, of all the swaggering crew, and tell them they must for all these come to judgment.

To the fashion-mongers, both the statelier sort and the light-headed, yellow-banded fools : tell the one, that the richest lining and inside is a good conscience ; and for the other, if thou wilt vouchsafe, tell them, that plain apparel and a good conscience will do them more honour than all these apes' toys.

As for the players, and jesters, and rhymers, and all that rabblement, tell them, thou wilt one day be in earnest with them, and though thou suffer them to personate thee upon their stages, and shew their wit, and break their jests on thee now, thou wilt owe it them, till they come upon the great stage, before God and all the world. Where my sides, memory, and knowledge fail, add, enlarge, and apply. Print it in the hearts of as many as thou canst, and the Lord grant thee grace and audience in their ears, that they may suffer the words of exhortation ; and so I end with the prayer after my text, which is like a rich garment, that hath facing, guards, and selvage of its own. 'The God of peace, that brought again from the dead our Lord Jesus, the great Shepherd of the sheep, through the blood of the everlasting covenant, make you perfect in all good works, to do his will,' &c.

Thou, O Lord, that hast wonderfully planted and formed our consciences within us ; that only knowest and searchest our consciences ; that hast thy chair in the heavens, and only art able to teach them and purify them ; thou which woundedst and healedst three thousand at one sermon; whose hand is not shortened; stretch out thine arm, and do the like in these latter times.

Forgive the sins against thee and our consciences, and the frequent checks of it and thy Spirit.

Overthrow the man of sin, that tyrant and usurper of conscience.

Mollify and enlighten the obstinate consciences of the Jews, Turks, and pagans.

Illuminate and sanctify all Christian princes, especially our sovereign, and fill the royal treasure of his conscience full of excellent comfort; and that he may as much excel in conscience all other kings of the earth, as he doth in science, without all comparison.

Comfort the afflicted, direct the doubtful and scrupulous, and remove all snares and scandals of weak consciences, which thou hast not planted, and which thou knowest are not for the peace of thy Sion.

The grace of our Lord Jesus Christ, and the love of God our Father, and the comfortable fellowship of the Holy Ghost, and the peace of a good conscience, be with you all, now and ever ! Amen.

Qu. ' Nooks ?'—ED.

JETHRO'S JUSTICE OF PEACE.

A SERMON PREACHED AT A GENERAL ASSIZES, HELD AT BURY ST EDMUND'S, FOR THE COUNTY OF SUFFOLK.

TO THE RIGHT HONOURABLE
SIR FRANCIS BACON, KNIGHT,
LORD CHANCELLOR OF ENGLAND, ETC.

WHEN we see one go or do amiss, though his feet or hands be the next actors and instruments of his error, yet we say not, Are you lame? but, Have you no eyes? or, Can you not see? Whatever swervings or stumblings any part of the body politic makes, the blame lights not upon the gentry or commonalty, the immediate delinquents, but on the principal lights in magistracy or ministry, which, being as guardians and tutors of the rest, should either prevent or reform their aberrations. And herein miserable is the condition of these two optic pieces, that they are more subject, and that to more distempers than other inferior parts; yet herein more, that, being hurt, they are more impatient of cure, not only of searching acrimonious waters (which yet oft are needful), but shy of the most soft and lawny touches; but most of all in this, that being once extinct, they leave a void darkness to the whole body, exposing it to the pits of destruction. As exceeding great, on the other hand, is the happiness, honour, and use of them, if clear and single. For this our national body, it will little boot either to applaud the one, or to bewail the other ; I rather wish and look about me for some eye-salve, which may help to descry and redress, if anything be amiss. And behold here (Right Honourable) a confection promising something thereto. It was prescribed first by Jethro, whom Moses calls the eyes of Israel, Num. x. 31 ; and newly compounded by an oculist, of whom as I may not, so I need not, say anything at all. Next under the sacred fountain of light (the light of our Israel), I worthily account your Lordship most sufficient in law to accept, to make use, to judge, to patronise it.　The subject of the book is the principal object of your office, to elect, direct, and correct inferior magistracy.　To which purposes, nature, literature, and grace have enabled you, that if you should fail the world's expectation, they will hardly trust any other in haste. Many in rising have followed the stirrup, pampered and jetting honour not standing the ground, but once seated have done renownedly.　But your Lordship had never any other graces than your birth and desert, to which hereditary dignity hath so gently tendered itself, that you have not let fall your name of religion in getting up.　Therefore, now you are in the top of honour, all that know you look you will be exactly honourable.　For my part, bounden to your lordship for a favour formerly received, greater than your honour knows of, or I can express, I shall leave Jethro to be your monitor, and myself remain ever an humble suitor to God, who hath made you a judge of conscience, that he would make you continue a conscionable judge, improving your place and abilities to the best advantage belonging to it, the furtherance of your reckoning at the last day.

Your honour's daily beadsman,

NATH. WARD.

JETHRO'S JUSTICE OF PEACE.

Moreover, thou shalt provide out of all the people able men, such as fear God, men of truth, hating covetousness, and place such over them, to be rulers of thousands, and rulers of hundreds, rulers of fifties, and rulers of tens. And let them judge the people at all seasons: and it shall be, that every great matter they shall bring unto thee, but every small matter they shall judge: so shall it be easier for thyself, and they shall bear the burden with thee. If thou do this thing, and God command thee so, then thou shalt be able to endure, and all this people shall also go to their place in peace.— Exodus XVIII. 21, 22, 23

If Jethro were, as the fashion of those times and the nature of his style will bear, and (as some conceit) both prince and priest,* then was he, beyond all exception, every way qualified for skill, as a judicious divine, and for experience as an aged governor, to give direction in matters of magistracy, and to cast Moses a mould for a polity in Israel. Sure I am, a godly and religious man he was, for he begins with prayer, and ends with sacrifice. And such as himself was his advice, sage and holy. And howsoever it passed from him at the first under God's correction, yet afterward allowed by God, and practised by Moses, becomes, of good policy, sound divinity; of private counsel, a general oracle; ruling for the substance of it all ages and persons.

Venerable it is for the very antiquity of it. What price do men set upon old copies, coins, and statues? Who passeth by a crystal fountain, bearing some ancient name or date, and tastes not of it, though no thirst provoke him?† Such is this, the clear head-spring of all ensuing brooks in Scripture and other writers concerning magistracy. All those texts (which I wish were set as a frontlet between the eyes, and as a seal upon the hearts of all in authority), Jehoshaphat's charge, 2 Chron. xix. 5, Job's character, chap. xxix, David's vow, Ps. ci., the scattered parables of Solomon, and passages of the prophets, chiefly that round and smart one, Isa. xxxiii. 14, are they not all branches of this root? In which respect it must needs be of sovereign use for the discovering and reforming of whatsoever error time hath soiled government withal. How are defaced copies and disfigured

---

* Cohen.

† Τ𝜘υς παριοντας και μη διψωσιν εφελκονται αρυσασθαι του ποτου. Ignat. ad Marian. Cassub.

pictures better amended than by reducing them to their original ?   If the pipe fail, go we not to the head ?

Here is the archetype or first draught of magistracy, worthy in this regard, chosen by judicious Bucer to press upon Edward the Sixth, for the purgation of his offices and laws from the dross and filth contracted under the Romish confusion, which considering, that worthy Josiah of ours took in such good part, and practised with such good success.   Yea, Moses himself, learned in all good literature, trained up in court, the greatest lawgiver that ever was, and father of all lawgivers, of the thrice great Hermes, Lycurgus, Solon, Plato, Justinian, and the rest, yea, God's familiar favourite, faithful in his house, known by name and face, honoured with miraculous power, &c., and that at the hands of one (age and fatherhood excepted) his inferior; I trust that none will dare to reject or slight it off, remembering that divinity, as the mistress, taketh upon her to direct her handmaid, and that the Scripture is the best man of counsel for the greatest statesman in the world, this little portion thereof containing in it more than all Lepsius's *Bee-hive*, or Machiavelli's *Spider-web*.   All which will best appear by the opening of this rich cabinet, and viewing the several jewels in it, which are these—

1. It first gives order for the care and circumspection in the choice. ' Provide.'

2. Secondly, it directs this choice by four essential characters of magisstrates :—(1.) Men of ability.   (2.) Fearing God.   (3.) Men of truth.   (4.) Hating covetousness.

3. Thirdly, it applies these four to magistrates of all degrees, in an exact distribution of them, by way of gradation, descending step by step, from the highest to the lowest.   ' And place such over them to be rulers :'   (1) of thousands ;   (2) of hundreds ;   (3) of fifties ;   (4) of tens.

4. Fourthly, it prescribes to the magistrates, thus qualified and chosen, their offices, viz., to judge the people in the smaller causes, &c., and their assiduity and industry therein.   ' And let them judge the people at all seasons, &c.   And it shall be that they shall bring every great matter to thee, but every small matter they shall judge.'

5. Lastly, it propounds the blessed fruit and emolument that will necessarily ensue thereupon.   *First*, to Moses himself, ' So shall it be easier for thyself, and they shall bear the burden with thee, and thou shalt be able to endure.'   *Secondly*, to the people, ' And all this people shall go to their place in peace.'

THE FIRST PART.

Techezeh, ' provide,' or look out.   A word implying all exactness and curiosity incident to elections, as inspection, circumspection, inquisition, suspicion, information, deliberation, coming of *Chozah*, to see or contemplate, whence the prophets were called *Chosi*, seers.   It is in a manner translated by a word of the like force, in a business of the like nature, Acts vi. 5, ἐπισκέψασθε, ' survey' the whole body of the people, and choose the best you can cull out.   It were somewhat strict and strange to say that prayer and fasting must be used.   And yet this I find practised in such cases, ' Let the Lord God of the spirits of all flesh set a man over this congregation,' Acts i. and Num. xxvii. 16.   Yea, Jethro himself sanctified this his advice with prayer, ' God be with thee,' ver. 19.   And good reason He should be called to counsel whose the judgment is, and whose providence is always very special in those elections, whether sought or no. If God supervise not, Samuel the seer shall take seven wrong before one right, 1 Sam. xvi. Some men's faults are palpable, and go before election; some are cunningly concealed, and break not out till after. First, therefore, look up to God, and then amongst the people. Have thine eyes in thy head, all the care that may be will be little enough. Say not there are no sufficient persons, nor yet think every one that thinks himself so, or commonly goes for such, is sufficient. Seek out such, and such may be found. Look among the olives, vines, and fig-trees. Such trees must be climbed. Brambles will lay hold on the sleeve for preferment. *Ne sit qui ambit.* Let him never speed that sues. Lay hands on none rashly. They that are fit and able must and will be sought to, yea, hauled out of their ease and privacy into the light of employment, the charge and danger whereof they weighing, as well as the credit or gain, and knowing them to be callings, will not meddle with them till they be called to them, which ambitious inconsiderates, not being able to ponder, much less to sustain, thrust their shoulders under, and either by hook or crook come in, or climb into the chair of honour, more tickle than the stool Eli brake his neck off: whither, when they have aspired with much trouble and cost, they sit as in the top of a mast, in fear and hazard, and often fall with shame and confusion, not unlike to some rash youth, that, having gotten a horse as wild as himself, with much ado backs him, sets him in a sweat, and comes down with a mischief.

For the prevention of all which evils unavoidably attending ambition, lighting partly upon the intruders themselves, partly upon the admitters, but most heavily upon the commonweal, see how needful Jethro's counsel was and ever will be. That such be provided, not as would have places, but as places should have. Which care, as Jethro commits to Moses, so both the Scripture and reason imposeth upon the superior magistrate, in whose power and place it is either to nominate or constitute inferior authorities; and whose fault chiefly it is, if they be otherwise than they ought, or the people injured in this kind. How circumspect and religious ought such to be in the performance of this greatest and weightiest duty.

Unless you will reply, as I fear many a fox doth in his bosom. Thus indeed you have heard it said of old, but those times were plain, and Jethro a simple-meaning old man. A beaten politician of our times, learned in the wisdom of newer state, and acquainted with the mysteries of the market, that knows how to improve things to the best, for his own time and turn, and to let the common body shift for itself, would have projected Moses a far more commodious plot, after this or the like manner. Now you have offices to bestow, a fair opportunity in your hand to make yourself for ever, to raise your house, to pleasure your friends; either proclaim it openly or secretly, set it abroad by some means or other, see who bids fairest, weigh the sacrifices, choose the men of the best and greatest gifts.

O gall of bitterness, O root of all evil to church and commonwealth! when authorities and offices of justice shall be bought and sold, * as with a trumpet or drum, to the candle or outrope. The particular branches whereof, when I seriously consider, I wonder not that Christ with such zealous severity brake down the banks, and whipped out the chapmen out of the temple; nor that Peter with such fiery indignation banned Simon and his money. For if such men and money perish not, kingdoms and churches must perish, and both civil and ecclesiastical courts will soon prove dens of thieves.

* Tanquam sub hasta.

Whose soul bleeds not to see men's souls bought and sold, like sheep at the market to every butcher ? Of this you lawyers much complain against the clergymen, for buying of benefices, which you might do the more justly, if you yourselves were not often the sellers of them. I would the fault rested only in benefices, and reached not into offices and civil dignities. Indeed that kind of purchase we call not *simony*, it may from his other name be fitlier styled *magic;* for by I know not what kind of witchcraft, men sin by leave and law in these civil purchases ; the laws and statutes provided for the remedy of the evil in some cases, tolerating it in other, and the practice by means of this allowance growing intolerable. Some of them (as the world reports) offices for life, and at pleasure, amounting to the rate of lands and inheritances.

I am not ignorant of the distinction of judicature, trust and pains ; but are they not all offices of justice ? Do they not prepare to judicature, and lies it not in them to guide or misguide, to hasten or delay justice, &c., which how can they freely give, which buy dearly ?

Doth not Bucer deal faithfully with his sovereign ? Offices are not livings and salaries, but charges and duties; not preferments for favourites, but rewards of deserts, &c. Doth Julius, Justinianus, or Theodosius their laws give allowance to any ? See then how providently Jethro provides against this hemlock root of justice ! out of whose proviso I conclude that which Augustine saw in his time, and dear experience confirms in others; that such as provide themselves places, are not provided for them ; come into them, and execute them, not with a mind of doing good, but domineering ; not of providing for others' welfare, but for their own turns. Let us pray that, if it be possible, this fault may be forgiven and amended.

And not this only, but another near of kin to this, met withal in the very next clause of my text, 'Among all the people' (*Micol Hagnam*). Where Jethro restrains not Moses to his own family, to any particular tribe, or to the richer sort ; but requires this freedom, as well as the former circumspection. Generality and impartiality being requisite to the good being of a choice ; and limitation and restraint the very banes of election, yea, contradictions to it. As if one should say, you shall choose amongst twenty, but you shall choose this or that one ; doth he not in effect say, you shall not have your choice ? Will a man, when he goes to market, be confined to any shop or stall, if he mean to provide the best ? How grossly is the country wronged and befooled, chiefly in the choice of such as into whose hands they put their lives and lands at parliaments, by a kind of *conye d' elire*, usually sent them by some of the gentry of the shires, persuading (if not prescribing) the very couple they must choose. Thus have we seen naturals tied to a post with a straw, which they durst not break.

This text bids you know and stand fast in your lawful liberties of election, which, that you may not abuse, I come to the second part of the text.

THE SECOND PART.

It teacheth you how to order and direct it by these four marks following, which I reckon as four supporters of the throne of justice, not altogether unlike to those four in Christ's throne, so often mentioned in the Old and New Testament, which, being properties of angels, are symbols both of magistrates and ministers.

These four, whosoever is compounded of, is a man after God's own heart, and is a star in his right hand. He that wants any of them is but a blazing comet, how high soever he seems to soar. These will not only serve for the trial of such as are *candidati*, and not to be chosen; but also of such as are invested and already in place, to approve or reprove their condition. And for this end and purpose, let us use them this day as four weights of the sanctuary, whereunto whatsoever officer here present, from the judges to the bailiffs, shall not answer, this text (as the handwriting on the wall) shall say unto him from God, ' Thou art weighed in the balance, and found too light, and thine office (at least, ought to be) taken from thee.'

1. The first and prime mark is ability (*anishi chaiil*). So our new translation expresseth it well in a comprehensive word, and so I find it in Scripture, signifying and comprising all the severals that belong to faculty or ability ; whereof I number, first, three complemental, for conveniency ; secondly, three substantial, and of necessity.

First, Chaiil includes strength of body and manhood, such as enableth them for riding, going, sitting, watching, and industrious execution of their place ; such as the Scripture commends in Caleb at fourscore and five ; and stories in Vespasian, our Alfred, Hardicanutus, Ironsides, &c.

Which our strait-buttoned, carpet, and effeminate gentry, wanting, cannot endure to hold out a forenoon or afternoon sitting without a tobacco bait, or a game at bowls, or some such breathing, to refresh their bodies and minds, little acquainted with the tediousness of wise and serious business. ' Woe to the people (saith Solomon) whose princes are children, and eat in the morning ; and blessed are the people whose governors eat in time and for strength,' Eccles. x.

Secondly, Neither is wealth to be excluded. That Diana of the world, which it only accounts ability, and calls it *opes et potentia*, which yet is better called *value* than *valour*, yet may it concur to make up that which our law term calls *mieux*, valiant ; and though at the beam of the sanctuary money makes not the man, yet it adds some mettle to the man.

And besides, there is some use of these trappings to the common sort ; *Ad populum phaleras*, which taught Agrippa to come to the judgment-seat with pomp, state, and attendance, like that of our sheriffs, not to be neglected, as that which procures some terror and awe in the people ; which Alexander, well advised of, left his gigantic armour behind him among the Indians, and used more state than at Greece.

Yet remembering that these compliments, without the substance, are but empty gulls and scarebugs of majesty, the sophistry of government,* as one calls them, and as Zechariah the prophet saith, the instruments of a foolish governor. And such as Jeremiah derides in Shallum the son of Josiah, Jer. xxii. 14, ' Thinkest thou to rule because of thy large building, cedar ceiling, painted with vermilion ? Did not thy father prosper when he did execute judgment and justice ?' which is indeed the truth and substance, the other but the flourish.

Thirdly, I exclude not birth and blood, which many times conveys spirit and courage with it. ' Blessed is the land whose princes are the sons of nobles,' Eccles. x. 17. Eagles produce eagles, and crows cravens, yet regeneration and education often corrects this rule ; and experience tells us, that cottages and ploughs have brought forth as able men for the gown and sword, as palaces and sceptres. Gideon came out of the poorest of the family of Manasseh, Judges vi. 15, and he the least in his father's house, a

---

* Σοφισματα μορμολυκεια. Cassa et hordeacea morionis sceptra.—Chap. Zac.

poor thresher. David was taken from the sheep-fold, &c. Yet both mighty men of valour, and special saviours of their people. And the wisdom of some of our neighbour nations is much to be commended in this, that if they discern an excellent spirit and faculty in any man, they respect not his wealth, or birth, or profession, but choose him into their magistracy and weighty employments.

But these three are but of the by and well-being, the three following of the main and essential to magistracy, all comprised under the word *chaiil*, as first wisdom and experience, which the preacher tells us is better than strength either of body or estate, Eccles. ix. 16. And of this ability, Moses expounds this word in his practice, Deut. i. 15, which is a good comment-ary upon his father's advice.

And indeed, without this, what is a magistrate, but a blind Polyphemus, or a monster without an eye?* If he want either skill in the laws, or observation of his own, must he not be tutored by his clerk, as it often falls out? Or shall he not be misled by some councillor, crossed and contradicted by every stander by, that shall tell him, This you cannot do by law, or, I take it, you are besides your book?

The second is strength of mind to govern and manage passion and unruly affections, which he that wields at will is stronger than he that subdues a city and conquers a kingdom. To bear and forbear, and to order the mutinous perturbations of the mind, is that ability which the Grecians call κράτος and ἐγκράτεια.

Very requisite in a judge, who must not suffer his affection to disquiet his judgment and understanding, in rising at the first complaint, nor at any accident or present miscarriage of either party, suddenly occasioned, which is collateral to the cause, and impertinent to the question; but he must be patient and meek towards their personal weakness. Likewise long-minded, to endure the rusticity and homeliness of common people in giving evidence, after their plain fashion and faculty, in time, and multitude of words, happily with some absurdities of phrase or gestures, nor impatient towards their foolish affected eloquent terms, nor anything else whereby the truth of their tale may be guessed at.

Lastly and principally, I understand with the Geneva translation, that fortitude, valour, and magnanimity, which we call courage and spirit; typified in Judah, the law-giving tribe, whose emblem or scutcheon was the lion *couchant*, that sits or lies by the prey without fear of rescue, that turns not his head at the sight of any other creature, Prov. xxx., which Solomon symbolised in the steps of his throne adorned with lions; the Athenian judges by sitting in Mars Street, ἐν Ἀρείῳ πάγῳ. Some think that from this virtue Constantine was termed, Rev. xii., the church's male or man-child; others apply it to Luther; others to Christ, the true Lion of Judah.

And though I regard not the *Salique law*, because the God of spirits hath often put great spirits into that sex, yet I mislike not Theodoret's observa-tion upon that in Leviticus, chap. iv. 22, 27, where the ruler, for his sin, is enjoined to offer an he-goat, the private man a she-goat.† The male suits the ruler best, and the female the ruled.

This ability is so requisite, that it is often put for the only quality, as if this alone would serve, as in Moses' charge to Joshua, and David's to Solomon. And experience hath taught, that where this one hath abounded,

* Monstrum cui lumen ademptum.

† πρόσφορον ἄρρεν τῷ ἄρχόντι τὸ δὲ θῆλυ τῷ ἀρχομένῳ.

though the other hath been wanting in some magistrates, they have done more good service to their country, than many others who have had some tolerable measure of the rest, but have failed only in this.

Had not the principal posts of an house need to be of heart of oak? Are rulers and standards, that regulate other measures, to be made of soft wood, or of lead, that will bend and bow at pleasure? Do men choose a starting horse to lead the team? Had not he need be of David's valour, and Samson's courage, that must take the prey out of the lion's mouth, and rescue the oppressed from the man that is too mighty for him? Had not he need to be of some spirit and resolution, that must neglect the displeasure and frowns, reject the letters and suits, of great men and superiors?

It is incredible to those that know it not, what strength great men will put to (especially if once interested) for the upholding of a rotten ale-house, countenancing of a disordered retainer, &c. The resistance whereof, requires it not some spirit? Had not the brain need to be of a strong constitution, that must dispel and disperse the fumes ascending from a corrupt liver, stomach, or spleen? I mean the clamours, rumours, and sometimes the flatteries of the vulgar, which often intoxicate able men, and make them as weak as water; yielding and giving, as Pilate, when he heard but a buzz that he was not Cæsar's friend, and saw that, in dismissing Christ, he should displease the Jews.

What heroical spirit had he need have, that must encounter the Hydra of sin, oppose the current of the times, and the torrent of vice, that must turn the wheel over the wicked; especially such roaring monsters, and rebellious Korahs, such lawless sons of Belial, wherewith our times swarm, who stick not to oppose with crest and breast, whosoever stand in the way of their humours and lusts! Surely if Jethro called for courage in those modest primitive times, and among a people newly tamed with Egyptian yokes, what do our audacious and foreheadless swaggerers require? Our lees and dregs of time, not unlike to those wherein God was fain to raise up extraordinary judges to smite hip and thigh, &c. What Atlas shall support the state of the ruinous and tottering world, in these perilous ends of time?

For all these fore-named purposes, how unapt is a man of a soft, timorous, and flexible nature! for whom it is as possible to steer a right course, without swerving to the left hand or right, for fear or favour, as it is for a cock-boat to keep head against wind and tide, without help of oars or sails: experience ever making this good, that cowards are slaves to their superiors, fellow-fools to their equals, tyrants to their inferiors, and wind-mills to popular breath, not being able to any of these to say so much as No!

Wherefore this text proclaims and speaks, as Gideon, in the ears of all the faint-hearted, 'Whosoever is fearful and timorous, let him depart' from Mount Gilead, Judges vii. 3, and there departed twenty thousand; and yet God the second time, out of the remnant, viz., ten thousand, defaulks all the lazy persons, and reduced that huge army to three hundred able persons.

It were excellent for the commonwealth, if such a subtraction might be made, and the weak-hearted would resign their rooms to able men. For what have servile cowards to do with the sword of the Lord and Gideon, with God and the king's offices?

On the contrary, it saith to all men of ability, as the angel to Gideon,

'The Lord is with thee, thou mighty man of valour; go on in this thy might, to save Israel,' &c.   What is our office, that are ministers, but as God's trumpeters and drummers to encourage, hearken, and put life in those that fight his battles, and do his work ?   By the virtue, then, of this my text, I say to every good-hearted magistrate, Proceed, and go on from strength to strength.

And if any ask me, Who, then, is sufficient for these things ?   Or where shall we get this strength, that are but flesh and blood, and men as others ? I answer, with Job, ' Silver hath his vein, and gold his mine where it is found ; iron is taken out of the earth, and brass molten out of the stone,' Job xxviii. ; but the place of this ability is not to be found in the land of the living.   Nature saith it is not to be found in me ; wealth and honour says not in me.   It is falsely said of Cato and Fabricius, that the sun might sooner be stayed or altered in his race, than they in the course of justice. The stoutest and the richest will yield.   But David tells his son Solomon, on his deathbed, where he shall find it, 1 Chron. xxix. 11, 12 : 'Thine, O Lord, is greatness and power ; thou art the head of all riches ; honour and strength are in thy hands ; it is in thee to make great,' &c.   This God hath taught David to break a bow of steel with his hands.   It is he that looseth the collar of princes, girdeth their loins, and ungirdeth them again, befools the counsellor, the judge, and the spokesman.   He it was that made the shoes of Joseph as strong as brass, Jeremiah as a wall of brass, Caleb as strong at fourscore and five as at forty.   If Samson's hair be off, and God departed from him, he is as other men, and he can strengthen him again without his locks at his pleasure.

If any man want wisdom or strength, let him pray, and he can make him wiser than the children of the east, and stronger than the Anakims.   Wherefore be strong in the Lord, faint not ; be not weary of well-doing, for fear of opposition and crossing.   Though in rowing this ship the winds blow, and the seas rage, Christ can straight send an halcyon, and set it on shore.

It is the fault of many Christian magistrates, ever to be complaining and groaning under the burthen, as if ease and delicacy were to be sought for in government.   What if there be a lion in the way ?   The righteous is bolder than the lion.   What if thou be weak ?   Is not God strength ? and doth he not perfect his strength in our weakness ?   What if there be many opposites in the way ?   True courage is strong as death, Cant. viii., and will trample all under feet without resistance.

Yea, but what if an host come against thee, and as bees encompass thee ? True faith sees more on God's side than against them, even guards of angels, as plainly as men do the sheriff's halberts, and doubts not, but in the name of the Lord, to vanquish them all.

One concluding place for all, out of a preacher's mouth, Eccles. vii. 15, that knew what he said : ' Wisdom strengthens one man more than twenty mighty potentates that are in a city,' he that feareth God shall come forth of all dangers.   Whence, by way of passage, note that the next point of the fear of God, is that which giveth life to the foregoing, and to the two following also : and is placed in the text, as the heart in the body, for conveying life to all the parts ; or, as a dram of musk, perfuming the whole box of ointment.

2. *Fearing God*.   Jethro must be understood, not of the poor, bastardly, slavish fear, which depraved nature hath left in all ; nor of any sudden flash of fear wrought by word or works, such as Felix, Belshazzar, and Caligula,

were not void of, and yet never the better magistrates; but such a filial fear as faith and the assurance of God's love and salvation breeds, such as awed Joseph, Cornelius, David, &c. This is the fear required by Jethro, εὐσέβεια, quæ parit εὐλαβείαν, godliness which breedeth an heedfulness in all our ways and actions.

Without this fear of God, what is ability but the devil's anvil, whereon he forgeth and hammereth mischief? What is wisdom but subtilty? What is courage unsanctified but injustice? Wherein is such skill in the laws commonly employed, but in colouring and covering bad causes and persons, and in making the laws a nose of wax to private ends? Other men have other bits and restraints; but men in authority, if they fear not God, have nothing else to fear. Wherefore Christ joins them well in the unrighteous judge, that he feared neither God nor man. If he be a simple coward, he fears all men; if a man of ability, he fears none at all.

What are the nerves and sinews of all government, the bonds and commands of obedience, but an oath? And what are oaths to profane men, but as Samson's cords, which he snapt asunder, as fast as they were offered him. The common sort of our people count the oaths that men take when they take offices, no other than formal; so they distinguish them (a strange distinction) from other oaths of contract, and dally with them accordingly.

They discern God no more in oaths than Christ in the sacraments, and therefore take them, and break them, rashly and regardlessly; which, when they have done, the devil enters into them, as into Judas, and runs them headlong into all perjured courses, which makes the land to mourn for the contempt of oaths and neglect of duties. What is the ground of all fidelity to king and country but religion? Well fare Constantius's maxim: 'He cannot be faithful to me that is unfaithful to God.' Why, then, what are oaths for atheists and papists, other than collars for monkies' necks, which slip them at their pleasure?* Such neither are, nor can be, good subjects, much less good magistrates. Papists will keep no faith with protestants, let protestants give no trust to papists, though they swear upon all the books in the world.†

Finally, what is the principal scope of magistracy in God's intention, whose creature and ordinance it is; but, to promote his glory, countenancing the gospel and the professors of it, safeguard of the church and commonwealth, the first and second table, and principally the former. Now, for all these, chiefly for the chiefest, what cares a Cato or a Gallio, who bears the sword in vain for God and his ends; who never minds anything but his own cabinet, or the ship of the commonwealth, at the best? For the other, sink they, swim they, all is one to him, he took no charge, nor will he take notice of them.

Wherefore I conclude, that the fear of God is the principal part, as of my text, so of a good magistrate, whom Christ calls a ruler in Israel, John iii.; Paul, God's minister and sword-bearer, Rom. xiii.; yea, the very form and soul of such an one; yea, it troubles me to make it, but a part which Solomon calls the whole of a man, Eccles. xi. 13, especially such a man who is sent of God, for the praise of the godly, and the punishment of evil-doers, 1 Pet. ii. In which respect, being the main of my text, give me leave to give you a short character of such a magistrate, as this quality will make him, wherever it is found in any good latitude.

* ὃς ἔτε βῶμος ἔτε ὁρκος.

† Nulla fides habenda papistis, etiamsi per omnes deos juraverint.

He is one that came into his place by God's door, and not by the devil's window; when he is in, he eyes him that is invisible, even God in the assembly of gods; and therefore sits on the judgment-seat in as great, though not in so slavish, a fear of offending, as Olanes upon the flayed skin of his father Sylannes, nailed by Cambyses on the tribunal; or as a Russian judge that fears the boiling cauldron or open-battocking;* or the Turkish senate, when they think the great Turk to stand behind the arras, at the dangerous door.

Who hath always (as God enjoineth, Deut. xvii. 18) a copy of the law of his God before him, and reads it all the days of his life, that he may learn to fear the Lord his God, and to keep the commandments, without turning aside either to the right hand or left.

If at all he be glad of his place, it is not as a chair of honour, or farm of commodity, nor sword of revenge; but only as a mean of furthering his reckoning and pleasuring his country. For his oath he remembers it, and trembles lest, if carelessly he transgress it, the winged flying book overtake him before he get home; if he cut but the skirt or lap of justice, his heart smites him with a privy pinch, till he sets all right again with God and man. He dares not so much as by countenance offend any of God's little ones, nor afford a good look to a varlet, nor yet to respect their persons as to wrong their cause, for he knows all these to be abomination to his Lord, into whose hands he dreads to fall, as knowing him a consuming fire, and one that hath provided Tophet for princes. When an unlawful suit is commenced† by power or by friendship, his heart answers (if not his tongue) with Job: 'How shall I do this, and answer God when he comes to judgment?'

As for bribes he dares not look on them, lest they blind his eyes before he be aware; such pitch he dares not touch, nor receive into his bosom, lest it defile him in the open sun; if tendered in closet or chamber, he fears the timber and stones in the wall would be witnesses against him.

When he comes in court, he fixeth his eye, neither before him on that person, nor about him on the beholders, nor behind him for bribes, but upward on God,‡ generally considering that Christ is Lord-paramount of all courts of justice, and that now his Father hath resigned all judgment into his hands. He stewards all to his content, promotes his profits without wrong to the tenant. Looks so to the church, that the commonweal receive no detriment; and so to the commonwealth as the church shall surely flourish; so countenancing the servants of God that he wrong not the worst worldling; maintains piety and neglects not equity; keeps his house well, but his church better; in frequenting whereof, he, with his family, are precedents to all the hundreds where he dwells; and, in a word, doth as much good by his example as by his authority.

This is the godly man, whom the Lord chooseth and guideth, whose praise and reward is of God, which David, having found true in this life, a little before his death recordeth to all ages. 'The Spirit of the Lord spake by me, and his word was in my tongue. The God of Israel spake to me, the strength of Israel said, Thou shalt bear rule over men, being just, and ruling in the fear of God. Even as the morning light when the sun riseth, the morning, I say, without clouds, so shall mine house be, and not as the grass of the earth is by the bright rain. For God hath

---

* That is, the bastinado—ED.   † Qu. ' Commended?'—ED.
‡ Summa boni judicis est neque respicere neque despicere, neque circumspicere, sed suspicere.—Ferus in John v. 30.

made with me an everlasting covenant, perfect in all points, and sure,'
2 Sam. xxiii. 2–4.

Let the devil and the world storm and burst with envy. One of these is
worth a thousand of the common sort, though men will see no difference,
but say, Are not all honest and sufficient men? Let men talk of their
quiet and peaceable neighbours, and good housekeepers, good commonwealth men; though these be good things, yet if religion come not in, as
a number to make them of some value, they are all but as cyphers in God's
account.

Now, if God think so meanly of these, who are either mere civil and
politic men, or idle, pleasurable gentlemen, what reckoning do we think he
makes of such profane, uncircumcised vice-gods (as I may, in the worst
sense, best term them) that sell themselves to work wickedness, that give
themselves to all good fellowship (as they call it), and to all excess of riot
(as the apostle calls it), and that hate to be reformed,—such, I mean, as
hold religion a disparagement to gentry, and fear nothing more than to
have a name that they fear God, who think when they have gotten an office
they may swear by authority, oppress by licence, drink and swill without
control.

What shall I say of such? Are these gods and children of the Most
High, or the characters of his most holy image? Devils are they rather
than deputies for him, imps of his kingdom, far better becoming an ale-
bench than a shire-bench, and the bar than a judgment-seat.

But what shall I say to such mock-god-like Esaus'? Shall I take up the
words of Moses, 'If thou wilt not fear this glorious name, The Lord thy
God, I will make thy plagues wonderful, and of great continuance?' or
those of David, which perhaps will fit them better, and these times of im-
minent changes, 'They know not, and understand nothing; they walk in
darkness, albeit the foundations of the earth be moved. I have said, Ye
are gods; but ye shall die like men, and fall like others.' Or will they suffer
the prophet's exhortation, Isa. lii. 8, 12, 13. 'Who art thou that dreadest
a mortal man, whose breath is in his nostrils, whom the moth shall eat
like a garment, and the worm like wool, and forgettest thy maker, that hath
spread the heavens, laid the foundations of the earth, that giveth the first
and latter rain, that hath set the bounds to the sea,' &c., Jer. v. 23, 24.
Or will they hear Solomon's end of all, ' Fear God, that will bring every
secret to judgment'? or a greater yet than Solomon, ' Fear him that is able,
when he hath killed the body, to destroy the soul also in hell fire for evermore'?

Well, the Lord cause them to hear, that hath planted the ear, and plant
his fear in their hearts where it is not, increase it where it is, that there
may be more holy magistrates, and that the holy may yet be more holy. And
then we hope the other two properties following will more abound, and we
shall spend the less time and labour about them; for men fearing God truly
will be also

3. ' Men of truth,' without which show of religion is but lying vanity,—
a glorious profession, but plain hypocrisy; and courage, if it be not for the
truth, and in the truth, is but either thrasonical audacity or wicked impudency.
And therefore this character, added to the former, joins those which are in
the form of jurates, and ought to be in all officers, ' good men and true.'

This style, ' men of truth,' admits two interpretations, both compatible
with the text and theme. A man of truth is either a true Israelite, a true
Nathanael, void of guile, as truth is opposed to hypocrisy, φιλαληθής; or

else a lover of the truth, as truth is opposed unto falsehood; one that, in particular cases, suits, and controversies between man and man, counts it his honour to sift out the truth, maintain the truth, stick to it, not suffering himself to be misinformed by tale-bearers, promoters, and sycophants, nor misled and perverted by the false pleading and colouring of conscienceless counsellors, but brings judgment to the balance and rule of righteousness, and delights (as the hound doth naturally in scenting out the hare) to search and trace out the truth out of all the thickets and dens of juggling and conveyance, labouring as much to bolt it out by examination *in hypothesi* as the philosophers by disputations *in thesi;* being of his temper that worthily said, Plato is my friend, Socrates my friend, but the truth is my dearest friend; or like Job, chap. xxix. 16, who covered himself with justice, and to whom judgment was as a robe and a crown, who, when he knew not the cause, sought it out diligently.

And, for this purpose, a man of truth keeps men of truth about him, and, with David, abandons all liars out of his household, Ps. ci. 7; whereas of a prince that hearkeneth to lies, all his servants are liars. And of such justice which is in truth and for truth, I say (as of old it was said) neither the evening nor morning star equals it in brightness.*

But withal I must complain, as of old, that truth is fallen in the streets, and utterly perished from among men, Isa. v. 44. Judgment fails, and stands afar off. Equity enters not, the common trade of the times being to weave lies in all cases, especially against the true servants of God, and the common weakness of the times to receive the slanders which are broached and bruited by tongues set on fire from hell, so that he that refrains from cunning makes himself a prey, the Latin whereof was all that Louis the Eleventh would have his son to learn,† and is all the policy that most study and practise; insomuch that the common bywords are, that when men swear by faith and truth, they swear by idols that are not. Names they are, and notions; things they are not, nor substances. Jewels they are, but such as use them die beggars; honourable ladies and mistresses they are, but such as follow them close at the heels may have their teeth dashed out of their heads.

Well, let deceivers thus deceive themselves; let cunning heads and glozing tongues make as much as they will of Tiberius's art, or the devil's rather, the father of the art of dissimulation. In the end, they shall prove it to be most pernicious to the students and masters of it. Let the children of truth justify their mother, which hath the reward of honour in her right hand, and of wealth in the left. And if it should be attended with hatred and crosses for a time, yet he that is *Amen,* the true witness, yea, truth itself, will reward them in the end; when he shall shut out with the dogs all such as love and make lies; with whose exhortation I close up this link, and knit with the following, 'Buy the truth, and sell it not;' which he that means to do must be,

4. A true 'hater of covetousness,' else will Solomon's several proverbs meet in him. 'The wicked gives heed to the false lip, and the liar to a naughty tongue,' Pro. xvii. 4. He taketh the gift out of the bosom to wrest judgment. Acceptation of gifts prove commonly prevarication to the truth.‡ It is impossible to be a champion to truth and a slave to Mammon; but he must love the one and hate the other. It is best, therefore, to hate the worst, yea, the worst of all vices incident to magistracy, the root of all evil, which, if it be not rooted out of the magistrate's heart, it alone will poison

* Nec Hesperus nec vesper formosior.   † Qui nescit dissimulare nescit vivere.
‡ Acceptatio muneris est prævaricatio veritatis.

all the three former qualities required in him. Neither strength, nor religion, nor love of the truth, shall be able to preserve him from enchantments of covetousness.

Which being an inordinate love of money, an evil concupiscence of having more than God hath allotted, or a lawful course affordeth, is such a kind of idolatry as transformeth the worshippers of this golden calf into idols themselves, making them to have eyes that see not, ears that hear not, only leaving them hands to handle that which perverteth the eyes of the wise, Deut. xvi. 19. It bores out their eyes, and maketh them as blind as ever was Samson and Zedekiah.

Eyes, you know, are tender things, and small motes annoy them; even handfuls of barley and morsels of bread make such men to transgress, Ezek. xiii. 8; and a dram's weight injected inclines the golden scales of justice to which side they please.

There is such a strange, bewitching power in Balaam's deceitful wages, that he that will admit them for justice shall soon take them for injustice.* If the right hand be full of bribes, the left hand must be full of mischief. The devil as well as the briber layeth his hooks in this shrap, whereof he that is greedy and will needs be rich falleth into his snare, and many other noisome lusts, which sink men into perdition, 1 Tim. vi., pierce their souls with sorrow, their names with reproach, cause them to swerve from the truth, and make shipwreck of a good conscience. Even the most precious things are vile and cheap in his eyes to whom money is dear. He will not stick, with Ahab, to sell even himself to work wickedness for the compassing of that his soul loveth and longeth after.

But thou, O man of God, flee these things, and hate covetousness with a perfect hatred. Hate it as Amnon did Tamar. First thrust it out of thy heart, and shut and lock the door after it. Secondly, let thy behaviour and conversation be averse and strange from the love of money.† Let all sordid and filthy lucre be abominable, all ill-gotten goods execrable. Let them stink in thy nostrils as ill as Vespasian's tribute of urine.

Shake thy lap of bribes with Nehemiah. Consider, as Bernard counsels Eugenius, how the people may grow rich under thee, and not thou by them.‡ Remember the end of Balaam's wages, and of Judas's bag. And wish with Damianus rather to have Gehazi's leprosy than his curse entailed to thee and thy posterity and inheritance after thee, fretting thine estate as a canker and moth, consuming your flesh as fire, and crying in the ears of the Lord of hosts for vengeance.

But what do I making myself ridiculous to this old, doting, covetous age of the world? This theme only made the pharisees laugh at Christ's woes, because they were covetous. And so do they serve all our caveats against covetousness, applauding themselves, and laughing in their sleeves when they behold their bags in the chest, and their lands from off their turrets, saying to themselves, What is a man but his wealth? What is an office but the fees.

There is a text in Isaiah, chap. xxxiii 14, that, if Paul had the preaching of it, he would make every gropping and gripping Felix to tremble. I mean such as the Scripture termeth roaring lions, ranging bears, horse-leeches, wolves, devouring all in the evening, and leaving none till the morning, as well judges that judge for reward, and say with shame, 'Bring you,'

---

* A venditione justi judicii venitur ad venditionem nequissimi.

† Heb. xiii. 5, ἀφιλάργυρος ὁ τρόπος.

‡ Præes ut de subditis crescas? nequaquam, sed ut ipsi de te.

such as the country calls capon-justices; as also such mercenary lawyers as sell both their tongues and their silence, their clients' causes, and their own consciences, who only keep life in the law so long as there is money in the purse, and when this golden stream ceaseth the mill stands still, and the case is altered; such extorting officers of justice as invent pulleys and winches for extraordinary fees, to the miserable undoing of poor suitors; such false perjured sheriffs, stewards of liberties, and their deputies, as for money falsify their charges; such corrupted jurates and witnesses of the post, which are as hammers and swords and sharp arrows in their brethren's hearts; such cheese-bailiffs and lamb-bailiffs as vex the poor countrymen with unjust summonses to the assizes and sessions, with the rest of that rabble.

These muck-worms of the world, which, like the gentles, breed of putrefaction, and beetles fed in the dung, relishing nothing else but earthly things, think there is no other godliness but gain, no happiness but to scrape and gather, to have and to hold. Let such consult shame to their houses. Let such make their offices as casting-nets for all fish that come, till they get the devil and all. Let them heap up treasures of wickedness and treasures of wrath withal.

But where there is any fear of God and love of the truth, let John's counsel prevail with them, to ' be content with their due wages.' Let Paul persuade them that godliness is gain with contentation; Solomon, that God's blessing maketh rich, and adds no sorrow therewith. So shall they follow Jethro's advice the better, and prove complete magistrates and officers, ' men of courage, men of religion, men of truth, hating covetousness.'

These are the four cardinal virtues of magistrates, of which, if all were compounded, and were as eminent for them as for their place, and did (as the great dictator of reason speaks in his politics) as far exceed the vulgar sort in those heroical virtues as the statues of the gods the statues of men, then would people become voluntary subjects, put the sceptres into their hands, and the law of commanding and obeying become easy, things thought irreparable would easily be reformed.

The Third Part.

But before I come to make use of what hath been said, let me, as the third part of my text and the distribution of magistracy requires, tell you to whom all this hath been spoken. Not to judges and justices of peace only, as I fear most have imagined in hearing it, but to all, from the highest and greatest to the lowest and least instrument of justice, from the governor of the thousand to the centurion, from him to the tithing man or deciner. To the which ancient division of the Jewish commonwealth our platform agrees in, substance. Their *Sanhedrim* or senate of seventy, to our parliament, council table, star chamber, exchequer chamber, &c. Our justices of assizes, in their circuit, and justices of peace, in their general commission or dominion, and high sheriffs in their shires, answering to the rulers of thousands.

Our justices in their several divisions, judges of hundred courts and turns, to their rulers of hundreds, to whom I may add high constables in their places; our court leets, and court barons, to their rulers of fifties; to whom I add ordinary constables in their offices; our chief pledges, tithing-men, or deciners, to their rulers of tens. Now all these Jethro means, and speaks of every one of them in their station and degree, conceiving the commonwealth as an instrument not well in tune, if but the least of these strings be false or naught.

Contrary to the common and dangerous opinion of the vulgar, who to their own injury think and say, that it matters not for petty officers, constables, and bailiffs, &c., though they be of the lees and dregs of men; nay, they hold that for some offices, it is pity any honest men should come into them. Alas! alas! the more subject to tentation and vice it is, the more needful it is that none other should have them.

O but (say they) a good judge or justice may help all. They err and are deceived ; it is no one beam, though never so bright, that enlightens all; it is not the light and influence of the fixed stars, though the greatest and highest, but of the sun and moon, and the lowest and nearest orbs, that govern the world. It is the ground wind, not the rack wind, that drives mills and ships. It is in the civil, as in the ecclesiastical body ; if bishops be never so learned, and the parishional ministers negligent, worldly, proud, or blind Sir Johns, ' the people perish for want of vision.'

What can the superior do, if the inferior inform not ? What can the eye do, if the hand and foot be crooked and unserviceable ? Yea, not only if such as be organs of justice, such as have places of judicature ; but if the media and spectacles of the sense will yield a false report, how shall the common sense make a right judgment? If pleaders and attorneys will colour and gloze, if the clerks and penmen make false records, may not any of these disturb or pervert justice ? If the least finger or toe of this body be distorted, I mean jailor or sergeant, or any other that should execute justice, be remiss and slack, then must the Dutchman's proverb be verified, Look what the bell is without the clapper, such are good laws and judgments without due execution.*

Thus we see in this curious clock-work of justice, the least pin or wheel amiss may distemper and disorder all; but if care were had to frame all these parts of the building according to the platform of this skilful architect, what an absolute harmony of the parts, what an exact perfection of the whole; yea, what golden times should we live to see!

Hearken, O ye mountains and little hills, you rulers of thousands, you rulers of tens, you reverend sages of the laws, you worshipful knights and gentlemen of the country ; yea, listen to this charge of Jethro, ye of the meanest places of the commonwealth, weigh not things nor persons at the common beam of custom and opinion, but at the golden standard of God's sanctuary, with these goldsmiths' weights of my text, which if I shall persuade you to do, I fear that we must say with the Psalmist, that sons of men *Beni-Adam*, yea, the chiefest men, *Beni-ish*, to be laid upon the balance, will be found lies, and lighter than vanity, Ps. lxi. 9; here money will not make the man, nor craft carry it away. Every Nabal of Mount Carmel, nor every Ahithophel may be admitted.

The text saith to every timorous, profane, false-hearted, covetous person, as Samuel to Saul, ' God hath rent thine office from thee, and bestowed it on thy better ;' or as the Scripture of Judas, ' Let another more worthy take his place ;' if this order and rule of trial might take place, how many would be turned out of commission ? how many would be *officii perdæ?* how would benches and shire-houses be thinned ?

As for this present, to the which God hath called me to speak (for if I had called myself, I could not nor durst not speak), give me leave without offence to speak that plainly and openly, which I conceive inwardly. When

* Quod campana sine pistillo, &c. Apud Bucolæum.

I have come into the shire-house sometimes to observe the state of it, it hath presented itself to my view, not unlike to that image in Daniel, or picture in Horace, or table of the popes of Rome, which for memory's sake I reduce to these two distichs :

> Ex auro caput est, argentea brachia, venter
> Æneus, admisto ferrea crura luto
> Divino capiti, ceruix humana, ferinus
> Assuitur truncus, Dæmoniique pedes.

The head of gold. And with such honourable judges God hath usually, and for a long time, blessed this circuit. If I had ever heard other of these present, I durst not give titles, lest my Maker should condemn me ; yet being unknown to me but by fame, which hath spoken all good, I desire you to prove and weigh yourselves by Jethro's weights, and accordingly to have peace and approof in your own consciences before the Judge of all judges.

The shoulders of silver. A worthy bench, yet mingled with some dross, and not so refined as I have known and seen it, like the sky in a clear evening bespangled with bright stars. Many such there be at this present. God be praised, religious and able justices, and so many, as I believe few other benches are furnished withal ; yet in this silver I fear some dross, some whose skill and ability the country doubts of, being conceived to be either so simple or so timorous, that they dare meddle with none that dare meddle with them ; or else so popular they will displease none. The devil himself, they say, may keep an ale-house under their nose. Others whose religion they call into question, at least for the truth, and for the power of it ; unless religion may stand with common swearing, with drinking, with familiarity with papists and recusants, with ungoverned and ungodly families, void of all exercises of religion, fraught with spirits of the buttery, ruffians, ale-house hunters, and such as are the sin-tutors and sin-leaders to all the country about them. I hope there be few such, I could wish there were none at all.

The breast and belly of brass, the strength of the country, in which rank I account the great inquest, jurymen, and constables, of which number how few make a conscience to present disorders according to oath, or that know and regard the bond of an oath !

The legs and feet of iron and clay, or mire. Indeed the very mire and dirt of the country, the bailiffs, stewards of small liberties, bum-bailiffs, jailors, &c. If Beelzebub wanted officers, he needed no worse than some of these ; what mysteries have they to vex the poor countrymen with false arrests ? and by virtue of that statute tying every freeholder of forty shillings *per annum* to attend the assizes ; but I list not to stir this sediment of the country, too unsavory to be raked up in a sermon.

O that some Jehoshaphat would visit and reform, or that you judges in these your days of visitations would redress some part of these grievances, and reduce all to this idea of Jethro's, which indeed would make a heaven upon earth amongst us. An Utopia, I fear some will say, too good to be true, objecting to me as to Cato, that, he not discerning the times he lived in, looked for Plato's commonwealth in the dregs of Romulus. And so that these magistrates, thus limned out, might be found in Moses' golden age of the world, but not in these lees of time.

To which I answer : that if Jethro were now to give advice, he would double the force of it. If David's reason be true, it is now high time for God to work, for men have destroyed his law. Was there ever more need

of courage than now, when sin is so audacious? of truth, when Esauism?
of religion, when hypocrisy and iniquity? of contentation, when the love
of the world so abounds? The only way to repair these ruins of the dying
world, is to renew government to the primitive beauty of it: the face
whereof I have now shewed in this excellent mirror or looking-glass; so
you go not away, and forget both the comeliness and spots it hath shewed
you, but wash and be clean, and such as it would have you to be.

THE FOURTH PART.

There being nothing else remaining to your perfection, and the peace of
the commonwealth, but this one item following in my text, requiring assiduity and diligence: ' Let them judge the people at all times,' &c.

A most needful caveat in times that love ease and private employments,
with neglect of public. Sitting in the gate is perpetually needful. Diligence in hearing and ending causes, would prevent that grievance of delays
which occasioned Jethro his discourse: how do you think it would have
affected him to have seen six or seven, I have heard sixteen, sums set upon
one suit? These our English delays being (as Marnixius complained) worse
than Spanish strappadoes.

And it is fit, though public and general courts have their terms, yet that
particular audience of petty grievance should have no vacation.

Many are the suits and controversies, many are the criminal offences,
that need continual inspection. Let him therefore that hath an office,
attend to his office with cheerfulness; he that hath no leisure to hear his
neighbour's causes, let him (as the woman said to Philip) have no leisure
to bear office. Cursed is he that doeth the work of the Lord negligently,
and withholdeth his hands therefrom.

You gentlemen complain often of idle shepherds, dumb dogs, &c., in
the ministry. But how many such in the magistracy! Some in commission, that never sit on the bench but for fashion; constables that are but
cyphers in their place. Forsooth they will be no pragmatical fellows, no
busybodies to trouble the country. Is there no mean between busybodies
and tell-clocks, between factotums and faineants?

From this neglect comes that wrong and injury to the assizes, that such
petty causes, trifling actions and complaints, trouble these grave and reverend personages, which a mean yeoman were judge fit enough to end in a
chair at home: when the whole shire must be troubled to hear and judge
of a curtsey* made out of the path, or a blow given upon the shoulder,
upon occasion of a wager, or such like bauble-trespasses which I shame to
mention. And to punish every petty larcenary, every small riot or disorder, which lighter controversies and faults, if particular officers would
compromise and redress in their spheres, these greater orbs should not be
troubled with them.

THE FIFTH PART.

Then indeed would that follow, which Jethro assures Moses of in the last
part of my text, ver 23 : ' If thou do this thing (God so commanding thee),
then shalt thou and thy people endure, and all this people shall go quietly
to their place.'

That is, ' a short-cut.'—ED.

An admirable emolument of magistracy, and sufficient reward of all the pains of it; that they and the people may go home in peace, sit under their vines and fig-trees, follow their callings, and, that which is the chief jewel of all, may lead their lives in all godliness and honesty. That the gold, blue, and purple silk might shine and glitter within the tabernacle, the outside was covered with red skins and goats' hair; such a shelter is magistracy to God's church and religion. Nebuchadnezzar was a great tree, and every particular magistrate a little one, under whose boughs people build and sing, and bring up their young ones in religious nurture, even foster-fathers as Joseph in Egypt. Such were the rich and religious times under David and Solomon, and under such as are described, Isa. xxxii., which whole chapter is worth the reading, as a just commentary upon this point; setting forth the felicity, quietness, plenty, virtue and piety of just governors, as are hiding-places from the wind, and refuges from the tempest, rivers of waters to dry places, and as the rain to the new mown grass, &c.

Such also were the times enjoyed by the church under Constantine, deciphered, as I take it, Rev. viii., when there was silence in the heaven about half an hour, the golden vials filled with sweet odours, the prayers of the saints ascending as a pillar of smoke up to heaven.

Of these times see panegyrical sermons, and encomiastical discourses storied of old, and one of them at large recorded by Eusebius,* which whole book is nothing but an eulogium of those peaceable days, wherein the church was edified and multiplied. The commonwealth being to the church, as the elm is to the vine, or as the garden to the bees; the flourishing of the one, the thriving of the other; and the disturbance of the one, the disquiet of the other.

How can men either attend God's service or their own work, when they are molested at home with drunkards, barretors, quarrellous persons? when hurried up to London with suits? As I have known a constable molested with five or six actions, for an act of justice in punishing vice according to his office. With what bitterness of spirit do men groan under delayed and perverted justice, when it is turned into hemlock, and turns them out of their wits, some of them swooning at the sight of their orders, as I have heard from credible eye-witnesses, others ready to destroy themselves, their adversaries, yea, and sometimes their judges!

Oh, the benefit of good magistrates. It is an unknown good, as the countryman in an ancient poet, when he had met withal, feelingly cries out, that he had found that *summum bonum*, which the philosophers so much sought after, he now enjoying more sweetness of little than of great revenues in troublous times. Surely, we Christians ought to prize it as the mean of our greatest good, of our peaceable frequenting of our churches, and our serving of God. Merchants make a higher use, and are more glad of a calm than common passengers; so should we Christians than heathens, by how much we may and ought to improve it for richer ends of God's glory, and the salvation of our souls.

Lord, what manner of persons ought we to be in all godliness and honesty, which enjoy such length and latitude of halcyon days, as we do; the tithe whereof, not only former days, but our neighbour nations, would now be glad of.

God give us the use and fruit of them, continue and increase them, which will then be when this text shall be most studied and practised. Then (as Amos speaks) shall judgment flow as waters, and righteousness run down

* Euseb. lib. 10

as a mighty torrent; or as David: ' Then shall the earth increase, all people shall praise God, and God even our God shall bless us, and all the ends of the earth shall fear him.' And so I make Jethro's preface my conclusion. ' I have given you counsel this day; hearken to my voice, and the Lord God be with you all.' Amen.

TO MY LOVING BROTHER

MR SAMUEL WARD.

BROTHER—If you meet with your Jethro's counsel, returned from beyond the seas, and as much beyond your expectation preserved alive as his son-in-law was against Pharaoh's injunction, marvel as much as you will, but be no more offended than you have cause. Joab sinned wider on the other hand in destroying David's Absalom, contrary to his serious charge, yet Joab was pardoned, and yet no brother. I have noted you hitherto inexorable for your own publishing of anything of your own; whether out of judgment, modesty, curiosity, or melancholy, I judge not; but when others have adventured them with fruit and acceptance into the light, I have seen you rest content with the public good. The like leave I have taken, expecting the like success; assuring you and myself of the general welcomeness and usefulness hereof to all whom it concerns, which are the greatest number of the land, even so many as have any reference to sessions and assizes, if not all sorts of Christians. Only I fear that the corruption of our times is grown so gross and Eglon-like, that it doth not Ehud-like enough sharpen the points, and send them home to the hilt, that they may reach to the quick. I had myself added thereto a project and persuasion for the redress of many abuses crept into offices and officers, having spent so much time in the study of the law, and execution of some offices, as made me weary of the errors I saw, and heartily wish the reformation of them; but fearing I have learned too much bluntness and plumpness of speech among the Lutherans, which is here as prime a quality as smoothness with you, as also loath to meddle out of mine orb, in my second thoughts I suppressed it. And so wishing unto this many diligent, conscionable, and ingenuous readers and appliers, and to them God's blessing and the fruit intended, I take my leave. From Elbing in Prussia.

Your Brother in the flesh, in the Lord, and in the work of the ministry,

NATH. WARD.

A PEACE-OFFERING TO GOD

FOR THE BLESSINGS WE ENJOY UNDER HIS MAJESTY'S REIGN;

WITH A THANKSGIVING FOR THE PRINCE'S SAFE RETURN, ON SUNDAY THE 5TH OF OCTOBER 1623.

IN A SERMON PREACHED AT MANITREE, IN ESSEX, ON THURSDAY THE 9TH OF OCTOBER, NEXT AFTER HIS HIGHNESS'S HAPPY ARRIVAL.

TO THE

KING'S MOST SACRED MAJESTY.

THE altar of incense was compassed about with a crown of pure gold. Gratitude is a rich and royal virtue, best beseeming the best princes, which have the best means to express, and the most cause to excite them thereunto. The meanest subject following the mill, may be as thankful as the greatest monarch sitting upon the throne. But between the effects of their thanks, there is as broad a difference, as between the acts of a giant and a cripple, whose fortitude may yet be equal. A private man praiseth God upon a ten-stringed, a king upon a ten thousand stringed, instrument, upon the loud-sounding organs, having so many millions of pipes, as there be men to whom his authority or example reacheth. The fruits of Constantine, Theodosius, and such good emperors' gratitudes, have been religion planted and promoted, churches erected, idolatry suppressed, wholesome laws enacted and executed, which makes divines doubt whether such kings were well advised,* though much applauded in story, who upon victories obtained, not laid down only, but wholly laid off their crowns, and resigned their kingdoms to God, not considering they might better have

* Elethan Rex Ethiopum (Niceph li. 17). Fernandus Rex Castiliæ (Rodericus de rebus Hispanicis, lib. 4. Fox, tom. i. Martyrolog).

paid their thanks to him in kind, as kings, than in private devotions, as monks. David was, therefore, a man after God's own heart, not because a king, but because a thankful king ; the sweet singer of Israel, not for his poetry or music, but for his grateful hymns, composed and sung to God's praise upon every fresh occasion ; and he calls upon princes and rulers three times in one verse, because they have three times the cause that subjects have, who have but a single share in those blessings, which jointly meet in the head of sovereignty. He often puts the thorn to his breast, as if he found some oblivion there, or unwillingness ;* yea, he often calls upon the angels, either implying the worth of the work, or else that the best alacrity may admit excitation. Alphonsus, that renowned king, † in a speech to the pope's ambassador, professeth he did not so much wonder at his courtiers' ingratitude to him, who had raised sundry of them from mean to great estates, as at his own to God. How acceptable an offering shall this be to God, if it may kindle the least spark, or rather blow those coals already flaming in your royal breast, or testify our gratefulness to him for his infinite old and new favours to your majesty's person, and thereby to your kingdoms! For all defects in it, the title pleads pardon and acceptance. Even God himself allowed a female in peace-offerings, not admitted in other kinds. Gratitude hath set a price upon mean presents. The form of a sermon will not disparage the subject-matter. The best monument of Constantine's government is a grateful sermon, recorded at large by Eusebius in his tenth, whose blessed and much honoured days, God make yours equal, and exceed in length and happiness ! So humbly and heartily prays,

Your Majesty's most loyal and thankful Subject,

SAMUEL WARD.

---

* Aug. in Ps. cxlv. Quasi tacentes invenerit angelos, hortatur qui tamen nunquam tacuerunt.

† Æneas Sylvius, lib. iv. de dictis Alphonsi.

A PEACE-OFFERING TO GOD;

OR,

A THANKSGIVING FOR THE PRINCE'S SAFE RETURN.

In all things give thanks, for this is the will of God in Christ Jesus our Lord towards you.—1 THESS. V. 18.

MAY an herald find out a rich coat of arms ungiven, then may a divine meet with a profitable subject unhandled. Gratitude, a virtue whose beauty so equally blazeth in the eyes of all,* whose name sounds so pleasantly in the ears of all, whose contrary is so odiously censured of all, to whom hath it been beholden for so much as a small tract or sermon?† What divine hath bestowed so much cost upon it, as to acquaint us with the nature, kinds, canons, and motives of it? Men, I confess, had the use of logic before the art was penned; and so David the king, of all grateful persons, with other the servants of God in all ages, have in abundant measure expressed their thankfulness; yet no man will deny, but that rules and directions orderly collected and compiled, do much conduce to a more lively and certain practice, than wild and unguided affections: and such helps God's Spirit in ordinary despiseth not.

All that I shall upon this sudden and extraordinary cause of public thanks undertake, is to be as the wheel to the bird, which with its coarse noise sets better music on work; and out of this short text of gratitude, endeavour to bring some light to the duty enjoined, 'Give thanks.'

Secondly, To shew the extent of its matter, 'In all things.'

Thirdly, To enforce the practice from this motive of motives, 'For this is the will of God in Christ Jesus our Lord.'

Fourthly, To bring it home and apply it, 'Towards you.'

In handling whereof, if I shall procure any whit the more tribute of thanks and praise to God, I shall attain that which is the queen of all causes, the end of my labour, yea, that which is the queen of all ends, God's glory.

'Give thanks.' The nature and grace of thankfulness consists in a kindly reflection of honour upon the benefactor for the benefit received.

* Virtutum lauditissima, &c.—Sen.

† Basil entitleth a homily, 'Of giving thanks,' but the subject-matter is of bearing afflictions cheerfully.

Look what perfection a solid body gives to the sunbeams, which having obscurely passed through the translucent air, are by it made to rebound with a spreading increase of their lustre and heat; look what such an echo as the sevenfold porch of Thebes is to the sound of a trumpet; such is thankfulness to the benefactor. And therefore, in reference to parents, is the sum of piety; to equals, of amity and humanity ; to God, of religion ; yea, the very prime and sum of all virtues and duties, because it most directly and fully promotes and achieves that which is the end and scope of all the Creator's works and gifts, ' his glory.' ' He that praiseth me honoureth me,' Ps. l. ; and contrariwise, ' They glorified not God, neither were they thankful,' Rom. i.

To discuss here these school queries,* whether it be a part of commutative or distributive justice, whether a general virtue or special, distinct or confounded with piety and justice, whether voluntary or bounden, whether of debt and by law or mere honesty, whether the innocent or the penitent be more obliged, whether it may adequate or surpass the benefit, were to trouble your heads with frigid subtleties, instead of warming your hearts with profitable matter. A thankful man had rather by ten times learn how to discharge this bond of needful duty, than to untie these knots of curious wit.

To such a one, I content myself to give the old tripartite rule, let him see that his soul, his tongue, and his life† bear their parts, discharge their several offices in glorifying God, that so his thanks being cordial, oreal, and real,‡ they may be complete and accepted of God. And first let them make sure of the first, especially when he hath to do with God, the maker, searcher, and judge of spirits, who in these kinds of offerings loves the fat, and the inwards, Levit. iii. ; the deeper and hollower the belly of the lute or viol is, the pleasanter is the sound ; the fleeter, the more grating and harsh in our ears: the voice which is made in the mouth, is nothing so sweet as that which comes from the depth of the breast. By how much spring water is better than plash water, by so much handy, hearty, than wordy thanks. ' Sing with grace in your hearts,' is the best tune to all the Psalms, without which, if one could descant with the voice of an angel, he were but as the sound of a tinkling cymbal. The very Alpha and Omega, the principal and total of our thanks with God, is as Bernard ends his epistles, and counsels to one that inquired of him what God required of man, ' Give me thy heart,' or keep all to thyself. If Benjamin come not, all the rest may stay behind. Unless, therefore, you mean to offer the sacrifice of fools, and the lips of calves, begin and end as David his Psalms, ' My soul, praise thou the Lord.' Take also David's commentary, Ps. ciii. ' And all that is within me, praise his holy name.'§ The first work is of the understanding, to judge of the worth of the benefit, to consider the unworthiness of the receiver, to study a *quid retribuam.* A fool cannot, and a proud man will not, be thankful ; the first, because he cannot estimate and weigh in the balance of judgment the value of the favour conferred upon him, or, through melancholy conceitedness, will not see what God hath done for him. The second, because he conceives it no more, if not less, than his due and desert, which is the reason that an heretic, overweening the strength of his naturals, or the merit of his works, cannot be thankful ; which taught Prosper wittily and wisely to entitle his poems, *Contra ingratos,*

---

* Vide Thomam secundæ secundæ questione centesima sexta.
† Corde, ore, opere. Bradward, lib. ii. c. 23.
‡ Conscientia lingua, vita. Aug. in Ps. cxlviii.
§ Tota estimatio ad animum redit. Sen.

without further naming the adversaries of God's grace. A rash man cannot be thankful, who for a fit only and brunt, sends up an extemporary 'God be thanked,' whereas he ought fixedly and seriously to study and devise how he might cast most honour upon his good God for his bounty to him.

The second care must be had of the memory, that a deep impression be made, frequent refreshing and refrication be used with David's watchword, 'My soul, forget not all his benefits,' which made him write down his passions, and give his Psalms the title of *Record*, or *Remembrance*. Oblivion is so far from excusing, that itself is the worst kind of ingratitude, excluding all hopes of future thanks, and arguing a slight esteem of favours past, which so soon have set them behind back, and out of sight in some blind corner of the mind. Our memory is a natural mother to injuries, a stepmother to benefits, for the help whereof our grateful forefathers were wont to erect pillars and monuments, stamp coins, give names to places, dedicate days, and keep anniversary feasts, that so they might preserve a vestal fire in their breasts, and not serve God with a flash of joy and blaze of thanks.

A third work is the warmth of the affections, which if dead and cold, how can any fumes of incense ascend ? Excess of joy and gladness is instead of thanks, which the nearer it comes to a rapture and ecstasy (such an one as Peter was in, when he wot not what he said, or the Jews coming out of captivity, faring as one in a dream) ; the more pleasing it is unto God, though it express itself in abrupt and exorbitant passions and gestures, such as David's dancing, unseemly in foolish Michal's, but most comely and kingly in God's eyes.

These acts of the soul are often all that God requires, but always the best fountain and spring of thanks, which sets the price upon the offering, and makes the turtle of the poor as welcome as the ox of the rich, the cruse and mite of the widow more worth than the rivers of oil and treasures of the wicked.

All this is intrinsical and immanent thanks ; but God's favours are too great for one man's heart to comprehend or requite ; and therefore he will not have them die in the breast of one man, and lie buried in silent admiration, but requires a transitive expression and publication of them. How many aids and witnesses doth David summon to assist him in this work, the mountains to leap, the floods to make a noise, the hills to clap their hands, and which of his musical instruments doth he not call upon ? Sundry helps and signs of thankfulness hath nature and art found out and used ; ringing of bells, displaying of banners, pomp and feasting, lights and fires, which while some condemn, they come near his fault that asked, ' What meaneth this waste ?' Yet are all these but a poor and senseless kind of sacrifice, performed by reasonless deputies, if the thanks determine and end in these without more significant expression. Cheer of the countenance, gestures of the body, leaping and dancing, are but dumb shows ; the best interpreter of the mind is the tongue, the glory of man and glorifier of God. ' My tongue shall tell of thy wondrous acts, and my lips shall never cease to publish thy praise.' This was all the fee Christ expected for his cures, ' Go and tell what God hath done for thee.' Words seem to be a poor and slight recompence, but Christ (saith Nazianzen) called himself the Word, and good words coming from a good heart are of great account and force with God and man.

David envied the birds, that might in their kinds sing God's praise in his courts ; and in imitation of them, who set themselves on the highest tops of trees, whence their notes may be furthest heard, he laboured to spread God's praises in the greatest congregations, in Saul's court, in all companies he came in, in the temple itself. By speech one man's heart conveys into another the cheerly conceptions and passions of his soul, and so multiplies praise, and sets others on work to bless God with him ; and the more the merrier ; and the more mirth, the more thanks ; the greater the flock, the cheerlier noise ; the fuller the choir, the louder the music, and one cheerly bird often sets all the flock a chirping. One man shouts and the whole host follows. John heard a voice from the throne saying, 'Praise ye our God, all his servants, small and great ; and immediately a noise as of many waters and mighty thunders saying, Halelujah, for the Almighty reigneth.'

Yet, because speech is transient, and of life for the present only, the pens and writings of thankful men have been of singular use to transmit and convey unto posterity the noble acts of God ; one generation teaching another to keep like praises in store, that God's thanks may be immortal in succession and propagation. Such fruit may our statute have in after ages, penned for the perpetuation of God's invaluable deliverance from the hellish powder-plot, were it as duly read as it was providently enacted.

When we have given God good words, it remains that we give him not words alone, but our real obedience, preferred by God to all our sacrifices ; slay not our beasts, but our beastly lusts ; give him not our goods, but ourselves ; not any dead, but a living and seasonable sacrifice. * He that in way of thankfulness vows and performs the mortification of one darling sin, the addition of one good duty, pleaseth God better than Solomon with his twenty thousand beeves and sheep. Would we know, then, how we should perfect our thanks, walk we with God, let us do righteousness, abound in alms and prayer, better our piety and charity, increase the works of our callings, bring forth more fruit in our kinds ; for with such sacrifices God is most honoured and best pleased. The ancient and wonted thanks after victories and blessings were reformation of vices, removal of idols, sanctions and executions of good laws, release of debts, bounty to the poor.† The life of thankfulness consists in the lives of the thankful ; otherwise it is but as one should sing a good song with his voice, and play a bad one on his instrument, which would make but a black *Sanctis*, and become such saints. He that saith, 'God be thanked' with his mouth, and his life remains reprobate to every good work, hath the show of thanks, but the power of ingratitude, and is near the curse of the fig tree, full of leaves and empty of fruit ; for God is not mocked with words. Wherefore, O thou vain man, justify thy words by thy works, and thou shalt be blessed in thy deeds, and God by the poor blessed for them, who hath himself no need or profit of our works ; but, as great men, turns over his fees and thanks to his poor followers and servants, and tells us in plain terms he reckons that done to himself which is done to the least of his ; and smells as sweet a savour of Cornelius's alms as of his prayers, and counts himself as much honoured by a good housekeeper as by a church-frequenter ; but best by him that is both in truth and from faith. A new song‡ becomes

---

* Per victimas caro aliena, per obedientiam, propria voluntas mactatur.

† Non sola vox sonet, sed et manus consonet ; verbis facta concordant, quando cantas halelujah, manum porrigas esurienti.—Aug. in Ps. cxlix.

‡ Canticum novum et vetus homo male concordant, cantet canticum novum qui nova est creatura, qui novam præstat obedientiam.—Aug. in Ps. cxlix. Cui lingua tua laudes Dei cantillat, cujus vita sacreligium exhalat.—*Idem.* in Ps. xxiii.

not the old man's mouth ; and let him sing a new song that leads a new life, and that's the best harmony, and makes the best music in God's ear.

'In all things.' Now I have shewed how thou mayest and must be thankful. If thou ask me wherein, or for what, I will ask thee what thou hast of thine own, and what of right and desert ? If nothing, then ' in all things give thanks.' We have heard that a thankful man needs a good judgment ; but we shall see that he needs no invention ; if his heart be in tune, all things will bring matter to hand. Gratitude is as large as logic, that hath for its object things that are, and that are not. There be favours privative, and favours positive ; there be good things bestowed and evils kept from us ; yea, the very evils that do betide us are turned to our good, and therefore we are bound to give thanks in all, and for all. Not with a collective thanks by lump and wholesale, with a ' God be thanked for all his benefits,' but distributively keeping a bill of the particulars, and duly thanking as we daily receive them. This distribution is best made by a just gradation and scale of discretion, ascending in our thanks according to the degrees of his favours.

First, he will be praised in all his creatures, whereof we have the sight or the use, even as if we had a propriety in them ; for every one of us have no less benefit by the sun and air, than if we saw and breathed alone. The Hebrews have a canon, that God would be praised in the least emmet or gnat, but magnified in the elephant and leviathan ; admired in the sun, moon, stars, comets, earthquakes, thunders, and such extraordinary works. The praise of his wisdom and power lies asleep and dead in every creature, till man actuates and enlives it.* The heavens and the earth, and all things therein, are said to praise God ; that is (saith Augustine) when thou considerest their order and beauty, and praisest the invisible Creator, they praise him with thy understanding and thy voice, which have none of their own, but are dumb and senseless.†

In all the works of his provident administration. And here let public blessings have the precedency in thy thanks. It is not only self-love, but want of judgment, that makes fools prize a domestical and private welfare before the commonwealth, and the good of the kingdom, which is in itself the greater, and would, in the long run, be greater to the particular man. Is any cost bestowed on the private cabin comparable to the saving of the whole ship ? The very heathens rejoiced more in their country's good than in their own ; let Christians much more praise God for their kings, princes, and rulers, by whose wise government they may live a quiet life under their vines and fig trees, and in all honesty and godliness worship God in their chapels and churches.

In all thy personal favours ; among which the privative challenge a place, that is, such evils as pass by and over thee. Famous is the story of the good bishop, that, seeing a toad by the way, lift up his heart unto God, that made him not such a creature. And Chrysostom wills us to walk into hospitals and lazar-houses,‡ that, by the sight of other's miseries, we may be occasioned to thanks for our own freedom. Every man that sees another stricken, and himself spared, is to keep a passover for himself.

In all the crosses that do befal us ; yea, happily more than in them we count and call blessings. To call for afflictions, we have no precedent or precept in Scripture ; but to praise God for them, store of both. To count

---

* Raymundus in Theologia naturali.
† August. in Ps. xlviii., Tua voce clamat, &c.
‡ Chrysost. ad Stagorium.—Epist. 3.

it exceeding joy because of the exceeding gain; to count it an honour that we are counted worthy to suffer, as the disciples that leaped and sung after their scourgings; and in this theme Basil spends all his sermon, which he entitles giving of thanks in all things.

In all the gifts of God, whether for necessity or pleasure, of nature or of grace, temporal or eternal, more for necessities than for delicacies, more for thy bread and water than for thy wine and oil, for thy clothes than for thy lace and ornaments, for thy health more than thy wealth, for thy good name above thy jewels, the goods of thy soul above all goods. Plato observed this order in his thanks, that he was a man, a Grecian, an Athenian, and Socrates's scholar; Alphonsus, that he was a king, a philosopher, and a Christian; Theodosius, more that he was a member of Christ in his church, than head of the empire; Paul best of all, 'Blessed be God, that hath blessed us with spiritual blessings in heavenly things.' One spiritual is better than all corporal, and one eternal than all temporal.

In all thy spiritual blessings, preparations, preventions, excitations, motions, acts, confirmations, consummations, give all to the praise of his grace, by which thou art that thou art; chiefly in those thou hast most wanted and earnestly begged, in these let thy praises answer thy prayers. Samuel and Augustine, children of many prayers and fears, were also children of many praises and thanks.

In all and above all, for him that is *all in all*, thanks and praises. For he is worthy who hath redeemed us, and made us kings and priests unto himself; and if thanks be the will of God in Jesus Christ towards us, then sure I am it is his will, that all thanks be given him for Jesus Christ, in whom all the promises are yea and amen.

In all things, in all times, and in all places; so the very context implies. Pray always, in all things give thanks. Wish with Epictetus, thou wert of the nightingale's unwearied spirit, ever to be singing day and night; at least, with Bernard, imitate the other birds, which morning and evening, at the rise and setting of the sun, omit not to praise their Creator. These must be constant, set, and inviolable times. Occasional times are when benefits are newly received, which otherwise soon wax stale, and putrefy as fish; no part of the thanks-offering might be kept unspent till the third day. Hezekiah wrote his song the third day after his recovery: 'The living shall praise thee as I do this day.' And if he had been as speedy in his thanks after his deliverance from Ashur, it may be (saith Lavater) his plate had never been carried into Babylon. All days of prosperity and mirth are seasonable for thanks, as birds sing more in clear days than in gloomy. Let him that is sad, pray, and he that is merry, give thanks. The Jews' three solemn feasts were to be kept in three cheerful seasons:* the passover, at the first riping of corn; Whitsuntide, at the first reaping; tabernacles, at the end of harvest. God loves a cheerful giver. Christ willed his passion should be remembered when our spirits are refreshed with bread and wine. 'I will take the cup of salvation,' &c. Our joy, which otherwise is a slippery passion, is then safe and sanctified, when it brings forth thanksgiving.

Were it not now superfluous to say to whom this thanks ought to be given? To whom, but to him of whom we have all things? Yet we had rather change the name, and shift the debt to any save the right creditor, ascribing events to nature, destiny, and fortune, rather than to the living God; which is as if one should say, he owed no money to Seneca, but to

* Isidor. in Levit. Theodoret.

Lucius Annæus, which are but blind names of the same man. What is more common than to rob God to pay the instrument? The fisher sacrificeth to his net, the husbandman will thank his dunghill for his crop, rather than him that gives the increase. God allows some praise to the instrument. The sword of God and the sword of Gideon; but when he hears us give more to the means than to the author, he is jealous, and offended more justly than Saul with the people, for singing of David's ten thousand, and Saul's thousand. Let Solomon have his thousand, and the keeper of the vine two hundred, Cant. iii. Adrian and Verus, emperors of old, Selimus and Ferdinand of late, are taxed in history for erecting monuments of victory to their horses, forgetting the Lord of hosts. Let us learn of Paul, in right down terms, in all things to bless the Father of our Lord Jesus Christ.

Thus all things invite us to thanks; and yet Paul, foreseeing our backwardness and excuses, opposeth to them all the will of God in Jesus Christ, 'For this is the will of God.' The ungrateful, like unto the sluggard, is witty in finding out pretexts and pretences, making a clog to hinder of that which should be his goad to quicken him. God's name, he will tell you, excels all thanksgiving, his blessings are innumerable, and why should he attempt impossibilities? And yet the same man, in seeking of wealth and honour, will shoot at the fairest mark, though he take up his arrow short. Here, unless he may do all, he will do nothing at all; but God's will is, thou shouldst do thy good will, and he will accept thy will for the deed. And if thou shouldst say in thy heart, What addition shall my praise make to his honour, that is infinite and self-sufficient?* was he not as happy before there was a man or angel to praise him, as since? I might answer with a schoolman,† he counts it an increase *ad extra*, in the notice and glory of his attributes, though *ad intra*, in the perfection and excellence of them, he cannot increase. But I had rather answer with our apostle, 'It is his will.' But we have need of his benefits; if he will allow us the profit, we may well allow him the praise; our emptiness calls for the one, and to his fulness belongs the other. Bradwardine, as thankful an English heart as ever wrote, knits and unties the knot thus: Why should I go about to pay that debt which is unpayable, and by paying whereof I run further in debt? for the grace and heart, the will and ability to be thankful, is his gift; and for that I must be further obliged, as David when he built the temple. But God forbid, saith he, that I should entangle mine heart in this chain of ingratitude, and break asunder this my bond of thanks, because I cannot unloose it. Let me rather know this to be my happiness, to whom I owe much, to owe more; to be as deep in his books as I can, who loves to water where he plants, to heap favour upon favour, till he overcome us with favour; to him let me be ever owing, and ever paying, never discharged, but ever becoming more and more thankful, till I be wholly transformed into thankfulness, and when all is done, account myself indebted and unprofitable.‡

'For this is God's will in Jesus Christ.' God's will hath binding authority enough; but he adds a winning word, his 'will in Christ,' commending the duty to us from God by that lovely name. The force of the persuasion is, as if God should say to us, Behold, I have so loved you, as

* Nec deterior si vituperatur, nec melior si laudatur.—Bernard.
† Raymundus de Naturali Theolog.
‡ Bradward. de causa dei, lib. 3, cap. 23. Gratissimis gratitudinis vinculis alligor ut gratior, et gratior fiam tandemque in gratias gratissimè transformer.

to give you my Son, and with him all things; and what return do I expect? what is my will, but that in all things you give me thanks in his name? Thanks is my will, and pleaseth my will, as sweet odours do man's nostrils. Gratitude needs not, as other virtues, letters testimonial, or commendatory. David often tells us it is comely and lovely enough of itself. Prayer is profitable, but praise is honourable. To ask is a troublesome thing,* and a mendicant word implying want, and therefore comes hardly and harshly from us; but praise becomes the angels, yea, the Son of God, and therefore should be welcome to us, It is a grace and praise to him that gives, as well as to him to whom it is given. How renowned in all story hath been the practice of this virtue in David to Jonathan's, Abimelech's, and Barzillai's posterity; in Joseph to his parents; in Hannah (more honoured for being the author of a song than the mother of a son); in Cromwell's to Frescobald; Agrippa to Thaumastus's servant, for a cup of cold water in his troubles; Egelred to the swineherd;† yea, in brute beasts, in lions,‡ dragons,§ eagles, and falcons; in elephants, fishes, dogs. The contrary most hateful: in Judas, Ahithophel, Pharaoh's butler, &c., not actionable, or finable by any legal or set mulct, as sufficiently censurable, but deserving, and left to excess of hatred by God's judgment, and so generally reputed of all, the sum of all disgrace, the worst, yea, all that can be said of a man; say this, and say all; the main sin of the apostate angels and damned spirits. Thanks the chief, if not the whole, work of the glorified seraphims, who vent and spend all their burning fire in the flames of God's praise. How cheerfully should we redeem time to this blessed work!|| which, because it is too large to be done in this span-long life, it shall ever be doing in that eternlty. What like evidence hath a saint, of God's free and princely spirit residing in his heart and tongue, to this frankincense, and free work, wherein our ingenuity is best tried, not extorted from us by our own necessities, as prayer; not exacted by law, or drawn by shame or penalty from us, but voluntary, and therefore best testifying us to be of God's willing people: which grace, where he gives, surely he will confer more of all kinds. For where do men delight to sow, but in fertile soils, where they reap most? Where do musicians delight to sound their instruments, but where the echo multiplies them most in their return? But our profit is too sordid a motive for this liberal virtue. Thanks is not thanks, if bribing and eyeing future favour, if anything more than the praise of past bounty, though there should never be need or receipt of any more afterwards. But our dulness hath need of all spurs. David, the nightingale of Israel, sets many a thorn to his breast; that vigilant cock clappeth oft his own wings. An ingenuous child desires no more but to know what his father loves. Isaac, if his diet be known, shall be sure of venison enough; and if Saul take delight in David's harp, he shall not want music. A grateful courtier desires but to know what the will and pleasure of his sovereign is: and this is enough, and above all other bonds, to a man sensible of the benefits of creation and redemption. What else is the difference and pre-eminence of the gospel above the law, but thanks the one and debt the other? Which made Ursinus judiciously give his book of obedience and good works the title of *Gratitude:* which whoso slights or neglects undoes

---

* Molestissimum istud verbum *rogo.*—Sen.
† Fox, tom. i.　　　　　　　　　　　　　　　‡ Agell. lib. x. cap. 5.
§ Pierius, lib. xix.　Strabo, lib. v.　Philarchus apud Athenæum.　Gesnerus, &c.
|| Sit illa meditatio frequens in hoc sæculo quod opus erit in futuro.—Aug. Ps. cxlviii.

and dissolves the whole bond of perfection, not of humanity alone, but of all Christianity. God abhorring all that we can do with other respect or end, bidding the proud man and his merits perish, done in way of desert or pay; only accepting that which is done in the name of Christ, in way of thankfulness for him and his merit, who is the altar which sanctifies and graceth the gold and the gift, to the horns whereof it is best binding with the cords of thanks all our offerings: who is the great master of requests, having a golden vial ready to offer up, and commend to his Father all the incense of his saints, and to give a sweet odour and perfume unto them, making the least cup of water tendered in his name of precious account, without which all is abominable. And therefore he that would set a special gloss upon his sacrifice of thanks, let him, with the acknowledgment of his vileness (as David, ' Who am I and my people ? '), crave acceptance in his name, in whom God is well pleased; for ' this is his will in Christ Jesus our Lord,' &c.

That thanks *in thesi* and general, is God's will, it is now out of question; but there is yet another clause in my text, ' towards you,' which bids us search what is God's will *in hypothesi*, in particular. ' Towards us :' even to uswards of this nation, this assembly, towards thee and me, all and every one of us jointly and severally. First, It is requisite that we take good notice of our receipts, and then balance them well with our returns; and so shall we see our arrearages best, and what remains for us to do. Mark we advisedly what our own writers, historians, poets, usually applaud in our nation. How they extol our climate, our soil, our native commodities, our policies, laws, orders, peace, plenty, prosperity, terming us *Albion, quasi Olbion; Angli, quasi Angeli*. Can too much in truth be spoken to the praise of God's bounty, and blot of our ingratitude ? How hath he lifted us up to heaven, severed this island with the seas of his mercies from all the world besides, and bordering kingdoms round about, setting it as a queen in the midst of them, to hear news of wars, pestilence, bloodshed, and desolations, not to feel the least disturbance from within and without, scarce to hear a dog bark against its long-lontinued peace, unmatchable in present or past examples. Above all, what a golden candlestick hath he placed in it, furnished with oil and lamps, I would I could say in every shaft and pipe of it; but so as I may well resemble it to a bright sky in a clear evening sparkling with stars, though not in every part, yet in every zone and quarter of it! What times can tell of the like light, learning, preaching, knowledge ? O that I could say practice and thankfulness answerable ! What a hedge or wall of fire and protection hath God made about us ! What glorious salvations from foreign invasions,* from domestical treasons,† such as will scarce be credible to after ages.‡ Was Israel itself ever honoured with more ? To all these, when for a while of late we were in a damp of grief and fear in the absence of our prince for a season, how suddenly hath he blown over that cloud ! How speedily and happily hath he returned him, that we fare as people as in a dream, can scarce tell how to believe ourselves, or how to express our joys enough ! How hath he filled our hearts with gladness ! O that I may be able truly to say, our tongues with praise, and our lives with duties. In this fresh and last favour of his, he deals, methinks, with us as creditors with slow debtors :

* 1588. (The year of the Spanish Armada.— ED.)
† 1605. (The year of the Gunpowder Plot.—ED.)
‡ Factum est hoc á Domino, mirifico in consiliis, magnifico in operibus, et est mirabile in oculis nostris.

where they have adventured much, they will sometime shoot another arrow, in hope to find and make good their former losses; as Seneca counsels his Ebutius to imitate the husbandman, who never leaves husbanding and manuring the barren ground, till he make it fertile, to heap benefit on benefit, till he awaken his unthankful friend, overcome him with kindness, and in the end, by some welcome good turn, excite his dulness, and extort thanks by that for all the former from him. I would I were as sure God should speed of his end, as I am sure this is his end, to put us to the blush for our former ingratitude, to win us at length to pay our debts and vows unto him. Some, and sundry of all sorts, great and mean, he hath, I doubt not, among us, grateful observers and receivers of his blessings, like a few berries after the shaking of a tree, which makes him forbear to lay the axe to the root for a while: but the common thanks which he reaps at the hand of the multitude, is lukewarmness and neutrality at the best; in many, lingerings after superstition and idolatry; in the worser sort, desperate swearing, dissolute Sabbath keeping, brutish drunkenness and uncleanness, falsehood in dealings till all burst again, vanity in fashion-following, without shame or modesty. These are the dregs of our times, and blots of our feasts, which, if not amended, may not a withdraught of all God's favours, a removal of his candlestick, the worst of all plagues, be as certainly foreseen and foretold, as if visions and letters were sent us from heaven, as to the seven churches of Asia? But I hope better things of our better sort, and love as little as may be to have mine eye and finger upon such sores, wishing we might see such a book-fire as we read of Acts xvii., made of all our clandestine libels, seditious and malcontented pamphlets. I speak not against the precious balm of reproof, no, not oil of scorpions. Let the righteous smite us with plain and faithful rebukes, and such smitings shall not wound the body, or break the head, but shew us our defects without rancour and malice, pouring in no poison and venom, but oil and wine to heal our wounds, to excite us to thankfulness worthy the blessings heaped and renewed daily upon us; and what is the best thanks, but national and personal amendment of life? And what thanks is enough, what hecatombs of sacrifices are sufficient for a God that hath done so much for us, and yet ceaseth not to do us good? I would know of the most ungrateful man, what he can require of us more than he hath richly and abundantly deserved, were it to half, yea, to all the wealth of the kingdom? I take not upon me to prescribe particulars. But suppose he should exact of us this particular, which, I dare say, would highly please him, and would, I am sure, be a most worthy and needful fruit of our gratitude to him. I will not mention a ceremonial, circumstantial, super-fluous matter of form and order, but a necessary substantial amends of what all confess to be amiss; a provision, I mean, of a sufficient mainten-ance and minister in every parish of the kingdom, a righting of what popery hath wronged, a restitution of what religion first consecrated, superstition misplaced, covetousness wholly alienated and impropriated. This could not in likelihood but prove a cure to all the maladies, spiritual and temporal, a dispelling of our Egyptian fogs, a dispersing of the frogs that yet remain as thorns in our sides, a quickening to all good works of piety and charity, a goad and spur to all kinds and fruits of thankfulness that God can require of us. Have I spoken of more than he requires, or we need, or of that which is impossible? The last will be the only plea, but withal the plea only of our ingratitude and infidelity, not disability. Is it harder now to restore, than at first to give? When God stirred up his people's affections, their princes and priests were fain to set mortmains and bounds to their bounty, and stay their hands from giving more. What were a subsidy or two for God and his church ? If God give us hearts, wood and the sacrifice will soon be found, and brought to hand; and till this be done, a just brand of ingratitude lies upon us. It is impossible for any explication to extend to every particular. If every soul would study thankfulness, God would direct to the best duties. If every Englishman would kindle a bonfire in his own heart, how would the flame break out, and shine abroad, and the smoke ascend up to the heavens ! If every thankful man would take up his harp, and sing and play with his tongue and hand a new song of thanks, how loud and full melody would it make ! what joy would be on the earth, yea, in the heavens, to see our thankfulness and amendment. It is but every man's labour to sweep before his own door, and every man's fagot to this fire, and the work were done, and God pleased. ' Give unto the Lord,' you potentates, ' glory and strength ;' give unto the Lord, ye sons of the mighty, worship and praise due to his name. You house of Aaron, and you that serve him in his courts, praise ye the Lord, and stir up others to praise him. Let Israel, and all that fear him, say, ' His mercy endureth for ever.' Whatever others shall do, ' My soul, praise thou the Lord.'

A POSTSCRIPT TO THE READER.

A THANKFUL man is worth his weight in the gold of Ophir. Could I be as thankful as I ought to be, which sure I am I never shall be, yet can the thanks of a mean man procure but mean honour to God. Could I be as thankful as is possible for any one man to be, yet single thanks is like a single voice, which makes but simple music. But could I stir up thankful intentions and affections in every reader,—for example, in thy heart whose eye is now upon this advice,—then wouldst thou also endeavour to work the like in others; and so a small number, by multiplication, might prove a large sum, as a great debt is often paid by a collection from many hands which one poor man's ability could never have reached unto. That we may be aright thankful, it is requisite that with one eye we observe our sins and evils, both public and personal, and with the other our favours and blessings, that the one may acquaint us with our unworthiness, the other may prevent malcontented ungratefulness. Many a man would be much more thankful than he is, if he had but a hint of excitation and help of direction ; as many a scholar, if he had but a few heads of commonplaces, would be rich in observations, which, for want of such a slight help, vanish in the reading and perish in the meditating. Behold, therefore, I give thee here a register or inventory, which I wish thee to keep and use as a table of thanks due to God in kind, and negligently by thee paid; which, when thou perusest, thou must, under every head in the space left of purpose, record, not all and every favour, which is impossible, but the most memorable and thankworthy, putting a special *Selah* of thanks upon them, as David upon his deliverance from the bear, lion, and Goliah. It cannot but revive thy memory and quicken thy affections so often as thou shalt seriously review it.

A THANKFUL MAN'S CALENDAR.

Public.—Consider in what times and places the lot of my life hath fallen ; in what king's reign, in what nation, in what town, under what magistracy and ministry.

Domestical.—What parents, schoolmasters, and tutors, what wife, children, and servants, hath God blessed me withal ?

Personal and Privative.—What sickness have I been delivered from ? What dangers, casualties by sea or land ? What suits and vexations by law or otherwise ?

Positive, Corporal.—What measure of health and strength of body ?

External.—What talents of wealth, birth, office, authority, repute ?

Mental.—What faculties of understanding, memory ? What helps of arts, sciences, education ? &c.

When and how my conversion to God was wrought ? What assurance of God's love in Christ, what peace and joy in the Holy Ghost ? &c.

What progress, growth, and increase have I made in grace, and in good duties of my place and calling ?

What victory over tentations and special sins, old and inveterate customs of evil ?

When thou hast written down some particulars, then minister these interrogatives between God and thyself to thy conscience :—

What times formerly, or now usually, do I take to ponder and take notice of God's blessings ? What daily observation make I of them ? How many hours spend I weekly or monthly in revolving the memory of them ? What occasion take I to speak of them in company, to God's glory rather than mine own ostentation ?

What gain have my talents brought into my Master's banks ?

What benefit have my brethren by them ? Of what use is my life, parts of mind and body, &c., to my country, church, or commonwealth ?

What alms and good deeds have I done or intend to do ?

What shall I render to God for all his benefits ? How shall I add to my former thankfulness ? What good service may I do him more than I have, that men may glorify my heavenly Father ?

BRADWARDINI GRATA AD DEUM PRECATIUNCULA, LIB. 3, DE CAUSA DEI.

DA mihi mendicanti et misero, qui tuus sum magis quam meus, imo non meus sed tuus, ut tibi Patri luminum, cujus dona gratuita sunt omnes boni motus, actus, habitus, carentiæ malorum actuum, bona positiva, privativa, gratias, quæ mihi posibiles sunt agam maximas gratissimus. Da ut facilius corde et opere faciam quam ore proferam. Da, iterum atque iterum precor, nihil ut mihi dulcius sit et delectabilius quam hæc effectuosissimè affectuosissimè adimplere, incessanter semper sed ubique ab æterno in æternum. Amen.

Quoties tentatio superatur, periculum declinatur, vitium subjugatur, annosa et inveterata animi passio sanatur, laqueus deprehenditur, aut multum cupita virtus obtinetur, toties personare debet vox laudis ad singula beneficia.—Bernardus in Cant. Serm. I.

AUGUST. IN PSAL.

Quid est, *tota die impleatur os meum laudibus?* Sine intermissione te laudem, in prosperis quia consolaris, in adversis quia corrigis, antequam essem quia fecisti, quum essem quia salutem dedisti, quum peccassem quia ignovisti, &c.

WOE TO DRUNKARDS.

To whom is woe? To whom is sorrow? To whom is strife? &c. In the end it will bite like a serpent, and sting like a cockatrice.—PROV. XXIII. 29, 32.

SEER, art thou also blind? Watchman, art thou also drunk or asleep? Isa. xxi.; or hath a spirit of slumber put out thine eyes? Up to thy watch-tower; what descriest thou? Ah, Lord! what end or number is there of the vanities which mine eyes are weary of beholding? But what seest thou? I see men walking like the tops of trees shaken with the wind, like masts of ships reeling on the tempestuous seas. Drunkenness I mean, that hateful night-bird, which was wont to wait for the twilight, to seek nooks and corners, to avoid the hooting and wonderment of boys and girls. Now, as it were some eaglet, to dare the sunlight, to fly abroad at high noon in every street, in open markets and fairs, without fear or shame, without control or punishment, to the disgrace of the nation, the outfacing of magistracy and ministry, the utter undoing (without timely prevention) of health and wealth, piety and virtue, town and country, church and com-monwealth. And dost thou, like a dumb dog, hold thy peace at these things? Dost thou, with Solomon's sluggard, fold thine hands in thy bosom, and give thyself to ease and drowsiness, while the envious man causeth the noisomest and basest of weeds to overrun the choicest Eden of God? Up and arise, lift up thy voice, spare not, and cry aloud. What shall I cry? Cry woe, and woe again, unto the crown of pride, the drunkards of Ephraim. Take up a parable, and tell them how it stingeth like the cockatrice, de-clare unto them the deadly poison of this odious sin. Shew them also the sovereign antidote and cure of it, in the cup that was drunk off by him that was able to overcome it. Cause them to behold the brazen serpent, and be healed. And what though some of these deaf adders will not be charmed nor cured, yea, though few or none of these swinish herd of habitual drunkards, accustomed to wallow in their mire, yea, deeply and irre-coverably plunged by legions of devils into the dead sea of their filthiness, what if not one of them will be washed and made clean, but turn again to their vomit, and trample the pearls of all admonition under feet, yea, turn again, and rend their reprovers with scoffs and scorns, making jests and songs on their ale-bench; yet may some young ones be deterred, and some novices reclaimed, some parents and magistrates awakened to prevent and suppress

the spreading of this gangrene, and God have his work in such as belong
to his grace. And what is impossible to the work of his grace ? Go to then
now, ye drunkards, listen not what I, or any ordinary hedge-priest (as you
style us), but that most wise and experienced royal preacher, hath to say unto
you. And because you are a dull and thick-eared generation, he first deals
with you by way of question, a figure of force and impression.* ' To whom
is woe,' &c. You use to say, Woe be to hypocrites. It is true woe be to
such, and all other witting and willing sinners ; but there are no kind of
offenders on whom woe doth so palpably, inevitably attend as to you drunkards. You promise yourselves mirth, pleasure, and jollity in your cups ;
but for one drop of your mad mirth be sure of gallons and tuns of woe, gall,
wormwood, and bitterness here and hereafter. Other sinners shall taste of
the cup, but you shall drink of the dregs of God's wrath and displeasure.
' To whom is strife ? ' You talk of good fellowship and friendship, but wine
is a rager and tumultuous make-bate, and sets you a quarrelling and med-
dling. When wit is out of the head, and strength out of the body, it
thrusts even cowards and dastards, unfenced and unarmed, into needless
frays and combats. And then to whom are wounds, broken heads, blue
eyes, maimed limbs ? You have a drunken by-word, ' Drunkards take no
harm ;' but how many are the mishaps and untimely misfortunes that betide such, which, though they feel not in drink, they carry as marks and
brands to their grave ? You pretend you drink healths, and for healths ;
but to whom are all kind of diseases, infirmities, deformities, pearled faces,
palsies, dropsies, headaches, if not to drunkards ?

Upon these premises he forcibly infers his sober and serious advice.
Look upon these woful effects and evils of drunkenness, and look not upon
the wine, look upon the blue wounds, upon the red eyes it causeth, and
look not on the red colour when it sparkleth in the cup, If there were no
worse than these, yet would no wise man be overtaken with wine; as if he
should say, What see you in the cup or drink, that countervaileth these dregs
that lie in the bottom ? Behold, this is the sugar you are to look for, and
the tang it leaves behind. Woe, and alas ! sorrow and strife, shame,
poverty, and diseases, these are enough to make it odious, but that which
followeth withal will make it hideous and fearful. For Solomon, duly considering that he speaks to men past shame and grace, senseless of blows,
and therefore much more of reasons and words, insisteth not upon these
petty woes, which they, bewitched and besotted with the love of wine, will
easily oversee and overleap, but sets before their eyes the direful end and
fruit, the black and poisonful tail, of this sin. ' In the end it stingeth like
the serpent, it biteth like the cockatrice' (or adder), saith our new translation.

All interpreters agree that he means some most virulent serpent, whose
poison is present and deadly.† All the woes he hath mentioned before
were but as the sting of some emmet, wasp, or nettle, in comparison of
this cockatrice, which is even unto death, death speedy, death painful, and
woful death, and that as naturally and inevitably as opium procureth sleep,
as hellebore purgeth, or any poison killeth.

Three-forked is this sting, and threefold is the death it procureth to all
that are stung therewith. The first is the death of grace, the second is of
the body, the third is of soul and body eternal. All sin is the poison

* Μεγάλη τῆς ἐρωτήσεως ἐνεργεια.—Basil.
† Φάρμακον Θανατήφορον, φθοροποῖον, δηλητήριον. ' Novissimo tanquam serpens
mordebit, et tanquam regulus punget.'—(Montanus et Mercerus.) ' Tamquam
hæmorrhois vel dipsas.'—(Tremelius.)

wherewithal the old serpent and red dragon envenoms the soul of man, but no sin (except it be that which is unto death) so mortal as this, which though not ever unpardonably, yet for the most part is also irrecoverably and inevitably unto death. Seest thou one bitten with any other snake, there is hope and help, as the father said of his son, when he had information of his gaming, of his prodigality, yea, of his whoring; but when he heard that he was poisoned with drunkenness, he gave him for dead, his case for desperate and forlorn. Age and experience often cures the other; but this increaseth with years, and parteth not till death. Whoring is a deep ditch, yet some few shall a man see return and lay hold on the ways of life, one of a thousand, but scarce one drunkard of ten thousand. One, Ambrose mentions, and one have I known, and but one of all that ever I knew or heard of. Often have I been asked, and often have I inquired, but never could meet with an instance, save one or two at the most. I speak of drunkards, not of one drunken,* of such who rarely and casually have, Noah-like, been surprised, overtaken at unawares. But if once a custom, ever necessity. Wine takes away the heart, and spoils the brain, over-throws the faculties and organs of repentance and resolution.† And is it not just with God, that he who will put out his natural light, should have his spiritual extinguished? He that will deprive himself of reason, should lose also the guide and pilot of reason, God's Spirit and grace; he that will wittingly and willingly make himself an habitation of unclean spirits, should not dispossess them at his own pleasure? Most aptly therefore is it translated by Tremelius, *hæmorrhois*, which Gesner confounds with the *dipsas*, or thirsty serpent, whose poison breedeth such thirst, drought, and inflammation, like that of ratsbane, that they never leave drinking till they burst and die withal. Would it not grieve and pity any Christian soul, to see a towardly hopeful young man, well-natured, well-nurtured, stung with this cockatrice, bewailing his own case, crying out against the baseness of the sin, inveighing against company, melting under the persuasions of friends, yea, protesting against all enticements, vow, covenant, and seriously indent with himself, and his friends, for the relinquishing of it; and yet if he meet with a companion that holds but up his finger, he follows him as a fool to the stocks, and as an ox to the slaughter-house, having no power to withstand the temptation, but in he goes with him to the tippling-house, not considering that its chambers are the chambers of death, and the guests, the guests of death; and there he continues as one bewitched, or conjured in a spell, out of which he returns not till he hath emptied his purse of money, his head of reason, and his heart of all his former seeming grace. There his eyes behold the strange woman, his heart speaketh perverse things, becoming heartless, as one (saith Solomon) in the heart of the sea, re-solving to continue, and return to his vomit, whatever it cost him, to make it his daily work. 'I was sick, and knew it not. I was struck, and felt it not; when I awake, I will seek it yet still,' ver. 34, 35. And why indeed (without a miracle) should any expect that one stung with this viper should shake it off, and ever recover of it again? Yea, so far are they from recovering themselves, that they infect and become contagious and pestilent to all they come near; the dragon infusing his venom, and assimilating his elves to himself in no sin so much as in this, that it becomes as good as meat and drink to them, to spend their wits and money, to compass ale-house after ale-house, yea, town after town, to transform others with their Circean cups, till they have made them

* De ebrioso, non de ebrio; cujus vivere est bibere.
† Principia lædit et cædit, hominem in fungum et testudinem vertit.

brutes and swine worse than themselves. The adulterer and usurer desire to enjoy their sin alone, but the chiefest pastime of a drunkard is to heat and overcome others with wine, that he may discover their nakedness, and glory in their foil and folly. In a word, excess of wine and the spirit of grace are opposites: the former expels the latter out of the heart, as smoke doth bees out of the hive, and makes the man a mere slave and prey to Satan and his snares; when by this poison he hath put out his eyes, and spoiled him of his strength, he useth him as the Philistines did Samson, leads him in a string whither he pleaseth, like a very drudge, scorn, and make-sport to himself and his imps, makes him grind in the mill of all kind of sins and vices. And that I take to be the reason why drunkenness is not specially prohibited in any one of the ten commandments, because it is not the single breach of any one, but in effect the violation of all and every one; it is no one sin, but all sins, because it is the inlet and sluice to all other sins.* The devil having moistened and steeped him in his liquor, shapes him like soft clay into what mould he pleaseth; having shaken off his rudder and pilot, dashes his soul upon what rocks, sands, and syrtes he listeth, and that with as much ease as a man may push down his body with the least thrust of his hand or finger. He that in his right wits and sober mood seems religious, modest, chaste, courteous, secret; in his drunken fits swears, blasphemes, rages, strikes, talks filthily, blabs all secrets, commits folly, knows no difference of persons or sexes, becomes wholly at Satan's command, as a dead organ to be enacted at his will and pleasure.† O that God would be pleased to open the eyes of some drunkard to see what a dunghill and carrion his soul becomes, and how loathsome effects follow upon this spiritual death, and sting of this cockatrice, which is the fountain of the other two following, temporal and eternal death.

And well may it be, that some such as are altogether fearless and careless of the former death, will yet tremble and be moved with that which I shall in the second place tell them. Among all other sins that are, none brings forth bodily death so frequently as this, none so ordinarily slays in the act of sin as this. And what can be more horrible than to die in the act of a sin without the act of repentance? I pronounce no definitive sentence of damnation upon any particular so dying; but what door of hope or comfort is left to their friends behind of their salvation? The whoremaster, he hopes to have a space and time to repent in age, though sometimes it pleaseth God that death strikes Cosbi and Zimri napping, as the devil is said to slay one of the popes in the instant of his adultery, and carry him quick to hell. The swearer and blasphemer hath commonly space, though seldom grace to repent and amend; and some rare examples stories afford, of some taken with oaths and blasphemies in their mouths. The thief and oppressor may live, and repent, and make restitution, as Zaccheus, though I have seen one slain right out with the timber he stole half an hour before; and heard of one that having stolen a sheep, and laying it down upon a stone to rest him, was ginned and hanged with the struggling of it about his neck. But these are extraordinary and rare cases. God sometimes practising martial law, and doing present execution, lest fools should say in their hearts, there were no God, or judgment; but conniving and deferring the most, that men might expect a judge coming, and a solemn day

---

* Omne vitium incendit et detegit, obstantem malis conatibus verecundiam removet.—(Senec. Epist. 84.) Ebrietas in se culpas complectitur omnes.

† Musto dolia ipsa rumpuntur, sic vino exæstuante quidquid in imo latet effertur. (Idem Ibidem.)

of judgment to come. But this sin of drunkenness is so odious to him, that he makes itself justice, judge, and executioner, slaying the ungodly with misfortune, bringing them to untimely, shameful ends in brutish and bestial manner, often in their own vomit and ordure; sending them sottish, sleeping, and senseless to hell, not leaving them either time, or reason, or grace to repent, and cry so much as ' Lord, have mercy upon us.' Were there (as in some cities in Italy) an office kept, or a record and register by every coroner in shires and counties, of such dismal events which God hath avenged this sin withal, what a volume would it have made within these few years in this our nation! How terrible a theatre of God's judgments against drunkards, such as might make their hearts to bleed and relent, if not their ears to tingle, to hear of a taste of some few such noted and re-markable examples of God's justice, as have come within the compass of mine own notice and certain knowledge; I think I should offend to conceal them from the world, whom they may happily keep from being the like to others, themselves.

An alewife in Kesgrave, near to Ipswich, who would needs force three serving-men (that had been drinking in her house, and were taking their leaves), to stay and drink the three *outs* first (that is, wit out of the head, money out of the purse, ale out of the pot), as she was coming towards them with the pot in her hand, was suddenly taken speechless and sick, her tongue swollen in her mouth, never recovered speech, the third day after died. This Sir Anthony Felton, the next gentleman and justice, with divers other eye-witnesses of her in sickness, related to me; whereupon I went to the house with two or three witnesses, inquired the truth of it.

Two servants of a brewer in Ipswich, drinking for a rump of a turkey, struggling in their drink for it, fell into a scalding caldron backwards; whereof the one died presently, the other lingeringly and painfully, since my coming to Ipswich.

Anno 1619. A miller in Bromeswell coming home drunk from Wood-bridge (as he oft did), would needs go and swim in the mill-pond. His wife and servants, knowing he could not swim, dissuaded him, once by en-treaty got him out of the water, but in he would needs go again, and there was drowned. I was at the house to inquire of this, and found it to be true.

In Barnwell, near to Cambridge, one at the sign of the plough, a lusty young man, with two of his neighbours, and one woman in their company, agreed to drink a barrel of strong beer. They drunk up the vessel. Three of them died within four and twenty hours, the fourth hardly escaped, after great sickness. This I have under a justice of peace's hand, near dwelling, besides the common fame.

A butcher in Haslingfield, hearing the minister inveigh against drunken-ness, being at his cups in the alehouse, fell a jesting and scoffing at the minister and his sermons. As he was drinking, the drink, or something in the cup, quackled him, stuck so in his throat that he could not get it up nor down, but strangled him presently.

At Tillingham, in Dengy Hundred, in Essex, three young men meeting to drink strong waters, fell by degrees to half pints. One fell dead in the room, and the other,* prevented by company coming in, escaped not with-out much sickness.

At Bungey, in Norfolk, three coming out of an alehouse in a very dark evening, swore they thought it was not darker in hell itself. One of them fell off the bridge into the water, and was drowned. The second fell off his

* That is, ' the others.'—ED.

horse. The third, sleeping on the ground by the river's side, was frozen to death. This have I often heard, but have no certain ground for the truth of it.

A bailiff of Hadly, upon the Lord's day, being drunk at Melford, would needs get upon his mare to ride through the street, affirming (as the report goes) that his mare would carry him to the devil. His mare casts him off, and broke his neck instantly. Reported by sundry sufficient witnesses.

Company drinking in an alehouse at Harwich in the night, over against one Mr Russel's, and by him, out of his window, once or twice willed to depart. At length he came down, and took one of them, and made as if he would carry him to prison, who, drawing his knife, fled from him, and was, three days after, taken out of the sea, with the knife in his hand. Related to me by Mr Russel himself, mayor of the town.

At Tenby, in Pembrokeshire, a drunkard being exceeding drunk, broke himself all to pieces off an high and steep rock in a most fearful manner, and yet the occasion and circumstances of his fall so ridiculous as I think not fit to relate, lest in so serious a judgment I should move laughter to the reader.

A glazier in Chancery Lane, in London, noted formerly for profession, fell to a common course of drinking, whereof, being oft by his wife and many Christian friends admonished, yet presuming much of God's mercy to himself, continued therein, till upon a time, having surcharged his stomach with drink, he fell a vomiting, broke a vein, lay two days in extreme pain of body and distress of mind, till in the end, recovering a little comfort, he died. Both these examples related to me by a gentleman of worth, upon his own knowledge.

Four sundry instances of drunkards wallowing and tumbling in their drink, slain by carts, I forbear to mention, because such examples are so common and ordinary.

A yeoman's son, in Northamptonshire, being drunk at Wellingborough on a market-day, would needs ride his horse in a bravery over the ploughed lands, fell from his horse, and brake his neck. Reported to me by a kinsman of his own.

A knight notoriously given to drunkenness, carrying sometimes pails of drink into the open field to make people drunk withal, being upon a time drinking with company, a woman comes in, delivering him a ring with this poesy, ' Drink and die,' saying to him, This is for you, which he took and wore, and within a week after came to his end by drinking. Reported by sundry, and justified by a minister dwelling within a mile of the place.

Two examples have I known of children that murdered their own mothers in drink, and one notorious drunkard that attempted to kill his father, of which being hindered, he fired his barn, and was afterward executed. One of these formerly in print.

At a tavern in Bread Street, in London, certain gentlemen drinking health to their lords on whom they had dependence, one desperate wretch steps to the table's end, lays hold on a pottle pot full of Canary sack, swears a deep oath, What! will none here drink a health to my noble lord and master? and so setting the pottle pot to his mouth, drinks it off to the bottom; was not able to rise up or to speak when he had done, but fell into a deep snoring sleep, and being removed, laid aside, and covered by one of the servants of the house, attending the time of the drinking, was within the space of two hours irrecoverably dead. Witnessed at the time of the printing hereof, by the same servant that stood by him in the act, and helped to remove him.

In Dengy Hundred, near Maldon, about the beginning of his majesty's reign, there fell out an extraordinary judgment upon five or six that plotted a solemn drinking at one of their houses ; laid in beer for the once, drunk healths in a strange manner, and died thereof within a few weeks, some sooner, and some later. Witnessed to me by one that was with one of them on his deathbed, to demand a debt, and often spoken of by Mr Heydon, late preacher of Maldon, in the hearing of many. The particular circumstances were exceeding remarkable, but having not sufficient proof for the particulars, I will not report them.

One of Aylesham, in Norfolk, a notorious drunkard, drowned in a shallow brook of water, with his horse by him.

Whilst this was at the press, a man eighty-five years old or thereabout, in Suffolk, overtaken with wine (though never in all his life before, as he himself said a little before his fall, seeming to bewail his present condition, and others that knew him so say of him), yet, going down a pair of stairs, against the persuasion of a woman sitting by him in his chamber, fell, and was so dangerously hurt, as he died soon after, not being able to speak from the time of his fall to his death.

The names of the parties thus punished, I forbear, for the kindred's sake yet living.

If conscionable ministers of all places of the land, would give notice of such judgments as come within the compass of their certain knowledge, it might be a great mean to suppress this sin, which reigns everywhere, to the scandal of our nation, and high displeasure of Almighty God.

These may suffice for a taste of God's judgments. Easy were it to abound in sundry particular casualties, and fearful examples of this nature. Drunkard, that which hath befallen any one of these may befall thee, if thou wilt dally with this cockatrice, whatever leagues thou makest with death, and dispensations thou givest thyself from the like. Some of these were young, some were rich, some thought themselves as wise as thou ; none of them ever looked for such ignominious ends more than thou, whoever thou art. If thou hatest such ends, God give thee grace to decline such courses.

If thou beest yet insensate with wine, void of wit and fear, I know not what further to mind thee of, but of that third and worst sting of all the rest, which will ever be gnawing and never dying ; which if thou wilt not fear here, sure thou art to feel there, when the red dragon hath gotten thee into his den, and shall fill thy soul with the gall of scorpions, where thou shalt yell and howl for a drop of water to cool thy tongue withal, and shalt be denied so small a refreshing, and have no other liquor to allay thy thirst but that which the lake of brimstone shall afford thee. And that worthily, for that thou wouldst incur the wrath of the Lamb for so base and sordid a sin as drunkenness, of which thou mayest think as venially and slightly as thou wilt. But Paul, that knew the danger of it, gives thee fair warning, and bids thee not deceive thyself, expressly and by name mentioning it among the mortal sins excluding from the kingdom of heaven, 1 Cor. vi. 10. And the prophet Isaiah tells thee, that for it hell hath enlarged itself, opened its mouth wide, and without measure, Isa. v. 14 ;' and therefore shall the multitude and their pomp, and the jolliest among them, descend into it. Consider this, you that are strong to pour in drink, that love to drink sorrow and care away. And be you well assured, that there you shall drink enough for all, having for every drop of your former bousings, vials, yea, whole seas of God's wrath, never to be exhaust.

Now, then, I appeal from yourselves in drink to yourselves in your sober fits. Reason a little the case, and tell me calmly, would you, for your own or any man's pleasure, to gratify friend or companion, if you knew there had been a toad in the wine-pot (as twice I have known happened, to the death of drinkers); or did you think that some Cæsar Borgia or Brasutus had tempered the cup; or did you see but a spider in the glass,—would you, or durst you, carouse it off? And are you so simple to fear the poison that can kill the body, and not that which killeth the soul and body ever, yea, for ever and ever, and if it were possible for more than for ever, for evermore? Oh, thou vain fellow, what tellest thou me of friendship or good fellowship? Wilt thou account him thy friend or good fellow that draws thee into his company that he may poison thee, and never thinks he hath given thee right entertainment or shewed thee kindness enough till he hath killed thy soul with his kindness, and with beer made thy body a carcase fit for the bier, a laughing and loathing-stock, not to boys and girls alone, but to men and angels? Why rather sayest thou not to such, What have I to do with you, ye sons of Belial, ye poisonful generation of vipers, that hunt for the precious life of a man? Oh, but there are few good wits or great spirits now-a-days but will pot it a little for company. What hear I? Oh, base and low-spirited times, if that were true! if we were fallen into such lees of time foretold of by Seneca,* in which all were so drowned in the dregs of vices, that it should be virtue and honour to bear most drink. But thanks be to God, who has reserved many thousands of men, and, without all comparison, more witty and valorous than such pot-wits and spirits of the buttery, who never bared their knees to drink healths, nor ever needed to whet their wits with wine, or arm their courage with pot-harness. And if it were so, yet, if no such wits or spirits shall ever enter into heaven without repentance, let my spirit never come and enter into their paradise; ever abhor to partake of their brutish pleasures, lest I partake of their endless woes. If young Cyrus could refuse to drink wine, and tell Astyages he thought it to be poison, for he saw it metamorphose men into beasts and carcases, what would he have said if he had known that which we may know, that the wine of drunkards is the wine of Sodom and Gomorrah, Deut. xxxii. 32, their grapes the grapes of gall, their clusters the clusters of bitterness, the juice of dragons and the venom of asps. In which words Moses, in a full commentary upon Solomon, largely expressing that he speaks here more briefly, ' It stings like the serpent, and bites like the cockatrice;' to the which I may not unfitly add that of Paul's, and think I ought to write of such with more passion and compassion than he did of the Christians in his time, which sure were not such monsters as ours in the shapes of Christians, ' whose god is their belly' (whom they serve with drink-offerings), ' whose glory is their shame, and whose end is damnation.'

What then? Take we pleasure in thundering out hell against drunkards? Is there nothing but death and damnation to drunkards? Nothing else to them, so continuing, so dying. But what? Is there no help nor hope, no amulet, antidote, or triacle? Are there no precedents found of recovery? Ambrose, I remember, tells of one that, having been a spectacle of drunkenness, proved, after his conversion, a pattern of sobriety.† And I myself must confess that one have I known, yet living, who, having drunk out his

---

* Seneca de Beneficiis, lib. i. cap. 10, Quum plurimum meri sumpsisse virtus erit, &c.

† Qui ludibrium fuerat ebrietatis, factus est postea sobrietatis exemplum.—Amb. de Hes.

bodily eyes, had his spiritual eyes opened, proved diligent in hearing and practising. Though the pit be deep, miry, and narrow, like that dungeon into which Jeremiah was put, yet, if it please God to let down the cords of his divine mercy, and cause the party to lay hold thereon, it is possible they may escape the snares of death. There is, even for the most debauched drunkard that ever was, a sovereign medicine,* a rich triacle, of force enough to cure and recover his disease, to obtain his pardon, and to furnish him with strength to overcome this deadly poison, fatal to the most. And though we may well say of it, as men out of experience do of quartan agues, that it is the disgrace of all moral physic, of all reproofs, counsels, and admonitions, yet is there a salve for this sore. There came one from heaven that trod the winepress of his Father's fierceness, drunk off a cup tempered with all the bitterness of God's wrath and the devil's malice, that he might heal even such as have drunk deepest of the sweet cup of sin. And let all such know, that in all the former discovery of this poison I have only aimed to cause them feel their sting, and that they might with earnest eyes behold the brazen serpent, and seriously repair to him for mercy and grace, who is perfectly able to eject even this kind, which so rarely and hardly is thrown out where once he gets possession. This seed of the woman is able to bruise this serpent's head. Oh, that they would listen to the gracious offers of Christ! If once there be wrought in thy soul a spiritual thirst after mercy, as the thirsty land hath after rain, a longing appetite after the water that comes out of the Rock, after the blood that was shed for thee, then let him that is athirst come, let him drink of the water of life without any money, of which if thou hast took but one true and thorough draught, thou wilt never long after thy old puddle waters of sin any more. Easy will it be for thee, after thou hast tasted of the bread and wine in thy Father's house, ever to loathe the husks and swill thou wert wont to follow after with greediness. The Lord Christ will bring thee into his mother's house, Cant. viii. 2, cause thee to drink of his spiced wine, of the new wine of the pomegranate. Yea, he will bring thee into his cellar, spread his banner of love over thee, stay thee with flagons, fill thee with his love, till thou beest sick and overcome with the sweetness of his consolations, Cant. ii. 4. In other drink there is excess, but here can be no danger. The devil hath his invitation, ' Come, let us drink;' and Christ hath his *inebriamini,* ' Be ye filled with the Spirit.' †￼
Here is a fountain set open, and proclamation made; and if it were possible for the brutishest drunkard in the world to know who it is that offereth, and what kind of water he offereth, he would ask, and God would give it frankly without money; he should drink liberally, be satisfied, and out of his belly should sally springs of the water of life, quenching and extinguishing all his inordinate longings after stolen water of sin and death.

All this while little hope have I to work upon many drunkards, especially by a sermon read (of less life and force in God's ordinance, and in its own nature, than preached). My first drift is, to stir up the spirits of parents and masters, who in all places complain of this evil, robbing them of good servants and dutiful children, by all care and industry to prevent it in their domestical education, by carrying a watchful and restraining hand over them. Parents, if you love either soul or body, thrift or piety, look to keep them from the infection. Lay all the bars of your authority, cautions, threats, and charges for the avoiding of this epidemical pestilence. If any of them be bitten of this cockatrice, sleep not, rest not, till you have cured

* Magna medicina tollit peccata magna.—Am.
† Habet Deus suum inebriamini, &c.—Bernard in Cant.

them of it, if you love their health, husbandry, grace, their present or
future lives. Dead are they while they live, if they live in this sin.
Mothers, lay about you, as Bathsheba, with all entreaties, ' What, my son,
my son of my loves and delights, wine is not for you,' &c.

My next hope is, to arouse and awaken the vigilancy of all faithful pastors
and teachers. I speak not to such stars as this dragon hath swept down
from heaven with its tail; for of such the prophets, the fathers of the
primitive, yea, all ages, complain of. I hate and abhor to mention this
abomination. To alter the proverb, ' As drunk as a beggar,' to a gentleman is odious; but to a man of God, to an angel, how harsh and hellish a
sound is it in a Christian's ears! I speak, therefore, to sober watchmen,
' Watch and be sober,' and labour to keep your charges sober and watchful,
that they may be so found of Him that comes like a thief in the night.
Two means have you of great virtue for the quelling of this serpent,—
zealous preaching and praying against it. It is an old received antidote,
that man's spittle, especially fasting spittle, is mortal to serpents.* Saint
Donatus is famous in story for spitting upon a dragon that kept a highway,
and devoured many passengers. This have I made good observation of,
that where God hath raised up zealous preachers, in such towns this serpent hath no nestling, no stabling or denning. If this will not do, Augustine
enforceth another, which I conceive God's and man's laws allow us upon
the reason he gives. If Paul (saith he) forbid to eat with such our common
bread in our own private houses, how much more the Lord's body in church
assemblies? If in our times this were strictly observed, the serpent would
soon languish and vanish. In the time of an epidemical disease, such as
the sweating or sneezing sickness, a wise physician would leave the study
of all other diseases to find out the cure of the present raging evil; if
Chrysostom were now alive, the bent of all his homilies, or at least one
part of them, should be spent to cry down drunkenness, as he did swearing
in Antioch, never desisting to reprove it till (if not the fear of God, yet) his
importunity made them weary of the sin.

Such Anakims and Zanzummims as the spiritual sword will not work
upon, I turn them over to the secular arm, with a signification of the
dangerous and contagious spreading of this poison in the veins and bowels
of the commonwealth, in the church's, and Christ's name also, entreating
them to carry a more vigilant eye over the dens and burrows of this
cockatrice, superfluous, blind, and clandestine ale-houses : I mean the very
pest houses of the nation. Which I could wish had all for their sign, a
picture of some hideous serpent, or a pair of them, as the best hieroglyphic
of the genius of the place, to warn passengers to shun and avoid the danger
of them. Who sees and knows not, that some one needless alehouse in a
country town, undoes all the rest of the houses in it, eating up the thrift
and fruit of their labours ; the ill manner of sundry places being there to
meet in some one night of the week, and spend what they have gathered
and spared all the days of the same before, to the prejudice of their poor
wives and children at home, and upon the Lord's day, after evening prayers
there to quench and drown all the good lessons they have heard that day
at church. If this go on, what shall become of us in time ? If woe be to
single drunkards, is not a national woe to be feared and expected of a
nation overrun with drunkenness ? Had we no other sin reigning but this,

---

* Ut serpens hominis quum tacta salivis,
　Disperit, ac sese mandendo conficit ipsa.—
　　　Lucretius : vide etiam Ophilium et Gesnerum, &c.

which cannot reign alone, will not God justly spew us out of his mouth for this alone ? We read of whole countries wasted, dispeopled, by serpents. Pliny tells us of the Amyclæ, Lycophron of Salamis, Herodotus of the Neuri, utterly depopulate and made unhabitable by them. Verily, if this cockatrice multiply and get head amongst us a while longer, as they have of late begun, where shall the people have sober servants to till their lands, or children to hold and enjoy them ? They speak of draining fens ; but if this evil be not stopped, we shall all shortly be drowned with it. I wish the magistracy, gentry, and yeomanry would take it to serious consideration, how to deal with this serpent, before he grow too strong and fierce for them. It is past the egg already,* and much at that pass, of which Augustine complains of in his time, that he scarce knew what remedy to advise, but thought it required the meeting of a general council.† The best course I think of is, if the great persons would first begin thorough reformation in their own families, banish the spirits of their butteries, abandon that foolish and vicious custom, as Ambrose and Basil calls it, of drinking healths,‡ and making that a sacrifice to God for the health of others, which is rather a sacrifice to the devil, and a bane of their own. I remember well, Sigismund the emperor's grave answer, wherein there concurred excellent wisdom and wit (seldom meeting in one saying) which he gave before the Council of Constance, to such as proposed a reformation of the church, to begin with the Franciscans and Minorites. You will never do any good, saith he, unless you begin with the Majorites first. Sure till it be out of fashion and grace in gentlemen's tables, butteries, and cellars, hardly shall you persuade the countryman to lay it down, who, as in fashions, so in vices, will ever be the ape of the gentry.

If this help not, I shall then conclude it to be such an evil as is only by sovereign power, and the king's hand, curable. And verily next under the word of God, which is omnipotent, how potent and wonder-working is the word of a king !§ When both meet as the sun and some good star in a benign conjunction, what enemy shall stand before the sword of God and Gideon ? What vice so predominant which these subdue not ? If the lion roar, what beast of the forest shall not tremble and hide their head ? Have we not a noble experiment hereof yet fresh in our memory, and worthy never to die, in the timely and speedy suppression of that impudent abomination of women's mannish habits, threatening the confusion of sexes, and ruin of modesty? The same royal hand and care the church and commonwealth implores for the vanquishing of this poison, no less pernicious, more spreading, and prevailing. ' Take us these little foxes,' was wont to be the suit of the church, for they gnabble our grapes, and hurt our tender branches ; but now it is become more serious. Take us these serpents, lest they destroy our vines, vinedressers, vineyards and all. This hath ever been royal game. How famous, in the story of Diodorus Siculus, is the royal munificence of Ptolemy, king of Egypt, for provision of nets, and maintenance of huntsmen, for the taking and destroying of serpents, noxious and noisome to his country. The like of Philip in Aris-

* Εγω δε επαινω μαλιστα εκεινους, οσοι υποφυομενα των κακων εγκοπτουσι. —Ælian. lib. 14. cap. 27.

† Tanta potentia hujus mali, ut sanari prorsus sine concilii autoritate non possit. —Aug. Ep. 64 ad Aurelium.

‡ Bibamus pro salute Imperatorum, comitum. Oh stultitiam, vitium sacrificium putant.—Amb. de Helia, &c. Basil. Hom contra Ebrios.

§ Where the word of a king is, there is power, Eccles. viii. 4.

totle, and of Attilius Regulus in Aulus Gellius. The emblem mentioned at large by Plutarch, engraven on Hercules' shield, what is it but a symbol of the divine honour due to princes following their Herculean labours, in subduing the like hydras, too mighty for any inferior person to take in hand? It is their honour to tread upon basilisks, and trample dragons under their feet. Solomon thinks it not unworthy his pen to discourse their danger.

A royal and elegant oration is happily and worthily preserved in the large volume of ancient writings, with this title, *Oratio magnifici et pacifici Edgari Regis, habita ad Dunstanum Archiep. Episcopos, &c.* The main scope whereof is, to excite the clergy's care and devotion for the suppressing of this vice for the common good. Undertakers of difficult plots promise themselves speed and effect, if once they interest the king, and make him party. And what more generally beneficial can be devised or proposed than this, with more honour and less charge to be effected, if it shall please his Majesty but to make trial of the strength of his temporal and spiritual arms. For the effecting of it, if this help not, what have we else remaining, but wishes and prayers to cast out this kind withal? God help us! To him I commend the success of these labours, and the vanquishing of this cockatrice.

THE HAPPINESS OF PRACTICE.

TO THE

WORSHIPFUL THE BAILIFFS, BURGHERS, AND COMMONALTY

OF THE TOWN OF IPSWICH.

SPEECH requires presence, writings have their use in absence; sermons are as showers of rain that water for the instant, books are as snow that lies longer on the earth: these may preach when the author cannot, and which is more, when he is not. Zisca desired his skin might serve the Bohemians in their wars, when his body could no more do it. Such is my affection towards you, that I ever desire to be sounding in your ears, and putting you in mind of these things, in season, out of season, in absence, in presence, whiles I remain in this tabernacle, and what I may, even after dissolution. For which purpose I have improved a little leisure, occasioned against my will, to whet upon you the scope and fruit of all my former labours, whose they are, and whose I am. To whom should I wish happiness but to you, whose happiness shall redound upon mine own head, and well-doing be put upon mine own account? And what other can be your happiness, but to be doers of what you are knowers? One-half of the Scriptures I have handled among you, endeavoured to acquaint you with the whole counsel of God; and what is now the top of all my ambition, but to make you doers of what you have been hearers? Wherein consists the delight of a husbandman? Not in his ploughing, sowing, or carting, but to see the furrows crowned, and barns filled, with the fruit of his labours.* When we preach we sow the seed; when we see good desires, then the corn sprouts up; when the people begin to do well, then it blades; but, when they are abund-

---

* Quum desideria bona concipimus, semen in terram mittimus; quum vero opera recta incipimus, herba sumus; quum ad profectum boni operis crescimus, ad spicam pervenimus; quum in ejusdem boni operis perfectione solidamur, bonum frumentum in spica proferimus.—Greg. in Hom.

ant in good works, then are the ears laden with corn ; when stedfast and perse-vering to the end, then are they ripe for God's barn. It was a pride in Montanus to overween his Pepuza and Tymium, two pelting parishes in Phrygia, and to call them Jerusalem,* as if they had been the only churches in the world. But this is the commendable zeal of every true pastor, to adorn his own lot, and to wish his garden as the Eden of God. Such shall you be, if God shall please to water the means you have with the dew of his Spirit, to continue and increase your love to hearing and doing; to the muzzling of the mouths of all scoffers and scorners at profession, to the joy, crown, and eternal happiness of your own souls, and such as God hath made watchmen over them, and of me the unworthiest of the rest.

SAMUEL WARD.

* Πέπουσαν κì Τυμιον Ιεϱουσάλημ ὀνομασας. —Euseb. 1. 5, cap xvii.

THE HAPPINESS OF PRACTICE.

These things if you know, happy are you if you do them.—
JOHN XIII. 17.

THE fastening nail of the chief Master of the assemblies, the great Shepherd's peg, driving home, and making sure, all his former counsels, chosen as a farewell close, making and leaving a deep impression of all his deeds and sayings, as the last strong and loud knoll of a bell, that ends all the peals going before. A text that puts life into all other texts, urging the life of them, which is the practice of them, and is therefore aptly and duly pronounced by many at the end of their sermons. A sermon upon which text the world hath as much need of as of any one yet extant; the multitude of them, as statutes and proclamations, wanting yet one to enforce the observation of the rest. The necessity of doing was the scope of our Lord's solemn and uncouth action of girding himself with a towel, rising from his magisterial seat, washing and wiping his disciples' feet. He had indeed two other by-ends: one mystical, intimated in his dialogue with Peter, typifying the great end of his descent from heaven, and begirding himself with our flesh, viz., that he might totally wash our souls in the bath of justification (ἐν ὁλονιπτρῷ) once for all, and partially in the laver of regeneration so often (ἐν ποδονιπτρῷ) as we soil our feet in the mire of this world by daily sins of infirmity. The other moral, to set his disciples a pattern of humility and love, stooping to the meanest offices of mutual service, without emulation or affectation of priority, which he foresaw would else be the bane of their sacred function. But his third and most principal aim was, by this his both verbal and real strange kind of lesson, to learn them not so much what they knew not as the use of doing that they knew, else would words only have served the turn, and not so much ado have needed; but he first does the things, and then expresses his intent, ' These things if you do,' &c.

In this conditional benediction, observe first the object on which happiness is conferred, and to which it is confined: ' These things.' Secondly, the two acts required hereto: ' if you know, if you do;' chiefly, the chief of them is, ' if you do.' To which happiness is fore-annexed specially: ' Happy are you if ye do,' &c.

' These things.' The knowledge and practice of these things only blesseth; these main arch-mysteries of faith, and these divine and cardinal virtues of love and humility, symbolised in their ablution, and not the doing or knowing of all the natural, moral, and manual sciences in the world besides.

If one knew all the circle of learning, and knew, as was said of Berengarius, all that was knowable, all the rules of policy, secrets of state, mysteries of trading, and could execute them all; yet in his such knowing and doing he might not bless himself, were not happy, nor so to be reputed of Christians. The right placing or misplacing of happiness is the rudder of a man's life, the fountain of his well or ill doing; according to which men take their marks, and shoot right or wrong, all the actions of their lives. He that admireth in his heart, and blesseth with his mouth, any other idol of good, instead of this only true good, must needs miss of his end, and be a miserable man, grossly mistaking his marks, as silly country people that oftentimes give terms of honours and majesties to mean persons. So do most people, when they transfer this transcendent word and stately thing happiness unto any shadow of skill save of these things to which it is perpetually restrained in Scriptures, Psalm i., Luke ii., James i. Insomuch that Christ himself was displeased when they bestowed it on the paps and womb of his mother, in comparison of hearing and keeping his Father's will. Here then, and here only, is to be found the lost jewel of happiness, which well may be likened to a stake set up in the midst of a field, which blinded men grope after, to make the beholders sport at their wanderings.

Augustine tells of a mountebank that undertook, in a city of great trading, to tell every man his wish, which was in his fallible conjecture, to buy cheap and sell dear. But here he who hath made, and knoweth the hearts of all, tells every man the end of his desire; and that which is more, shews him the way of attaining them. 'These things if you know, and if you do them, happy are you.'

The first if, providently premixed, and cautelously presupposed by Christ, intimates that knowledge must be the pilot, guide, and usher of practice, else superstitious deeds done by rote and random, the blind whelps of ignorant devotion, God regards not. Good works, the fruits of faith, and children of a believer that knows what he does, such are only pleasing in his sight. Christ divinely foresaw the devilish policy of subtile worldlings, that would cry up practice to cry down knowledge, as cunning papists will extol St James to disparage St Paul; praise good meanings and works, with an evil eye to hearing sermons and reading good books; and carnal protestants be ever commending reading to disgrace preaching; and another sort ever talking of a good heart, a good meaning, and the power of religion, ever disliking all show and profession of it; which, if well observed, are the least and worst doers in a country. Which Satanical sophism St James deeply prevents; who, though the chief aim of his epistle was to urge hypocrites to be doers, and vain boasters of justifying faith to justify their faith by their works, yet forelaid this caveat, 'Be swift to hear:' needful even in these hearing and knowing times, wherein though knowledge cover the earth as waters the sea, yet may the Lord have justly a controversy with the land, or a great number at least in it, like dry rocks in the midst of this sea, who have not a dram of saving and well-grounded knowledge. But this is but a pre-requisite to the main thing here required, which happiness is intendedly fore-placed, knowledge being but a step to this turret of happiness, 'happy are you if you do them,'

Here is the labour, here is the difficulty, here is the happiness, in the conjunction of doing with knowing, to practise that we know; to perform the duties prescribed in the gospel; to believe the things to be believed, and to do the things to be done; the sum of faith and love, sweetly coupled in this significant ablution of his disciples' feet.

Three noble ends divinity propounds to her followers: the first and greatest, God's glory; the second, next to that, man's own content here, and salvation hereafter; the last like to the former, the edification and conversion of our neighbours. In the attainment of these is a Christian's perfection and happiness, none whereof bare theory shall ever more than come near. All three practice, joined thereto, fully apprehends.

Of these three, that must needs be the noblest which God primarily intended in the revelation of his will to mankind, and Moses oft tells us, is that we might observe to do them. For if (as Wolphius reasoneth by a distribution) he had given us his laws to preserve only, he safelier might have committed them to iron coffers and marble pillars; if only to talk and prate of them, better to geese and parrots; if only for contemplation, to owls in ivy-woods, or to monks in cloisters, and not to all sorts of people. His scope sure was not to make trial of the wits of men, who could sharpliest conceive; nor of their memories, who could faithfulliest retain; of their eloquence, who could roundliest discourse; but of their wills, who would most obediently do them: this being his chief honour, to have his throne and command, not in the head and brains, but in the strongholds of their hearts and lives. For what shall God reward thee, O man, but for that which men praise God for in thee? Now for admirable gifts of science and learning, men may admire thee, but they give God thanks only for the good they receive from thee. The sun itself, if it did not shine and give warmth unto the creatures, were the glorious hue of it ten times more than it is, none would half so much bless God for it.

The men for whom our heavenly Father is glorified, are such whose works shine afore men, who warm the loins of the poor, and with their knowledge are an eye to the blind. I can hardly believe that God ever made any creature only to behold; neither star, pearl, flower, or feathered fowl, only to shew their glorious outsides, but to have influence, virtues, qualities, beneficial to mankind; much less a man to know only, or an art only to be known, but all to his glory, and man's service, which to effect is all the glory of men and arts. Some sciences, I know, in comparison of others more operative, are termed speculative; but not one of these, whose speculation tends and ends not in some operation, by which man is profited, and God honoured; specially divinity, which makes us his workmanship, not to knowledge; but to good works, to the praise of his grace. Who commends a schoolmaster, whose scholars can say and understand their rules, but speak not and write not any good styles by them? A captain, whose soldiers can skill of military terms and orders, unless their arts and exploits of war be suitable? Who praiseth a horse that feeds well, but is not deedy for the race or travel, speed or length? Little says the Scripture of the learning of the apostles, but much of their *acts*. These are the richest, and usual styles of commendation in Scripture. Moses, ' a man mighty in words and deeds;' Cornelius, ' a man fearing God, and giving much alms;' the Centurion, worthy of favour, for ' he hath built us a synagogue;' Dorcas ' made thus many coats for the poor;' Gaius, the ' host of the church,' &c. Such benefactors their works shall follow them, and praise them in the gates here, yea, at the great day obtain that, ' Come, you blessed of my Father: for I was naked, and you clothed me.' For such men God is blessed of men, and such men shall be blessed of God in their deeds; and as the more knowing without doing shall procure the more stripes, because God for them is the more blasphemed; so the more doing with knowing, shall have double honour, because God was doubly honoured in them. 'Behold I come quickly, and my reward is in mine hand, to give every man according to his deeds.' Blessed are they that do my commandments. If you know them, and do not, miserable are you; but these things if you know, and do them, you are the happiest men living.

The second branch of happiness, wherein doing hath the advantage of knowing, is in the personal benefit, consisting in the present sweetness, and future gain accruing thereby. Some luscious delight, yea, a kind of ravishing douceness there is in studying good books, ruminating on good notions, not unlike that which is in tasting and swallowing sweet meats, which made the epicure in Ælian wish his throat as long as the crane's; but all the benefit is in the strength and nourishment it breedeth after concoction, when thoughts breed works, and studies turn into manners, when the fat pasture is seen in the flesh and fleece of the sheep. One apple of the tree of life hath more sweet relish, than ten of the tree of knowledge of good and evil; which yet we fondly prefer in our longing, ever since our first parents' teeth were set on edge therewithal. For instance, thou findest thine ear tickled with an elaborate discourse of temperance, but try the practice of it, and tell me if it bring thee not in sundry real commodities to body and mind, beyond a poor, auricular transient titillation. Were it not for the different energy and efficacy in the heart and life, there might be well near as much pleasure in reading the witty commendations of folly, or pride, as in the sound tractate of wisdom, and humility; I had almost said in the language of fools; in the reading of Sir Philip, as St Peter.

All discourses of faith and hope are but dry things, in comparison of the acts and practice of them, which are delicate above the honey and the honeycomb, sweeter than the taste of any nectar. Some say, the study of the law is cragged, that if the gain of practice did not sweeten it, few would plod upon Ployden. But, I believe, few would study Saint Paul, and preach as Saint Paul did, instantly in season and out of season (quaintly and rarely they might for credit and preferment), but painfully and profitably, I hardly believe they would; fervently and feelingly they cannot, except the sweetness of their practice drives and constrains them. Of all men I hold them fools that bend their studies to divinity, not intending to be doers, as well as students and preachers; not much wiser, such as will be professors of religion and not practitioners. The parables in the Talmud fit their folly well, resembling them to such as plough and sow all the year, and never reap; to the grasshopper that sings all the summer and wants in the winter; to women ever conceiving, and ever making abortion, never coming to the birth; and, best of all, that of Christ, distinguishing hearers into foolish, that build on the sand of hearing, and professing, blown down with every puff of trouble; and the wise, that build on the rock of doing, unshakable. Search all the Scripture, and see if any covenants or grants were made to knowing, and not all to doing. Is not the ancient tenor of the law, 'Do this and live?' and the gospel, 'Believe and live?' which implies an act to be done, and that act implying sundry consequents and fruits of it: 'He that doth my Father's will, he is my brother and sister.' 'Not every one that saith, Lord, Lord, but he that doth my Father's will.' To him that doth ill shall be tribulation and anguish, to every soul, of Jew and Grecian; to him that doth well shall be honour and peace upon all the Israel of God. Unto whom shall that *Euge* be given at that great day but the doer; and in what form, but, ' Well done, good servant,' that hast not buried thy talent in a napkin? He himself expresseth the manner: ' Behold, I come quickly ; my reward is in my hand, to give every man according to his works. Blessed is every one that doth my commandments, that he may eat of the tree of life, and enter through the gates into the city.' In all which, happiness in this life and that to come, is conferred upon the living acts and exercises, not upon the dead habits of any grace whatsoever. In all labour there is abundance, but in the conceits of the brain and talk of the lips, nothing but emptiness and misery. If one could do as much as Mr Stoughton prints, and many credible witnesses report of the young gentlewoman of nine years old, that can say every syllable of the New Testament by heart, and, upon trial, not fail in returning a line without the right chapter and verse, and yet practise never a jot nor tittle of it, happier were such as never heard word of God's word. If one should take pains to get together a great number of songs, curiously set, artificially composed, yea, and knew how to sing or play them, and yet never heard them sung or played, what pleasure had he of them? The practice and use of all operative arts is all in all ; in divinity, the chief of all, which else is as the vine, excellent only in the sweet juice of it, otherwise fit not so much as for pin or peg.

Next to God's glory and a man's own good, a Christian placeth much happiness in winning and edifying others ; to which purpose a speechless life hath more life in it than a lifeless speech. Irresistible is the *Suada* of a good life above a fair profession. Chrysostom * calls good works unanswerable syllogisms, invincible demonstrations, to confute and convert pagans. Withal, tells us they have a louder language than the sun and moon, whose sound yet goes over all the world, publishing God's glory, not in Hebrew, Greek, or Latin, which many barbarous nations understand not, but in an oratory they can better skill of. An archer puts not more force into an arrow he shoots, than the life of the speaker into his speech ; whence it comes that one and the same sermon, or counsel, in several men's mouths, differ as much as a shaft out of a giant's, or child's, shooting. Miracles (says he) are now ceased, good conversation comes in their place ; the apostles might have preached long enough without audience, or acceptance, had not their miracles, as bells, tolled to their sermons, and as harbingers, made way into men's hearts for their doctrine ; by such weapons they conquered the world, as Gideon's soldiers the Midianites, carrying in one hand the burning lamp of a good life, and in the other the loud, shrill trumpets of preaching ;† otherwise, plain men will answer as Jovinian, to the orthodox and Arian bishops contending about the faith. Of your learning and subtle disputations I cannot so well judge, but I can well mark and observe which of your behaviours is most peaceable and fruitful ; and as one, Moses,‡ renowned for piety, to Lucius, reputed an Arian bishop, tendering the confession of his faith to clear himself: Tush, says he, what tellest thou me of the faith of the ears ? Let me have the faith of the hands. I will rather go without my instalment than take it of hands imbrued in blood, bribery, and injustice, as all know and report thine to be. Arguments are dark, and persuasions dull things, to lives and actions ; and most people are like sheep, easilier following example than led or driven by pre-

* In 1 Cor. i. 10, συλλογισμους ἀναντιρρητους, φωνην λαμπροτεραν.

† Theod. in Jud., φέροντες λαμπάδας πραγματῶν ἐν τῇ δεξίᾳ, καὶ σαλπιγγας κηρυγμάτων ἐν τῇ λαιᾷ.

‡ Ruffium eccles. hist. lib. ii. c. x.

cepts and rules. Let any make proof of both. Let a gentleman or minister persuade parishioners to contribute liberally to a brief, and set a niggardly example, and see how much less will come of it, than if he said less and gave more. What else moved Christ and the prophets so frequently to use that potent figure, which rhetoricians, from the special usefulness of it, call χρεια, that is, when the orator seconds and enlives his speech with some action ; as Christ, when here in my text, he girds himself with a towel; and elsewhere, when he took the child and set him in the midst of the apostles ; the prophet when he took Paul's girdle, and the old divine in Dorotheus, that had his auditor pluck at a great old tree, which he could not stir, and at a young sprout easily plucked up, to shew the difficulty of rooting out an old habit, in comparison of its beginnings.

The reason is, words are but wind, and vanish into the wind, leaving no print or impression more than a ship in the sea, in comparison of actions, which men take marks and notice of. This same inartificial argument of examples, though scholars less regard it as having less art in it, yet is it all the countryman's logic ; as the martyr that answered Bishop Bonner, ' My lord, I cannot dispute, but I can die for the truth,' moved the spectators as much as many learned discourses. By this, Christ demonstrated to John's disciples his Messiahship, ' Go and tell, not what you heard me preach, but saw me do ; how the blind receive sight,' &c. If I do not such works as none other hath done before me, I desire not men to believe in me. By these courses, Peter would have Christians win their neigh- bours, and wives their husbands, rather than by tutoring of them. Then would neighbours follow one another to the right religion and the true church, as tradesmen do to those markets where they see them gather wealth; yea, imitate their lives, and bring forth fruits as Jacob's sheep, if they saw their rods speckled with works, as well as with words. Thus Monica, Saint Augustine's famous mother, taught one of her neighbour gentlewomen, complaining of her churlish Nabal, and wondering how she won her perverse husband. Why, says she, I observed his mind, pleased him in all indifferent things, forbore him in his passions, gave him all con- tent in diet, attendance, and so have made him first God's, and then mine by degrees. These are the arts and charms that, if now used by preachers and professors, would convert multitudes of people, and cover multitudes of sins, and cause themselves to shine as stars. These things mind and exer- cise. These things, if you know and do, you shall save yourselves, and those you live withal, and so be every way happy men.

Thus in all these three references, you see that doing only brings in the happiness ; without which, all our knowing makes and leaves us but dis- honourable to God, uncomfortable to ourselves, scandalous to others, in no nearer terms of happiness, than Balaam, Judas, and the devil himself, who, the more they know, the worse for them ; the more sin, and the more pun- ishment. They do but teach God how to condemn them.

Use 1; *of reproof.*—If knowing made up happiness, England were an happy nation, our times as happy as ever any ; but if doing be required, great is the felicity of both. Of which, shall I complain in the words of Seneca ? Men now-a-days choose rather to discourse than to live ;* study styles rather than deeds ; or in Bernard's, men desire knowledge to be known by it ;† or as Anacharsis taxed the Athenians for using their money to count withal, and knowledge to know withal ;‡ or as Tully of the philo-

---

* Malint disputare quàm vivere.   † Scire ut sciantur.
‡ Nummis ad numerandum, scientia ad sciendum.

sophers, that their lives and their discourses miserably crossed one another.*
The truth is this, a plethory and dropsy there is of hearing and reading;
a dearth and consumption of doing; most ever gathering, never using; not
unlike some old university drones, ever in studying and learning, never
preaching or venting their studies. Like tedious musicians, ever tuning
and never playing, or like the changeling Luther mentions, ever suckling,
never battling; or like dying men, and sick of apoplexies, with speech, but
no faculty locomotive, no power to stir hand or foot. Few (I confess)
troubled in these times with the deaf and dumb spirits, but most having
withered hands, and dried arms, and lame feet.

This same want of doing what we know, what does it else but make common people blaspheme God? doubt whether all divinity be but policy, and
the Scriptures a fable? Verily, the atheism of the times hath this for its
principal fountain and pretext. There was a woman lately living, much
spoken of in some parts of this land, living in professed doubt of the Deity,
after illumination and repentance hardly comforted, who often protested,
that the vicious and offensive life of a great learned man in the town where
she lived occasioned those damned doubts. This opens men's mouths,
and gives the hint of all blasphemies, scorns, and scoffs of religion; such
as he broke upon the Jesuits, whom in foreign nations they call apostles.
' The apostles, indeed, shewed the world heaven, left the earth to earthly
men, got heaven themselves; but we are more beholden to our new ones;
they shew us heaven, leave it to us to purchase, and cozen us only of
earthly possessions in the mean time.' This made Linacre, reading upon the
New Testament the fifth, sixth, and seventh chapters of Saint Matthew, and
comparing those rules with Christians' lives, to throw down the book, and
burst out into this protestation, ' Either this is not God's gospel, or we are
not Christians and gospellers.' Questionless, the more any men know, or
profess to know, and the less they do, the more do they dishonour God.

And what are such themselves the better for their knowledge? but as
the preacher experimentally speaks, ' He that increaseth such knowledge,
addeth sorrow.' Their folly I cannot better express than Erasmus, in his
dialogue of a carnal gospeller, whom he calls *Cyclops Evangeliophorus*, a
swaggering ruffian, affecting yet the name of a gospeller, whom he describes,
having by one side hanging a bottle of rich sack, and by the other a Testament of Erasmus's translation, richly bound and bossed, the leaves gilt
over as fair as his life was foul, and conditions base. This man he discovers by certain interrogatories, to have no inward knowledge or affection
to the gospel, nor better proof of his love thereto, than that he carried it
always about him, and had laid it upon the pate of a Franciscan, that had
railed on Erasmus and the new gospellers. To convince him, he asks
him, What if he were tied ever to carry the bottle at his girdle and never
to taste of it; or but to taste only and never to drink it down? His
answer is, that were but a punishment, Tantalus-like. But what if he did,
as his manner was, drink deeply of it? He then answers, it would warm
his heart, refresh his spirits, cheer his countenance. So, says he, would
that little book, if thou didst eat it down; concoct, digest, and turn it into
nutriment in thy life and practice. My meaning is not in this relation to
tax Bible carrying, which I hold a better grace than rapiers or fans of
feathers, but only to shew the foppery of them that carry them in their
hands, or in their memories or understandings, as asses do dainty burdens
and taste not of them, have no fruit of them themselves. Verily, a man

* Cum Philosophorum vita miserabiliter pugnat oratio.

knows no more rightly than he practises. It is said of Christ, he knew no sins, because he did no sin ; and in that sense, he knows no good that doth no good. He that will obey shall know my Father's will, and such as will not do what they know to be good, shall soon unknow that which they know, and become as if they never had known any such matter ; it being just with God to punish shipwreck of a good conscience, with loss of the freight of knowledge ; according to that imprecation of the Hebrews, that if they should abuse their skill in music, their right hand might forget its cunning, and their tongue cleave to the roof of their mouths. From which just judgment, I persuade myself, it comes to pass that many become in matters of religion mere sceptics, because they would not be practics, and that the commonest religion of our times is Socrates's uncertainty. Men know nothing now-a-days. It is become a disputable problem whether the Pope be antichrist, Rome a good church ; whether a man may worship God before pictures, play upon any part of the Sabbath as well as upon the week days ; whether election be of foreseen faith ; whether the true believer may apostatise ? Shortly, I think, whether the Scripture be scripture, and whether there be a God or no ? To conclude, a good understanding have all they that do thereafter ; and cursed are all such as know these things and do the clean contrary.

Cursed (I say) are they, because they lay a stumbling-block before others, both weak ones within and bad ones without ; such, I say, as know God, and yet deny him in their lives, and are reprobate to every good word and work ; such as buy by one balance and sell by another, have a form of knowledge which they prescribe to others and live themselves by contrary rules. Of such I would I could speak with as much detestation, as Paul writes of them, Phil. iii., friends in show, but enemies in truth to the cross of Christ. Unclean beasts, for all their chewing of the cud, repeating of sermons, because they divide not the hoof, walk without all differences, and judgment, as if God had given them their lights to tread in puddles and gutters withal, to walk and wallow in the mire of all filthiness, which makes men mislike not only their persons, but the very religion which they retain too. Some few wise and grounded Christians will do as they say, and not as they do ; hear them, because they sit in the chair of Moses ; but the greatest number will loathe their sayings for their doings, as men the good light of a candle for the ill savour the stinking tallow yields, resolving as the Indians of the Spaniards, whatever their religion be, they will be of the clean contrary ; if such go to heaven, they will go to hell. I wonder with what face such can call themselves Christians, or with what ears hear themselves so called.* Does any man look to be called a carpenter that never squared timber, or erected frames ? What if never so skilful ? I say of all such skill, as Cato of superfluous useless trifles, they are dear of a farthing that are good for nothing.

Oh ! rather let us all lay claim to that honourable name, do the works of Christians, and thereby approve ourselves to God and man, as the angel to Manoah, who, being asked of his name, made answer, It was wonderful, and did wonderfully, ascended in the flame and made good his name by his action. Here is the labour, and here lies all the difficulty ; the maxims and sanctions of things to be done and believed are but few, contained in brief summaries ; but the incentives, motives, directions, reproofs, and such like appurtenances of practice, these make volumes swell, these lengthen sermons, and multiply books.† The art of doing is that which requires

* Greg. Nyssen. de nomine Christiani.   † Sic Epictetus de Philosophia.

study, strength, and divine assistance. Do the sins that swarm in our times proceed from ignorance, or incontinence rather, and wilfulness? It were happy if men had that plea; if the light were not so great, the times and the nation had not sin. May we not use the apostle's ordinary increpation and exprobration? Know you not that idolatry, swearing, Sabbath - breaking, drinking, and whoring are sins? Know you not that for these things comes the anger of God? Is any so simple that h knows not the ten commandments, and the sum of the gospels? yet how desperately do men rush upon these pikes, carelessly, wittingly, and willingly, seeing the gulf, and yet leaping into it! Many condemning them selves in Medea's terms, see the better and yet follow the worse, having no heart to leave that they see to be evil: as if men thought that ignorance only should condemn; as if God should only come in flaming fire to render vengeance upon poor pagans, savages, and Indians, or heretics, that know not the truth, and not much more upon his own servants, that knew and refused to do his will.

The infidel disputes against the faith, the impious lives against it ; * the one denies it in terms, the other in deeds ; and therefore both shall be held as enemies to the faith, and never attain salvation : of the two, it is worse to kick against the prick one sees, than to stumble in the dark at a block one sees not. But here is the chief cause of all impiety ; illumination is easy, sanctification is hard to flesh and blood, requires crossing and mastery, yea, crucifying of our lusts, wills, and affections, which is not done without much prayer and travail ; and therefore men neglect that, and content themselves with the easier and cheaper work. Upon this therefore do I wish Christians would set their prizes, and spend their studies, even about the art of doing. But how shall we attain this facility and faculty of doing? I answer : to wish it and heartily to desire it is half, yea, and the best half, of the work ; as Socrates was wont to say, He that would be an honest man shall soon be one, and is past the hardest part of the work. To affect goodness above cunning is a good sign, and a good help, and step to be such an one, especially when this desire breeds prayer for power to do, knowing that without Christ we can do just nothing, but lie becalmed and unable to move or promove ; as a ship on the sea, a mill on the land, without the breath of the Spirit. And this I commend as the best and first general help of practice, that every morning, and in the enterprise of all thy affairs, thou acknowledge thine own disability, or rather deadness, to every good work, and commend thyself to the work of his grace for the will and the deed : for preventing and subsequent, operating and co-operating, preserving and perfecting grace : entreating him not only to regenerate thee, and give thee new principles of motion, but to renew his inspiration upon every new act of thine, that by Christ, or rather Christ by and in thee, may do all things, pray as if thou hadst no will, vow as if there were no grace, that is seriously both.

Secondly, in the use of all means of practice, when thou goest to hear, read, or meditate, pray and desire thou mayest light upon profitable and pertinent themes, books, and sermons, applicatory, and levelling at thyself, and orations as if made for thee rather than for anybody else : desire not to gather flowers, but pot-herbs and fruit. Charms are said to have no effect unless one go with a belief unto them : I am sure no means ordinarily will do thee any good unless thou go with a mind to be bettered by them.

* Aug. lib. iv. contra Donat.

Thirdly, In the use of these, attend to thyself as well as to the matter, have one eye and ear fixed on what is said, and another on thyself; lay thyself to the rule, and say, What is this to me? how do I and that agree? Be not as little children, who, while they are looking in the glass, think only it is the baby's face, and not their own. Observe not, in hearing a sermon, the pleasing sound of the pipe, but how thou dancest thereunto; in reading of the Scriptures, at the end of every period ask thy heart, How do I practise this? or, How does this reproof tax me? This promise comfort me? When thou art well persuaded to do anything, resolve thoroughly to do it; and when resolved, dispatch and execute it speedily.

Fourthly, After the sermon is ended, say not, as the common manner is, Now the sermon is done; but consider it is not done till thou hast done it. After reading and hearing do as men do after dinner, sit a while, concoct it, by pondering of it, digest it, and after draw it out into action. So do such as learn music or writing: they play over their lesson, write after the copy. This, I think, Paul meant when he saith, ἀσκῶ. I exercise myself to have an inoffensive conscience, &c. Most err grossly in the fail of this, thinking it enough to retain it in memory, to repeat it over, serving divinity as absurdly as the countryman his physic, who, being bidden to take his bill or receipt, took it home, and carried it in his pocket, and after finding no ease upon his complaint, being directed to take it in posset ale, put the bill in a cup, but never took the ingredients prescribed into his body. And look how much good his physic did him, so much good will divinity do us, taken into our memories and tongues, and no further.

Fifthly, In all thy talk, discourses, and counsels to others, lick first thine own fingers. That wise man is a fool that is not wise for himself. And yet many such there be that can preach and write good books, like Tusser, that wrote well of husbandry, and was the most unthrifty husband himself that ever water wet.

Sixthly and lastly, In all thy privy reckonings with thyself, which must be duly observed at the close of every week, month, and year, less and more solemnly, observe what thou hast done, consider if thou shouldst keep a diary or journal, as many thriving Christians do, what acts it would record when I go out of the world. What, shall the world say, hath this man done singular or memorable? Take such accounts of thyself daily as masters of their journeymen and apprentices. As Pharoah's taskmaster of the Israelites, Where is the work done this day? lest thou be as huntsmen and falconers that have toiled all the day and have no quarry or roast at night.

A WORD OF APPLICATION.

If now, at the end of my sermon, my several hearers and readers would do, as St John Baptist's did, ask, What shall I do? and what shall I do? You have said much in the general of doing, what say you in particular to this nation, and to the several conditions of men in it?

I answer: What can I say to these knowing times, which hath not been said before me. What new doctrine, unheard of before, is it possible for me to broach? I will, therefore, say no more but 'do that which you know you should do.' If you know that Baal be God, if Rome be the church, let us return to it again. If you know that swearing, Sabbath-breaking, and fashion-following be good things, let us all fall to do these things. But if God hath given us the truth and the light, let us walk in it, and work by it while it is to-day, lest, if we play revel and riot by it, the candlestick be removed, and the light put out. If purity, sanctity, and sobriety be known to you to be good things, and pleasing to God, ' happy are you if you do them.'

Certain things there are known and acknowledged at all hands as meet to be done, that an able minister might be provided for every parish, that popery, swearing, and drunkenness would be suppressed. But why are they ever spoken of and never done ? How did they, in superstition, maintain so many idle bellies ? How was the head of the beast cut off at the first in this nation ? Is it harder for us to cut off the friggling tail of that hydra of Rome ? How was the infinite swarm of rogues and beggars suppressed by good laws ? Verily, nothing is hard to industrious and active spirits, God assisting ; and now it is high time, and God looks that these things should be done.

To the reverend clergy, and such as carry holiness in their fronts. Let such be sure to have Thummim as well as Urim on their breasts ; their right thumbs and feet anointed with holy oil, as well as their right ears ; their fruitful pomegranates on their skirts, as well as their bells to ring and make a sound withal, lest they be as tinkling cymbals to God's and men's ears. You know better than I can tell you what should be done. Happy are you if you do what you know.

To nobles and great persons. It is not your countenancing of religion will serve the turn, which yet were well if many of you would afford but your practising of it, not the having of a chaplain to say and do you such service as Ahab's four hundred did, but a faithful Micaiah to direct you, what God would have done, whom you may hear as Cornelius did Peter, with an intent to obey, not him, but the message he delivers out of God's book unto you.

To gentlemen. For God's sake, do something, besides hawking and hunting and living upon your lands and patrimonies. You have better means of knowing and doing than meaner men. Happy if you do what you know.

To lawyers and soldiers. I remit you to St John's counsel, which will serve you both. And happy should they and their clients be if they would practise it, be content with their wages, and do no wrong.

To merchants and tradesmen. If you believe there be a country and city that lies eastward, a new Jerusalem, where there are rich commodities, as rich as any in the East Indies, send your prayers and good works to factor there for you, and have a stock employed in God's banks to pauperous and pious uses ; and think of religion as of tradings that will bring no gain unless diligently followed and practised. It is not a nimble head, but a diligent hand, that maketh rich.

In a word, to all hearers and goers to sermons. Play not the fools, as most do. Hear not to hear. Go not to church as many now-a-days do to universities and inns of court, neither to get learning, law, nor money, for mere form or fashion ; or as boys go into the water to play and paddle there only, not to wash and be clean. To all sorts : I say not a word more ; but do that which you know to be good, and happy are you.

Brevis predicatio, longa ruminatio, actio perpetua.
Denique, quid verbis opus spectemur agendo.

A POSTSCRIPT.

READER, if thou hadst read over a treatise of physic, polity, mathematics, or any other mystery, earnestly promising thee health, wealth, or special benefit, wouldst thou not long till thou hadst made some trial of it in practice? Here, if thou wilt be persuaded to do the like, without all *if* or *and*, happy shalt thou be. To conclude: before thou be tired, consider well much reading is a weariness to the flesh, but much doing a refreshing to the spirit. The general complaint of the world is that there is no end of making many books, because there is little or no fruit in those that read them, but as the grass on the housetop, which withers before it cometh forth, whereof the mower filleth not his hand nor the gleaner his lap, neither they which go by say, The blessing of the Lord be on you, or, We bless you in the name of the Lord. Thou, therefore, who desirest to be a wise reader, one of a thousand, read to some purpose; that is, intend of a reader to become a doer. So shalt thou avert this curse and reproach from thee. So shall God and man call thee blessed; and blessed shalt thou feel thyself in so doing. Do, then; and so he hath done, that layeth no heavier burden on thee than on himself, nor wisheth other happiness than to himself.

SA. WARD.

GENERAL INDEX.*

* It is not considered necessary to give an Index of Scripture Texts, as there are only a very few quoted, and the remarks upon them are not of much importance.—ED.

ERRATA.

P. 23,	line 42,	*for* Zaccheus the jailor,	*read*	Zaccheus, the jailor
30	last,	... *suader*	...	*suadeo*
38	5,	... Chistians	...	Christians
52	17,	... president	...	precedent (?)
53	8,	... shoulst	...	shouldst
88	33,	... ἡδυσμασι x	...	ἡδυσμασι και
89	10,	... lias	...	Elias
106	28,	... ὑωοστασις	...	ὑποστασις
115	34,	... Τχυς	...	Τους
136	30,	... *lauditissima*	...	*laudatissima*
139	last,	... Cui...sacreligium	...	Cur...sacrilegium
147	38,	... posibiles	..	possibiles

March 2024
Bought after reading
Banner of Truth
"Voices from the past" Vol I.